SOVIET COMBAT AIRCRAFT
of the Second World War

Volume One
Single-Engined Fighters

SOVIET COMBAT AIRCRAFT
of the Second World War

Volume One:
Single-Engined Fighters

Yefim Gordon and Dmitri Khazanov

Midland Publishing
Limited

**Soviet Combat Aircraft
of the Second World War**
Volume One – Single-Engined Fighters

ISBN 1 85780 083 4
© 1998 Yefim Gordon and Dmitri Khazanov.
All illustrations via authors unless noted.

Published by Midland Publishing Limited
24 The Hollow, Earl Shilton
Leicester, LE9 7NA, England
Tel: 01455 847815 Fax: 01455 841805

Design concept and editorial layout
© Midland Publishing Limited and
Stephen Thompson Associates.

Edited by Philip Jarrett and Ken Ellis

Printed in Hong Kong via
World Print Limited

Worldwide distribution (except Nth America):
Midland Counties Publications (Aerophile) Ltd
Unit 3 Maizefield, Hinckley Fields
Hinckley, Leics., LE10 1YF, England
Tel: 01455 233747 Fax: 01455 233737
E-mail: midlandbooks@compuserve.com

North America trade distribution by:
Motorbooks International
Wholesalers & Distributors
729 Prospect Avenue, PO Box 1
Osceola, WI 54020-0001, USA
Tel: 715 294 3345 Fax: 715 294 4448
US/Canada orders/service: 800 458 0454

Photograph on half-title page:
**Major I Vishnyakov, Deputy Commander
of the 171st Fighter Regiment, in his La-5FN.**

Title page:
**Yak-9Bs of the 18th Guards Air Regiment,
summer 1943. The aircraft carry the legend
'From the Maly Theatre to the Front Line'.**
Philip Jarrett collection

Right:
MiG-3 on the Leningrad front, 1941.
Philip Jarrett collection

Contents

Introduction

BILL GUNSTON
OBE FRAeS

Stalin's domain was a fairly closed society. The rest of the world had little idea of what went on in the Soviet Union, and even after Operation *Barbarossa* – the invasion by Nazi Germany on 22nd June 1941 which launched what the Soviet Union called The Great Patriotic War – for several months nearly all the information on Soviet aircraft was gleaned from propaganda material put out by the German enemy. Checking through a 1941 volume of *The Aeroplane Spotter* I found only one photograph of a modern Soviet aircraft that had not been captured by the enemy. It showed a MiG-3. Never having heard of such an aircraft, the caption-writer said it was an 'I-18...armed with eight machine guns'!

Today we can put such nonsense behind us. In compiling this book Yefim Gordon and

Dmitri Khazanov have had the benefit not only of long experience studying Soviet aircraft but also of access to the archives of the various design bureaux. Even after the collapse of the rigid Soviet system in 1990 quite a few errors persisted where Soviet aircraft were concerned.

Soviet aviation

One of the few things that the outside world did know about Soviet aviation was that in a Communist state there were no 'companies'. I apologise for retracing what may be familiar ground, but the system was so unlike that in other countries that it may need to be explained yet again.

In the early days of the Soviet state several of the most experienced aircraft designers

Well-known, but very evocative, state information photograph, showing 'Soviet fighter planes on an airfield'. MiG-3s in a variety of colour schemes.
Philip Jarrett collection

emigrated. The few that were left were organised into groups called an OKB (experimental construction bureau), administered by the centralised Glavkoavia, from 1939 renamed the MAP (Ministry of Aviation Industry). Despite the word 'construction', the real purpose of these bureaux was to design aircraft. If they had the facilities, they also built prototypes of their designs.

Each bureau was allocated a few technical staff and a larger number of mostly unskilled workers. Everyone, especially senior designers, was allocated to a particular OKB, but to a very limited degree individuals could choose to work elsewhere.

These bureaux undertook hardly any research. That was left to centralised establishments, such as the Central Aviation and Hydrodynamics Institute (which had wind tunnels) and the Central Institute of Aviation Motors. Even more surprisingly, not only did the OKBs not build aircraft in quantity but they had almost no say in where the aircraft they had designed were built. If an aircraft was deemed worthy of being made in quantity – in some cases after competitive trials between rival prototypes – the MAP would arrange for it to be put into production at a selected GAZ (State Aviation Factory)

Stalin was intensely concerned with modern weapons, such as aircraft. He took a close personal interest in their design, and in the designers. Though he was a hard man to work for, and often thought that designers would work harder if they were put in prison, he did try to give the VVS (air force) the best aircraft, and he did try to build up the USSR's

The I-15*bis*, continued development of the biplane fighter, but there was more to come from Polikarpov. *Philip Jarrett collection*

production capacity. After 1934 some of the largest new factories were built far to the East, in such places as Irkutsk, Gorkii, Rybinsk, Khabarovsk and Novosibirsk. However, on 22nd June 1941 very few of these new plants had been completed. More than 90% of the Soviet aircraft industry was still in European Russia, and by 1943 almost every factory except those within the cities of Moscow and Leningrad had been overrun by the Germans.

Thus, of the aircraft in this book that finally made it to production before June 1941, almost every type was held back by the need to evacuate the factory and re-establish production east of the Urals. The effort this entailed can be left to the imagination. It was not a case of simply loading everything on trucks and driving off. East of Moscow most of the roads petered out and became mere tracks, thick mud in summer and rock-hard rutted ice in winter. Most of the evacuated factories and OKBs found that they had been allocated an unsuitable existing building, or a fine new factory that was not yet half-finished.

Once the evacuated design teams and the production factories had actually been able to resume work they had one big advantage. The Soviet Union was a gigantic country, and the new locations were beyond the reach of

almost all the Luftwaffe's bombers. Hitler never intended to make his armies march 5,000 miles across Siberia to the Pacific. His reason for attacking the Soviet Union was in order to take over the oil-producing region of Azerbaijan. He then intended to set up a guarded frontier on or West of the Urals, and then carry on the war against Britain.

We British thought he would be able to accomplish this. To quote the 'The Spotter' again, on 3rd July 1941 it said 'While the Luftwaffe is primarily occupied on the Russian front, an immediate invasion of this country does not seem likely. Such a state of affairs cannot be expected to last... there seems little doubt that Germany will be able to turn from Russia to the one other remaining front in Europe before the autumn is far advanced... We must be prepared to meet and defeat the full fury of the German onslaught, turned from the East to the West...'

This pessimistic belief stemmed from the colossal German victories of the first week of *Barbarossa*, which transcended anything seen before in warfare. They strongly reinforced the previously-held opinion in Western countries that Soviet weapons might be available in impressive quantity, but that they were generally inferior and obsolete.

Polikarpov's I-153 could pose quite a handful to a Bf109E pilot. *Philip Jarrett collection*

The requirements

Though Czarist Russia was home to a large number of pioneer designers, in the 1920s most aircraft in the Soviet Union were of foreign origin. Even those in production were to a large extent based on foreign designs. However, to a far greater extent than the outside world realised, these early types were replaced by aircraft of totally Soviet design. Though obviously constrained by the available engines – and to a considerable degree the engines that were available for front line service did remain derivatives of foreign designs even to the end of the Great Patriotic War – the Soviet designers were forced to create aircraft able to meet a particularly challenging set of requirements. Merely copying Western aircraft would have been shortsighted, as proved by the fact that many British and American aircraft supplied in 1941-44 proved unable to stand up to the environment.

From its birth, the Soviet state was preoccupied by the idea of attack by a hostile neighbour (as indeed happened). The entire country was divided into Military Districts, and the Commander of each was an army officer with authority over all arms in that region. The VVS (air force) was thus from the outset seen as an adjunct to the army and other ground forces. Indeed, in the 1920s the first Soviet air operations were in support of forces brought against internal rebels, notably in Turkestan. Thus, the primary mission was close air support of ground troops. Air operations became polarised around the idea of a battlefront.

Where fighters were concerned, the primary requirements were seen as speed, rate of climb and, especially, manoeuvrability in close combat. Where Soviet aircraft differed from most others was in the environment. Nowhere else might fighters have to operate in ambient temperatures ranging from 40° (104°F) in summer to –50° (–58°F) in winter.

This posed severe problems to aircraft with liquid-cooled engines, and to the lubrication of every moving part. It also meant that in winter any aircraft, even a fighter, might have to operate on skis.

Consideration of landing gear was made more difficult by the fact that in a land war the battlefront is unlikely to stay in the same place. Even the unique experience of static trench warfare in the First World War did not blind the Soviet commanders to this fact. In the Great Patriotic War the front often moved 30 miles (48km) in a day, and altogether moved East 1,000 miles (1,600km) and then back again. In such an environment all combat aircraft had to be able to operate from hastily prepared airfields.

Between September 1941 and April 1945 the VVS construction battalions created 8,545 front line airfields (in addition to over 1,300 much better ones elsewhere in the Soviet Union). Usually the surface of the front-line airfield was grass, sand or earth, often freshly cleared of scrub or even trees. Over vast areas the surface in summer was soft mud or bog, and over four million straight treetrunks were used to make runways. Such surfaces were too severe for Western fighters, such as the Vickers-Supermarine Spitfire (the Bell P-39 Airacobra was a welcome exception).

A major problem was the fact that in 1941-44 more than two million men and women joined the VVS in various ground duties. A few had experience with trucks and tractors, but most had no technical training whatsoever. Despite sustained attempts to rectify this situation, it had always been taken for granted that the general level of training of servicing personnel would be extremely basic. Even as late as 1943 many aircraft were unwittingly rendered unserviceable by 'brute force and ignorance' methods, and the basic design of the aircraft always had to bear this possibility in mind.

Even the pilots often had only a rudimentary idea of how engines and aircraft systems actually worked, and this handicap was accentuated in the Great Patriotic War. Most of the shattering losses in the first two weeks were sustained not in air combat but on the ground. This usually left the pilot intact but unemployed, but such was the Luftwaffe's command of the air that by 1942 over 70% of the pre-war pilots had been killed or captured. VVS flying training schools found the only way they could cope with demand was by shortening the period of instruction (this policy was fairly soon reversed).

In general the Soviet fighters were not designed for inexperienced pilots, and indeed were particularly challenging. Accordingly, by any standard the number of serious accidents was unacceptable.

Aircraft design

Any objective study of the aircraft in this book must make it clear that the Soviet designers did not, as was commonly supposed by Western observers in June 1941, merely copy the creations of their foreign counterparts. Whilst pursuing all the expected configurations, Soviet designers tried many others. For example, the Kozlov EI had a variable-incidence wing, and the Nikitin IS family had retractable lower wings. Several fighter prototypes had booster rockets (two, the La-7R and Su-7, are featured here) and the BI rocket interceptor had no parallel elsewhere except the much more tricky and dangerous Me 163 Komet. Polikarpov's last aircraft, left incomplete at his death, was the Malyutka (little one), an attractive rocket-engined fighter. Perhaps even more advanced in technology, ramjet engines were tested on several Soviet fighters, including the La-7PVRD included here.

The authors deliberately confined themselves in this book to types that were actually built. Had they included unbuilt projects they could have added many more that nobody could ever have said were the result of plagiarism. For example, Belyayev's never-completed EOI seated the pilot in a totally glazed nose with the engine behind him. Moskalyev, who had in 1935 actually flown his completely tail-less SAM-7 Sigma, almost completed the push/pull SAM-13 (which had a tail) before having to evacuate to Omsk.

In 1941 the most experienced Soviet fighter designer was Nikolay Polikarpov. In the mid-1930s VVS fighter pilots were no different from those in other countries in liking agile biplanes with open cockpits, and hating monoplanes with enclosed cockpits. Caught in the middle, our Nikolay did himself no favours by creating, in the TsKB-12, which led to the I-16, an unnecessarily tricky monoplane. He probably was influenced by Boeing's P-26, which was tricky enough, but I can't help feeling one only had to give the I-16 a single glance to say 'Not for me!' Half a century later designers began deliberately to create fighters that were longitudinally unstable, but in 1933 such aircraft were liable to crash, even without the assistance of an enemy.

In parallel, Polikarpov continued with his biplane fighters, and took this technology further than in any other country. Versions of his I-153 not only had retractable landing gear but also 20mm cannon, rockets, a turbosupercharger and a pressurised cockpit, though not all at once on the same aircraft! In the hands of a skilled and aggressive pilot, the Polikarpov I-153 could pose quite a handful to the pilot of a Messerschmitt Bf109E, and was far superior to the Italian Fiat CR.42 which stayed in production even longer.

Despite the attractions of the biplane, by 1935 it was fast becoming accepted all over the world that the way to design a fighter was to put the most powerful available engine in the front of the fuselage, driving a tractor propeller, and put a monoplane wing in the low position, with an enclosed cockpit above the trailing edge. The vast majority of Soviet wartime fighters adopted this layout, but with particular national characteristics incorporated. These are examined under the following subheadings.

Airframe

It seems common sense for a fighter designer 60 years ago to have made his airframe the smallest possible structure that could still house the engine, fuel, pilot and armament. This tendency showed in Soviet fighters more than in any other country. Of course, there were a few exceptions, but in general the aircraft in this book were characterised by big engines in small airframes.

To get a lot of information into a small space the following table compares some mass-produced Soviet fighters with important counterparts in other countries.

Soviet Fighters and their Contemporaries

	Engine Capacity in³ (litres)		Wing Area ft² (m²)	
MiG-3	2,847	(46.66)	187.7	(17.43)
Spitfire	1,649	(27.0)	242.2	(22.5)
La-5	2,514	(41.2)	186.0	(17.27)
A6M 'Zero'	1,696	(27.8)	241.5	(22.43)
Yak-3	2,142	(35.1)	160.0	(14.86)
P-51 Mustang	1,649	(27.0)	233.0	(21.64)

These figures inevitably suggest that, having massive engines in small airframes, the Soviet fighters must have had poor manoeuvrability, very high take-off and landing speeds (implying the need for a long run) and very short radius of action, suffering all these penalties in order to achieve fantastic speed. To some degree this assessment was indeed true of the MiG, but the Lavochkin and the Yakovlev had excellent manoeuvrability, and could operate from the same kind of front line airstrip as any other wartime fighters.

Moreover, the most surprising thing is that, despite bolting huge engines into small airframes, the Soviet fighters were if anything slower than average. Of the aircraft picked out for comparison, the slowest was the Japanese A6M, which at its best height could reach 351mph (564km/h). This is because it had the least powerful engine. At their optimum altitudes the three Soviet fighters had maximum speeds of 397, 375 and 401mph (638, 603 and 645km/h), whereas the Spitfire IX and P-51D reached 408 and 437mph (656 and 703km/h) respectively. This matter is discussed later under the heading 'Engines'.

The I-16 took the Polikarpov small fighter formula into monoplane format, with equal success. *Philip Jarrett collection*

Apart from the basic characteristic of a big engine in a small airframe the most outstanding feature of the Soviet wartime fighters was the widespread use of wood, and wood-derived materials. This reflected the fact that the Soviet Union, while it had limitless forests and quite a lot of iron ore with which to make steel, had very limited indigenous supplies of bauxite with which to make aluminium. In 1942-44 the Western Allies shipped to Murmansk and Archangel over 250,000 tons of aluminium ingots, but this could not have been foreseen. Accordingly, even though the Soviet Union had made great strides in developing a wide range of light alloys, fighter designers were strongly motivated to use wood as much as possible.

By 1941 teams at the VIAM (All-Union Institute for Aviation Materials), and in several GAZ, had developed wood construction further than in any other country. Apart from traditional techniques with machined solid wood and ordinary ply, there were two new techniques. One, called shpon, consisted of thin (typically 1mm) veneers, usually of birch, wrapped to form a skin over a male die (sometimes over the actual underlying structure of frames and stringers). A second sheet, like the first – a long band perhaps 20-40cm wide – would then be glued over the first, with the grain running in a different direction. The finished structure might have as many as six layers.

The other technique, delta drevesina (delta wood), involved impregnating each layer of veneer with resin adhesive. After this had soaked in, the plies were then bonded together under pressure. This was used mainly for stiff primary structures, such as wing spars. In about December 1940 the imported resin was replaced by locally produced sheets of phenol-formaldehyde adhesive with a trace of borax. After bonding at 150°C the material was called bakelite-ply.

The operating environment of what was called the Eastern Front in the Second World War was the harshest to which aircraft have ever been subjected. It is remarkable that wooden structures could stand up to it, especially as they frequently had to spend long periods in the open. In winter great care had to exercised to try to keep aircraft clean, because slush, mud and oil would freeze rock-hard, adding weight, causing aerodynamic turbulence and preventing landing gear retraction or control surface movement.

Of course, it was also essential to devise safe front line methods for repairing damage. This was crucial where the damage was to primary structure, such as a delta wing spar or a steel tube fuselage. Damage repair and the quick return to operational service of combat aircraft was brought to a fine art, even in the front line in winter.

Engines

Despite sustained efforts by the engine design bureaux and the central institutes, it was probably in the matter of engines that Soviet fighter designers found it most difficult to compete. The most important engine family for fighters in 1941-45 was that derived by V Ya Klimov from the French Hispano-Suiza 12Y of 1934. This had 12 cylinders in V-form, and though a refined engine with a 20-year heritage behind it, it was fundamentally unable to sustain the rotational speeds and boost pressures of the British Rolls-Royce Merlin. In 1941 the typical fighter Merlin (not the new 60-series with a two-stage supercharger), of 1,649in³ (27 litres) capacity, had a maximum power of 1,470hp (1,230kW) at 3,000 rpm. On fuel of 94/95 octane, the Soviet engine made in the greatest numbers, the VK-105, could not give more than 1,260hp (940kW) and usually only 1,150hp (858kW), at 2,700 rpm, despite having a capacity of 2,141in³ (35.09 litres).

The only other family of liquid cooled engines available from production were even less suitable for small fighters. A A Mikulin's 'AM' series had the same V-12 layout, but used cylinder blocks derived from the German BMW VI, with a capacity of 2,847in³ (46.66 litres). Such a big engine ought to have been in the 2,000+ hp (1,490+ kW) class, but in fact they were designed originally for bombers, and even at full throttle had low crankshaft speeds. Other things being equal, an engine's power is proportional to the speed of rotation of its crankshaft. The AM-35 had a governed speed of only 2,050rpm (compared with 3,000 for the Merlin), and thus despite its size and massive weight gave only 1,200hp (895kW). The AM-35A was rated at 1,350 hp (1,007kW).

One of the unexpected major success stories was A D Shvetsov's 14-cylinder radial, originally designated M-82 and in 1941 – in conformity with the new designer-based scheme – rechristened the ASh-82. This had air-cooled cylinders based on those of the American Wright R-1820 Cyclone (which had a single row of nine cylinders) but with considerable development by Shvetsov, in the course of which he reduced the stroke from 174.5mm to only 155mm. This resulted in a compact engine with an overall diameter of only 49.6in (1,260mm). With a capacity of 2,514in³ (41.2 litres), the ASh-82FN was qualified in early 1942 at 1,630hp (1,215kW), rising to 1,850hp (1,380kW) on 100 octane fuel.

A vital factor in any radial-engined fighter was the way the engine was installed. For example, even though the first Bristol Centaurus-engined Tornado in 1941 was faster than any previous Hawker fighter, after a captured Focke-Wulf Fw190 had been studied the installation was redesigned, leading to the

Tempest II and Fury which were some 50mph (80km/h) faster. In just the same way, when a team under I G Lazarev hastily fitted an M-82 (ASh-82) into a MiG-3 the result was a great disappointment. Later in 1942 a properly engineered installation was achieved in the Aircraft Ye, or I-211, and this was the fastest Soviet fighter ever flown at that time.

A particularly instructive comparison can be made between the LaGG-3 and the La-5. The LaGG was a typical Soviet fighter of the 1939-40 era, with a small wooden airframe and a big M-105 (VK-105) engine. Despite frantic improvements it was indifferent in combat, and large numbers of LaGG pilots were killed during training. 'LaGG' was said at the time to mean Lakirovannii Garantirovannii Grob, meaning 'varnished guaranteed coffin'. After Lavochkin replaced the VK-105 by an ASh-82 the aircraft was transformed, eventually becoming a fighter in which a skilled pilot could rack up a good score even against '109s and '190s (Ivan Kozhedub scored 62).

One cannot help but be bemused by a widespread belief, even in the Soviet Union but especially in Britain and France, that fighters had to have liquid-cooled engines. Properly installed, the air cooled radial was less vulnerable, lighter, offered roughly equal drag, worked better in cold environments, and probably was shorter and thus enhanced dogfight manoeuvrability. Towards the end of the war the British Hawker and Japanese Kawasaki companies were surprised to find the radial engine to be superior, while Yakovlev put an ASh-82FN into a Yak-3 to create – so he told the writer – the best of all the wartime fighters.

Armament

It always amazed the writer that, lacking neither money nor design and development capability, the British and Americans should have fought their greatest war with aircraft guns designed in the First World War. Even stranger, the British selected foreign designs. The Soviet Union, like the Germans, recognised that it is not against the laws of nature to design one's own guns, and try to make them the best in the world.

Thus, designers had a large and growing range of weapons to choose from. In the 1930s the ShKAS was the rifle calibre weapon. This took a 0.30 cal (7.62mm) cartridge fed by a belt at the outstandingly high rate of 1,800 rounds per minute. A British fighter of 1940 with five ShKAS would have had greater hitting power and more strikes per second than with eight Brownings, besides saving over 66lb (30kg) in weight. In 1937 the lightweight Ultra ShKAS fired at 2,700 rounds per minute, a remarkable figure for a single barrel gun, but by this time it was recognised that heavier calibres were needed.

First of the Soviet cannon, and the family of related designs made in the greatest numbers, the 20mm ShVAK was introduced from 1936. The designation came from designers Shpital'nyi and Vladimirov and Aviatsionnyi Krupnokalibre (aviation, large calibre). Again, this gun was dramatically superior to the RAF's ancient Hispano, firing projectiles of the same calibre at approximately the same muzzle velocity, at a higher cyclic rate (800 rounds per minute instead of 650), yet being much more compact and weighing 92.6lb (42kg) compared with 109lb (49.4kg). Variants of this extremely reliable gun were fitted to something like 85% of all Soviet wartime fighters.

To provide an intermediate calibre, the Beresin came into use in 1940. M Ye Beresin quickly developed it as the UBS for synchronized installations, the UBK for wing mounting and also the UBT for bomber turrets. Though it had the same 12.7mm calibre as the '50-calibre' Browning, it weighed only 47lb (21.4kg) compared with 64lb (29kg), and yet fired projectiles weighing 1.7 ounces (48g) at the rate of 1,050 rounds per minute with a muzzle velocity of 2,789ft/sec (850 m/sec), compared with the Browning's 1.1 ounces (33g) projectiles fired at 750 rounds per minute with a muzzle velocity of 2,749 ft/sec (838m/sec).

In the Great Patriotic War the Beresin and the ShVAK were overwhelmingly the most important fighter guns. The main problem was that the small Soviet fighters found it difficult to accommodate them in numbers. In Britain in 1941 it was decided that, where possible, RAF fighters would have six 20mm Hispano cannon. Later in 1941 it was decided that four would be adequate, and this remained standard British fighter armament until 1955. This was impossible with the Soviet fighters until late in the war, when three or four ShVAK, or even three or four of the new 23mm NS-23, were fitted to the La-7 and La-9, but they were the exceptions. The problem was not so much shortage of guns as the fundamental difficulty was installing cannon in the small airframes.

Most of the USSR's wartime fighters powered by a single liquid cooled engine had a cannon fitted in the traditional Hispano-Suiza fashion between the cylinder banks of the engine, with the barrel passing through the reduction gear and propeller shaft. As this meant that the gun's recoil force was on the aircraft centre line, passing close to the centre of gravity, it became possible to install guns of tremendous power.

The first move in this direction was the VYa of 1940, a gun whose power was far greater than the small change in calibre to 23mm suggests. Compared with the 20mm ShVAK, it fired a projectile more than twice as heavy with higher muzzle velocity, at a cyclic rate of 500 rounds per minute. Using AP ammunition, it could pierce 1in (25mm) of armour even at a range of about 0.6 miles (1km).

Soviet leaders always liked bigness, especially in weapons, and before the end of the war various fighters had tested guns of up to 2.24in (57mm) calibre. In my opinion, the awesome 57mm guns were not practical, but the 37mm and 45mm calibres were not only tested but used in action. The main reason for such guns was to destroy tanks, but they were also used in air combat. A single hit on a hostile aircraft, even on a wingtip, was usually enough.

In 1941 the Western Allies were intrigued to hear that Soviet aircraft were attacking tanks with rockets. Such weapons had been developed in the USSR ahead of all other countries, and by 1941 they had been made to fly in a predictable manner, stabilized by spinning about the longitudinal axis. The commonest pattern, the RS-82 (3.23in, 82mm, calibre), was used by the million. Most of the mass-produced Soviet fighters were cleared to launch these weapons, which were on occasion used against enemy aircraft. The Yak-9B even had an internal bomb bay.

I have no hesitation in claiming that this volume, together with the one dealing with twin-engined fighters, attack aircraft and bombers, are the first to cover the Soviet aircraft of the Great Patriotic War comprehensively and without errors.

Lavochkin La-7 with a Polikarpov UTI-4 lead-in trainer behind. *Philip Jarrett collection*

Glossary

A-VMF Aviatsiya Voenno-Morskovo Flota
– Naval Air Force.

B Bombardirovschik – as a prefix, bomber.

BB Blizhnii Bombardirovshchik
– as a prefix, short range bomber.

bis as a suffix, literally from the French or Latin 'again' or encore, more practically, a rethought or developed version, or even Mk.2. The use of this form of designation applied to only a few OKBs, MiG still used this with their MiG-21 jet.

cg Centre of Gravity.

D Dalny – as a suffix, long range.

EI Eksperimentalyni Istrebitel
– experimental fighter.

F Forsirovanny – as a suffix, enhanced, or literally 'boosted'.

GAZ Gosudarstvenny Aviatsionny Zavod
– state aircraft factory.

GKAT Gosudarstvenny Komitet Aviatsionnoi Teknniki
– State Committee for Aviation Equipment.

GKO Gosudarstvenny Komitet Oborony
– State Committee for Defence.

GUPA Glavnoye Upravleniye Aviatsionnoi Promyshlennosti
– Chief Directorate of the Aircraft Industry.

HSU Hero of the Soviet Union.

I Istrebitel – as a prefix, fighter, or 'destroyer'.

IS Istrebitel Skladnoy
– as a prefix, literally 'foldable fighter', see Nikitin, page 84.

ITP Istrebitel Tyazhely Pushechny
– fighter, heavy gun. See also TP.

K Krupnokaliberny
– as a suffix, fitted with large calibre gun.

KOSOS Konstruktorskii Otdel Opytnovo Samolyotostroyeniya
– Experimental Aircraft Design Section.

L Lyukovy – as a suffix, literally 'doors', fitted with an internal bomb bay.

LII Letno-Issledovatel'skii Institut
– Ministry of Aviation Industry Flight Research Institute.

M Modifitsirovanny – as a suffix, modified.
Ministerstvo Aviatsionnoi Promyshlennosti
– Ministry of Aircraft Production.

NII Nauchno Issledovatelyskii Institut
– scientific and research institute.

NKAP Narodny Komissariat Aviatsionnoi Promyshlennosti – State Commissariat for the Aviation Industry Promyshlennosti
– People's Commissariat for Heavy Industry.

NKTP Narodny Komissariat Tyazhyoloi

NKVD Narodny Komissariat Vnutrennikh Del
– People's Commissariat of Internal Affairs.

OGPU Obedinyonnoe Gosudarstvennoe Politischeskoe Upravlenie
– Amalgamated State Political Directorate.

OKB Opytno Konstruktorskoye Byuro
– experimental construction (but in effect, design, see Introduction, page 6) bureau.

P Pushechny – as a suffix, literally 'gunship', high calibre armed fighter.

PVRD Pryamotochnii Vozdushno-Reaktivnii Dvigatel – as a suffix, pulse jet engine.

R Reaktivny – as a suffix, literally, 'reaction' meaning rocket or jet.

ShKAS Shpitalny-Komaritski Aviatsionny Skorostrelny – rapid-firing machine gun (designed by Shpitalny and Komaritski).

ShVAK Shpitalny-Vladimirova Aviatsionnaya Krupnokalibernaya
– large calibre aircraft cannon (design by Shpitalny and Vladimirov).

SK Skorostnii Krylo - high speed wing.

T Tyazhelowooruzhenny
– as a suffix, heavily armed.

TP Tyazhely Pushechny – fighter, heavy gun. See also ITP.

TsAGI Tsentral'nyi Aerogidrodynamichesky Institut – Central Aerodynamic and Hydrodynamic Institute.

TsIAM Tsentral'nyi Institut Aviatsionnogo Motorostoeniya
– Central Institute of Aviation Motors.

TsKB Tsentral'nyi Konstruktorskoye Byuro
– central, ie state, design bureau.

U Uluchshenny – as a suffix, improved.

UT Uchebno-Trenirovochny
– as a suffix, trainer, ie primary trainer.

UTI Uchebno-Trenirovochny Istrebitel
– as a suffix, training fighter.

V Vysotnyi – as a suffix, literally height, or high altitude. See also V - vyvozny.

V Vyvoznoy – as a suffix, introductory, or in Western terms, advanced or conversion trainer. See also V - vysotnyi.

VIAM Vsesoyuzny Institue Aviatsionnykh Materialov – All-Union Institute for Aviation Materials.

VNOS Vozdushnogo Nabludeniya, Opoveshcheniya, Sviazy – Air Observation, Information and Communication Service.

VVS Voenno-vozdushniye Sily
– air forces of the USSR.

Note:
Combinations of suffix letters can be used, eg Yak-9PD, Yak-9TD.
See also Yak-9DD on page 150.

Airframe and Engine Design Bureaux

Accepted abbreviations to denote airframe (surname only used for the abbreviation) or engine design (first name and surname) origin within this volume are as follows:

AM Alexander Mikulin.
ASh Arkadi Shvetsov.
Gu Gudkov, Mikhail (see also LaGG).
Il Ilyushin, Sergei.
La Lavochkin, Semyon.
LaG Lavochkin and Gorbunov, Vladimir.
LaGG Lavochkin, Gorbunov and Gudkov (see also Gu).
MiG Mikoyan, Artyom and Gurevich, Mikhail.
Su Sukhoi, Pavel.
VD Viktor Dobryin.
VK Vladimir Klimov.
Yak Yakovlev, Alexander.

Note:
Nikolay Polikarpov's designs did not carry his abbreviated name as a suffix, except for later versions of the U-2, which became the Po-2. In the perhaps unlikely role as a bomber (in which it was widely used) it is featured in Volume Two.

Notes

Measurements

In the narrative, all measurements are given in Imperial figures (of British FPSR – foot, pound, second, Rankine) and then decimal units (or SI – Système International d'Unités, established in 1960) second in brackets. The states that comprised the Soviet Union embraced the decimal system from the earliest days, although it should be noted that power was measured up to the Great Patriotic War, and beyond, using the established Western horse power measurement. The following explanations may help:

aspect ratio wingspan and chord expressed as a ratio. Low aspect ratio, short, stubby wing; high aspect ratio, long, narrow wing.

ft feet – length, multiply by 0.305 to get metres (m). For height measurements involving service ceilings and cruise heights, the figure has been 'rounded'.

ft² square feet – area, multiply by 0.093 to get square metres (m²).

fuel measured in both gallons/litres and pounds/kilograms. The specific gravity (sg) of Soviet fuel varied considerably during the war and conversions from volume to weight and vice versa are impossible without knowing the sg of the fuel at the time.

gallon Imperial (or UK) gallon, multiply by 4.546 to get litres. (500 Imperial gallons equal 600 US gallons.)

hp horse power – power, measurement of power for piston engines. Multiply by 0.746 to get kilowatts (kW).

kg kilogram – weight, multiply by 2.205 to get pounds (lb).

km/h kilometres per hour – velocity, multiply by 0.621 to get miles per hour (mph).

kW kilowatt – power, measurement of power for piston engines. Multiply by 1.341 to get horse power.

lb pound – weight, multiply by 0.454 to get kilograms (kg). Also used for the force measurement of turbojet engines, with the same conversion factor, as pounds of static thrust.

litre volume, multiply by 0.219 to get Imperial (or UK) gallons.

m metre – length, multiply by 3.28 to get feet (ft).

m² square metre – area, multiply by 10.764 to get square feet (ft²).

mm millimetre – length, the bore of guns is traditionally a decimal measure (eg 30mm) and no Imperial conversion is given.

mph miles per hour – velocity, multiply by 1.609 to get kilometres per hour (km/h).

Russian Language and Transliteration

Russian is a version of the Slavonic family of languages, more exactly part of the so-called 'Eastern' Slavonic grouping, including Russian, White Russian and Ukrainian. As such it uses the Cyrillic alphabet, which is in turn largely based upon that of the Greeks.

The language is phonetic – pronounced as written, or 'as seen'. Translating into or from English gives rise to many problems and the vast majority of these arise because English is not a straightforward language, offering many pitfalls of pronunciation!

Accordingly, Russian words must be translated through into a *phonetic* form of English and this can lead to different ways of helping the reader pronounce what he or she sees.

Every effort has been made to standardise this, but inevitably variations will creep in. While reading from source to source this might seem confusing and/or inaccurate but it is the name as *pronounced* that is the constancy, not the *spelling* of that pronunciation!

The 20th letter of the Russian (Cyrillic) alphabet looks very much like a 'Y' but is pronounced as a 'U' as in the word 'rule'.

Another example, though not taken up in this work, is the train of thought that Russian words ending in 'y' are perhaps better spelt out as 'yi' to underline the pronunciation, but it is felt that most Western speakers would have problems getting their tongues around this!

This is a good example of the sort of problem that some Western sources have suffered from in the past (and occasionally some get regurgitated even today) when they make the mental leap about what they see approximating to an English letter.

Designations of German aircraft

Is it 'Bf' or 'Me' for the Messerschmitt designs? This work has used official documentation and Reichsluftfahrtministerium (RLM – Reich Air Ministry) nomenclature has been adhered to. The RLM transition from 'Bf' to 'Me' occurs between the unsuccessful Bf162 Jaguar (whose number was subsequently allocated to the He162 Volksjäger) and the Me163 Komet; all Messerschmitt types below the RLM number 162 being prefixed 'Bf' and all those from 163 and upwards being prefixed 'Me'.

Design and Illustration considerations

In this work we have utilised our well-proven format, aiming as always to provide a high level of readability and design.

A conscious decision was made to include peripheral details where they appear on the original illustrations; photographs have not been printed across the fold and cropping virtually eliminated.

Unfortunately, in this instance, many of the photographs were obtained from copies of those from official sources and have proved to be lacking in definition and tonal range, and although no effort has been spared to achieve the highest standard of reproduction, priority for inclusion has, of necessity, been given to historical significance over technical perfection.

Overleaf: **The Soviets produced millions of posters and displayed them widely as a constant reminder of the importance of Soviet air power. This particular design, which featured stylised Polikarpov-type aircraft, was released in 1941, just as the Soviet counter-offensive against the German invasion was getting underway. The message translates as 'Glory to the Heroes of the Patriotic War – Glory to Stalin's Falcons'.**

Bereznyak-Isaev

BI

The liquid-propellant rocket motor had been designed in the USSR before the outbreak of the Second World War, and by the early 1940s a number of such powerplants had been developed and were successfully used on rockets. In the spring of 1941 the Viktor Bolkhovitinov Design Bureau began to design an aircraft powered by the D-1-A liquid-propellant rocket motor, which delivered a thrust of 224.1lb (1,100kg) The programme leaders were Alexander Bereznyak and Alexey Isaev.

The extremely high fuel consumption of the rocket motor predetermined the combat application of that aircraft, which was to be an interceptor fighter operating on a ground-alert system. Its high thrust-to-weight ratio endowed it with high speed and climb rates.

To accelerate the design of the interceptor, work on the airframe, armament and engine was conducted in parallel. The airframe was developed and tested in towed flight with the engine inoperative, the armament was tested by pilot Boris Kudrin, and the powerplant was ground tested on a test-bench.

A year after design had begun, the first interceptor fighter was complete. On 15th May 1942 it took off for its first powered flight, with test pilot Captain Grigory Bakhchivandzhi at the controls. Bakhchivandzhi wrote in his re-

port: '...during take-off and in flight the engine operated normally. In-flight engine shut-down did not cause any lateral deviation, and the aircraft performed stable decelerations, gliding and handling like any ordinary aircraft'.

Both the first prototype of the BI (for Bereznyak and Isaev), as it was designated, and the following machines were rocket powered. The interceptor was very light, having an empty weight of 1,774lb (805kg) and a take-off weight of 3,637lb (1,650kg). It was fitted tailplane endplate fins and an additional dorsal fin. There was no unnecessary material used in its structure; this was a true 'austerity' fighter. The fuselage was a fabric covered plywood semi-monocoque structure, of which the fin was an integral part. The wing and tailplane had two wooden spars and plywood skins, while the control surfaces were made of duralumin and fabric covered. Kerosene was used as fuel, with concentrated nitric acid as an oxidiser, the engine being fed by means of high pressure air bottles. A retractable landing gear was fitted, and armament consisted of two 20mm guns in the forward fuselage. The maximum design speed was 559mph (900km/h). The maximum climb rate achieved during the test flights was three times greater than that of the best piston-engined aircraft, and the landing speed was 91.9mph (148km/h). A small batch

of rocket interceptors, designated BI-1, was produced at one of the plants.

A version of the BI with spherical fuel tanks, giving a 30% increase in flight endurance, was also under development, as was another with ramjets installed on the wingtips to double endurance. A version of the BI with an armoured cockpit was developed in early 1943.

On the whole, the flight tests bore out the designers' estimates. However, during a test flight on 27th March 1943, while undergoing horizontal acceleration up to 497mph (800 km/h) at 6,500ft (2,000m), the third prototype entered a dive from which it failed to recover. Captain Grigory Bakhchivandzhi died, and was posthumously made a Hero of the Soviet Union for heroism displayed during the air combats at the beginning of the war and during the testing of the first rocket-powered aeroplane. Testing was continued by Konstantin Gruzdev and Boris Kudrin.

The development and testing of different BI versions allowed the designers to gain valuable experience which was later used in jet fighter design.

For technical data, see Table E, page 177.

A view of the fifth BI, fitted with a retractable ski landing gear.

Top left: **A view of the fifth BI, fitted with a retractable ski landing gear.**

Centre left: **Soviet test pilot Grigory Bakhchivandzhi, giving scale to the BI rocket fighter. Bakhchivandzhi was killed when a BI failed to recover from a dive on 27th March 1943.**

Bottom left and top right: **Two views of the BI experimental fighter, showing nose guns and ski undercarriage.**

Above right: **One of the BI prototypes following a crash-landing.**

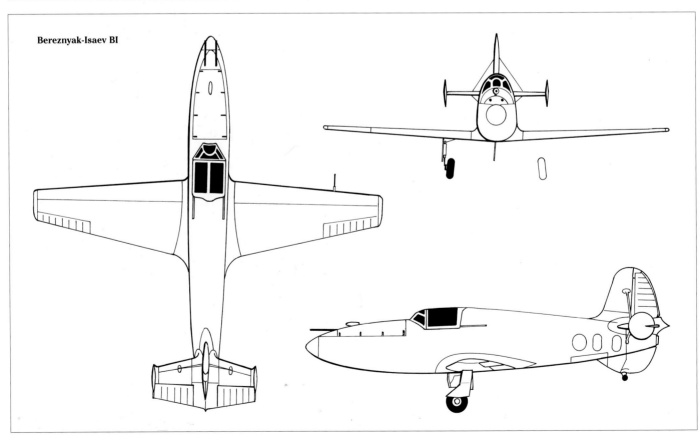

Bereznyak-Isaev BI

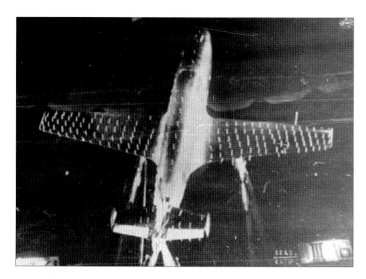

A BI, tufted to show flow patterns, in the Central Aerodynamic and Hydrodynamic Institute (TsAGI) wind tunnel in Moscow.

It was intended to equip the sixth BI with a mixed powerplant with a ramjet engine on each wingtip. TsAGI wind tunnel tests illustrated.

Bisnovat

SK

Two high-speed prototypes were designed and built by a team headed by Matus Bisnovat during 1939-40. The first, designated SK, Skorostnoye Krylo - high speed wing) was intended for flight investigations of different wing configurations and aerodynamic characteristics such as stability and controllability. High speed was obtained with a production 1,100hp (820kW) Klimov M-105 engine and a very clean aerodynamic configuration, with high wing loading and a retractable cockpit canopy which did not protrude above the fuselage contours in flight, but was opened during take-off and landing to form a windshield. The pilot's seat was raised hydraulically to improve his view during these phases.

The aircraft was built in early 1939, and it was tested on a ski undercarriage in February 1940 and on a wheeled one in May. No information regarding the test results has been found, and only the following estimated data is available: maximum speed 370.9mph (597 km/h) at sea level and 441.1mph (710km/h) at 17,200ft (5,250m); service ceiling 34,300ft (10,450m); take-off weight 4,629lb (2,100kg).

Side view of Matus Bisnovat's SK fighter prototype showing the 'buried' cockpit, behind the trailing edge of the comparatively small wing.

Just visible above the leading edge of the wing, the SK's cockpit in landing and take-off mode, with a retractable windshield to protect the pilot when his seat was raised to provide a better view.

SK-2

The second prototype, designated SK-2, was really a back-up aircraft for the first, but had a slightly different structure. It had a conventional cockpit canopy and the same engine installa-

tion and configuration as many of the monoplane fighters of the early 1940s. It was planned to arm the SK-2 with a pair of 12.7mm UBS synchronised machine guns and thus convert it into a fighter. Such a version was tested, but due to the series production of Lavochkin/

Gorbunov/Gudkov, Mikoyan-Gurevich and Yakovlev fighters the SK-2 remained only a prototype. It is known that it underwent flight testing at the Letno-Issledovatel'skii Institut (LII – Ministry of Aviation Industry Flight Research Institute) in the winter of 1940-41.

At a take-off weight of 5,070lb (2,300kg) without armament it had a maximum speed of 363.5mph (585km/h) at sea level and 410.1 mph (660km/h) at 16,000ft (4,900m), the SK-2 climbed to 16,400ft (5,000m) in 4 minutes 20 seconds. All of the test flights were conducted by G Shiyanov.

For technical data, see Table E, page 177.

Above left: **Trials were undertaken with skis replacing the retractable undercarriage on the SK.**

Left and above right: **Two views of the SK-2, with a more conventional cockpit placed even further back on the fuselage. Unlike the SK, the SK-2 was armed with a pair of 12.7mm BS machine guns.**

Borovkov-Florov

I-207

In 1935 young engineers Alexey Borovkov and Ilya Florov proposed an original biplane fighter, and this was produced in 1937 as the 'Type 7211'. Later, in 1938-39, new biplane fighter based on this machine and designated I-207 (I - istrebitel, fighter, or literally 'destroyer') was developed.

By the spring of 1939 the two prototypes had been built, the first powered by a 900hp (671kW) Shvetsov M-62 and the second by an M-63 of the same power. The third prototype, powered by an ungeared M-63, was ready by the autumn. The first two had a fixed undercarriage, while the third had retractable gear. All three had open cockpits.

In the spring of 1941 the fourth I-207 prototype, powered by a geared M-63 and fitted with an enclosed cockpit with a sideward-hinged canopy was completed. All of these aircraft had four 7.62mm ShKAS machine guns, and two 551lb (250kg) bombs could be carried beneath the lower wings.

When tested, they bettered the Polikarpov

I-15 biplane and I-16 monoplane in climb rate and service ceiling, and were superior in manoeuvrability to the I-15 but inferior to the I-16. During flight tests in 1940 the third prototype reached a speed of 301mph (486km/h) at 17,400ft (5,300m), which for that period was inadequate. Moreover the configuration was also out of date, and for these reasons the type did not go into production.

For technical data, see Table E, page 176.

Front view of the second prototype I-207 showing the exceptionally clean lines and the unbraced biplane wing.

Above: **The second prototype Borovkov-Florov I-207 with open cockpit and fixed undercarriage.**

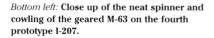

Right: **The third prototype I-207 featured retractable undercarriage. Note the bombs carried underwing.**

Bottom left: **Close up of the neat spinner and cowling of the geared M-63 on the fourth prototype I-207.**

Bottom right: **Main undercarriage on the fourth prototype I-207. Retraction was upwards into the fuselage sides.**

Gudkov

Gu-37 / Gu-1

In 1940 well-known designer and engineer Mikhail Gudkov began design of the Gu-37 (later re-designated Gu-1), which was to have the water-cooled Mikulin AM-37 engine. Its configuration was similar to that of American Bell P-39 Airacobra, with a nosewheel undercarriage and the powerplant mounted behind the cockpit, driving the propeller via a long shaft and gearbox. The 20mm diameter shaft also doubled as the cannon barrel. The Gu-37's structure was mixed, but wood pre-dominated. The forward fuselage was a welded truss of steel tubes with duralumin skinning, while the rear fuselage, wing, and tail were made of wood, although the wing centre section spars were metal. The wing had a automatic slats and the main radiators were also mounted in the wing. An intermediate water/air cooler with a separate surface intended for cooling the centrifugal blower was mounted between the engine cylinders. The oil coolers were installed in the engine bay on both sides of the fuselage over the wing. The armament consisted of Ya Taubin 37mm cannon provided with 81 rounds, firing through the propeller boss, and six fuselage and wing-mounted machine guns.

Upon completion the fighter was painted red and buffed to a high gloss finish, and on 12th June 1943 test pilot A Nikashin took it on its maiden flight, which ended in disaster. After a long take-off run the aircraft climbed to 650ft (200m), stalled and dived into the ground, killing the pilot. As a result, all development work on the Gu-37 was halted.

For technical data, see Table E, page 177.

Ilyushin

Above and below: **Two views of the Ilyushin Il-2I anti-bomber fighter - during state trials at the NII VVS in the summer of 1943.** *Opposite page:* **The Il-1, a refined and improved follow-up to the Il-2I.**

Il-2I

Of all the many and varied duties performed by Sergei Ilyushin's Il-2 attack aircraft during the war, the most unusual was its operation as a fighter. While this large Soviet attack aircraft was inferior to the Messerschmitt Bf109 and Focke-Wulf Fw190 in dogfights, it outperformed all other Luftwaffe aircraft. At the very beginning of the war Luftwaffe front line units equipped with the Henschel Hs126 suffered most of all from the ravages of Il-2s, and they often attacked close formations of Junkers Ju87 dive bombers, knowing that the 7.92mm machine guns of the German aircraft were ineffective against the Soviet armoured attack aircraft. Once their close formations were broken up and their concentration of fire was lost, the Ju87s became easy prey to Soviet fighters and even to Il-2s.

In the winter of 1941-1942 Il-2s were used against Luftwaffe transport aircraft, and became the most dangerous threat to the Junkers Ju52 tri-motor. The initiative was held by the pilots of the 33rd Guard Attack Air Regiment, but no less successful were the Il-2s operated against German transport aircraft near Stalingrad. Their targets were not only Ju52s but also the Heinkel He111s and Focke-Wulf Fw200s which supplied the German troops encircled in that region.

As a result of the combat experience thus accumulated, the government decided to initiate production of a fighter version of the Il-2, and in response to a request by the State Defence Committee, Sergei Ilyushin's team produced a modified Il-2I anti-bomber fighter (I - istrebitel, fighter, or literally 'destroyer'). This was a single-seat Il-2 powered by a Mikulin AM-38F engine, modified from a production two-seater as produced by a majority of the aircraft factories.

The ShKAS machine guns, internal bomb load and the attachment points for rocket launchers were removed, leaving only two VYa guns, each provided with 150 rounds and having a weight of fire of 4.0kg/sec. This was considerably greater than the firepower of all the modern Soviet production fighters. Moreover, each of the Il-2I's external bomb racks could carry bombs of up to 551lb (250kg).

In July-August 1943 the Il-2I underwent state trials at the Air Force Nauchno Issledovatelyskii Institut (NII - scientific and research institute) under the charge of pilot Major A Dolgov and engineer V Kholopov. Compared with the two-seater, the perfor-

mance of the updated single-seat aircraft was slightly better, the speed having increased by 8.6 to 11mph (14 to 18km/h). It was noted that the Il-2I could be used against some types of low speed bomber and transport aircraft at altitudes up to 13,000ft (4,000m).

Bearing in mind that the Junkers Ju88 and Dornier Do217 high speed bombers could be successfully attacked by Il-2s only by chance, and that the aircraft's attack capabilities were inferior to those of the standard Il-2, the commander-in-chief of the Voenno-vozdushniye Sily (VVS - air forces of the USSR) considered its further production unnecessary.

Il-1

To counter the latest high speed German bombers and fighters the Ilyushin Bureau designed a new aircraft, the Il-1 armoured low and medium altitude single-seat fighter. It

had an estimated maximum speed of 372 mph (600km/h) and sufficient manoeuvrability to allow it to engage in dogfights with Bf109s and Fw190s.

In accordance with a government decision the Il-1 was designed to have the new AM-42 liquid-cooled engine designed by the Alexander Mikulin Design Bureau, delivering 2,000 hp (1,492kW) at take-off. The pilot's position, engine, engine cooling and lubrication systems and fuel tanks had to be armoured like those of the Il-2I.

From the outset Sergei Ilyushin did not agree with the concept of a dedicated armoured fighter, and the Il-1 was therefore designed to be capable of the additional role of a high speed and manoeuvrable attack aircraft. The main design object was to make it aerodynamically efficient, and this was achieved by using high speed aerofoil sections of different thicknesses; the deepest in the wing centre section, where the wheels of the main undercarriage retracted, and the shallowest

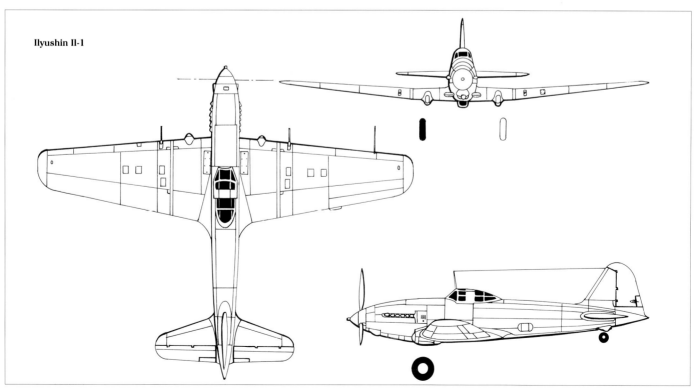

Ilyushin Il-1

in the detachable outer wing panels. Considerable attention was paid to improving the shape of the armoured fuselage, and this was achieved by housing the water and oil coolers in the fuselage, behind the front spar of the wing centre section. Cooling air was passed through the fuselage and emitted through a controllable slot in the fuselage underside, the size of the opening being regulated in accordance with the engine's operating mode. Consequently the fuselage contours were smoother than those of the Il-2, and the dimensions of the coolers were reduced.

A new system was devised for the main undercarriage legs, which retracted rearwards into the wing centre section, the wheels turn-

ing through 90° during retraction. As a result the drag of the undercarriage fairings was greatly reduced compared with those of the Il-2. Overall, drag was reduced by 30%.

The Il-1 had metal wings and empennage, while its tail was made of wood. Its attack armament was similar to that of the Il-2I, but its tail was protected from hostile fighter attacks by an AG-2 aerial grenade launcher. After release the grenades exploded while suspended beneath a parachute, damaging the attacking fighter. The Il-1 had no bomb load.

Test pilot Vladimir Kokkinaki undertook the maiden flight of the Il-1 on 19th May 1944. During production tests at 11,728lb (5,320kg) it reached a speed of 360mph (580km/h) at

10,700ft (3,260m). Its manoeuvrability was good; it took only 20 seconds to complete a 360° turn and climbed 3,000ft (900m) in a combat turn. All manoeuvres were performed smoothly and easily.

Although it was a worthy challenger to the German aircraft, the Il-1 could not compete with the new generation of aircraft that appeared in summer of 1944, such as the Lavochkin La-7 and the Yakovlev Yak-3 and -9U.

For technical data, see Table E, page 177.

Kozlov

EI

In 1939 the new EI (Eksperimentalyni Istrebitel – experimental fighter) single-seat prototype was designed by Sergei Kozlov's team in the Nikolay Zhukovskii Air Force Engineering Academy in Moscow. The EI was a low wing monoplane with a variable incidence wing, and it was intended to install Alexander Mikulin's new M-107 engine, which was still under design at that time. The aircraft was not completed by the agreed time, and because of the start of the evacuation of Moscow in mid-October 1941 it was destroyed together with its drawings.

Lavochkin

The destiny of one of three fighters put into series-production in the Soviet Union before the Second World War was unusual. Vladimir Gorbunov was chief of one of the departments of the People's Commissariat of the Aircraft Industry and because of his position took part in many meetings and was well informed of the situation in the aircraft industry. His concept, forwarded in 1939, was an aircraft having an all-wood structure, realising the necessity of greatly increasing the output of combat fighters as soon as possible, and the limitations that might be imposed on this process by the lack of aluminium. 'Even if only one small grove of trees is left in Russia,' thought Gorbunov, 'even then we shall be able to build fighters.'

The main contributor to the design study for the new aircraft was Semyon Lavochkin, who carried out the work under Gorbunov's direction. He had already gained extensive practical experience when working under of P Rishar, Vladimir Chizhevsky and Dmitry Grigorovich.

During the preparation of conceptual studies one more engineer from the department of the People's Commissariat of the Aircraft Industry, Mikhail Gudkov, joined in the research, thus creating a triumvirate of aircraft designers. In the spring of 1939 the group reported the results of their work to the then People's Commissar of the Aircraft Industry, M Kaganovich, who is often criticised, not without good reason, for making incompetent decisions. This time he very quickly realised the advantages of the design. After receiving his approval, Vladimir Gorbunov, Mikhail Gudkov and Semyon Lavochkin were appointed the heads of a newly established Opytno Konstruktorskoye Byuro (OKB - experimental design bureau) in May 1939.

The use in the aircraft's structure of a material hitherto unavailable in the USSR, a phenol-impregnated modified wood similar to wood plastic which had been examined during investigations of German wooden propellers, was to give impetus to the new fighter. At that time Leonty Ryzhkov, the chief engineer of the propeller and ski production plant in Kuntsevo, a district of Moscow, had been developing a process for the fabrication of modified wood impregnated with birch veneer tar. Such impregnation made wood heavier, much stronger and more fire-resistant. The co-designers of the project offered to use the modified wood for primary load-bearing structural elements such as the wing spar caps and fuselage longerons, where its use promised certain advantages compared with ordinary wood.

The interests of Ryzhkov and the triumvirate coincided, and it was therefore no surprise that the Kuntsevo plant became the first production facility of the new design bureau. The project approved by the People's Commissariat could be considered only a conceptual design. Only the centre of gravity (cg) position had been calculated and the maximum speeds were estimated; the prospect of the intensive task ahead had resulted in the establishment of the nucleus of the future design bureau. The personnel of this bureau were largely those of the A Silvanskii OKB, reformed after the failure of the I-220 fighter.

Eventually the conceptual design was completed and generally approved. In late June 1939 the Government had already issued a decree calling for the urgent manufacture of two prototypes of the new fighter. To accomplish this, an appropriate production plant was required, as the Kuntsevo factory was totally unsuitable for aircraft production.

Plant No.301 (GAZ - state aircraft factory), to which the new bureau was transferred, had not been set up for aircraft production either, having formerly been a factory making furniture for the Palace of the Soviets. The plant was already re-oriented in 1938, and was preparing to manufacture variously modified Caudron aircraft under a French licence. To set up the necessary engineering for these aircraft, an OKB headed by A Dubrovin had been established there.

When Gorbunov, Gudkov and Lavochkin arrived at GAZ-301 in the summer of 1939, the programme for the French licence-built aircraft had been cancelled and Dubrovin had been sent to Kharkov. However, most of the design bureau staff were retained and joined the design programme for the new fighter. Plant director Yu Eskin made an effective contribution to this work.

I-301 (LaGG-1)

The final version of the preliminary design, designated 'Type K', was approved by the Nauchno Issledovatelyskii Institut Voenno-vozdushniye Sily (NII VVS – scientific and research institute of the air forces of the USSR) in January 1940. While the aircraft was under construction it was referred to in documents as a 'high-speed armed fighter with structure featuring compressed wood', but after it was approved by the design bureau of Plant No.301 it was given the designation I-301, effectively fighter from GAZ-301 (I - istrebitel, fighter, or literally 'destroyer'). The I-22 fighter, to which reference has been made in previous accounts, is not mentioned at all in contemporary documents, and it can be argued that it never existed.

Design studies of the I-301 advanced with difficulty. Although the bureau had 93 workers in December 1939, it was still disorganised. Unlike the Yakovlev OKB it had not gained experience by producing trainers, and it did not enjoy the support of a production plant, like Mikoyan's OKB. Other designers were using used new and advanced components, but in the case of OKB-301 the aircraft's basic structural material was still experimental, not having been tried under normal conditions for any length of time.

There were unavoidable conflicts between the three leaders; frequently their decisions were far from being mutually agreed. For example, in the course of manufacturing the aircraft, Gudkov insisted on a metal tailplane, and other problems arose during the work. For this reason the Administration of the People's Commissariat urged that one of the three designers be appointed to take responsibility. Semyon Lavochkin was chosen as being the most competent.

Development of the aircraft was difficult. The VIAM-B-3 adhesive used was still in the experimental stage, and produced an unpleasant surprise. It contained much phenolic acid and irritated workers' skin. Extensive and urgent work was carried out at Plant No.301 by the All-Union Aircraft Materials Development Institute (VIAM), and the necessary handling instructions for the adhesive were drawn up.

There were also pleasant surprises. The new adhesive made it unnecessary to fit surfaces precisely, even allowing a clearance of up to ⅛in (3mm), as it penetrated deep into pinewood and the strength of bonded joints proved to be high.

The fighter was completed in March 1940, about 12 months after the work had begun. The I-301 was aerodynamically clean, and was covered with deep cherry paint and polished to a lustre finish. I Rabkin, NII VVS chief engineer, recalled: 'The open-work wooden parts of the I-301's structure looked durable and fine at the same time. They were a pleasure to behold owing to their design and the harmonious combination of their elements, and perhaps because of this they did not appear strong, though in reality they were'.

The I-301 was a single-seat, low wing monoplane. Its fuselage was a wooden semi-monocoque structure, skinned with birch veneer and plywood, like the wings. Phenol-impregnated modified wood was mainly used for the wing spars and local re-inforce-ment of the structure. The two spar wing comprised a centre section attached to the fuselage and two detachable outer panels. Three self-sealing fuel tanks were located between the spars of the centre section and the panels. Riveted metal split flaps and ailerons with a metal framework and fabric covering, like the elevators and rudder, were arranged in the wing trailing edge. The tailplane included two panels attached to the fuselage. Armament consisted of a Ya Taubin MP-6 23mm cannon mounted in the 'vee' of the engine cylinders and two synchronised M Berezin 12.7mm large calibre machine guns. Later, this armament was supplemented by two ShKAS 7.62mm synchronised machine guns installed beneath the engine.

The I-301's structure was well designed, and its airworthiness as a fighter seemed to cause no special concern. Perhaps no modern designs have undergone so many investigations and checks, but in many instances unfortunate events have revealed unforeseen shortcomings!

Successful completion of a task always requires an element of luck. In OKB-301's case it was undoubtedly associated with the appointment of A Nikashin, a leading engineering test pilot, to conduct the manufacturer's tests. He performed his task very well, and the

The first I-301 was painted in a deep cherry red colour. Its clean lines are evident.

Two views of the I-301 prototype following the accident of 11th August 1940.

personnel led by Semyon Lavochkin became much obliged to this short, reserved man; a great professional and a pilot with a high degree of engineering knowledge.

The first flight of the I-301 fighter prototype was made on 30th March 1940. Having performed several more flights, Nikashin found the behaviour of the aircraft satisfactory and its handling simple and within the capabilities of pilots of average and below average skill. Failures were inevitable during these flights (the engine had to be removed twice, the hydraulic system failed three times), but there were no serious accidents. On 1st May 1940 the I-301 was among other new Soviet aircraft taking part in the flying parade over Moscow's Red Square.

The flight tests proceeded at a good pace, and were completed on 12th June. Two days later the aircraft was sent for its official state tests, for which M Tarakanovsky was assigned leading engineer and Peotr Stefanovsky and Stepan Suprun were to be the pilots. During these tests, at a flying weight of 6,543lb (2,968kg), the fighter attained 320mph (515

km/h) at sea level and 363.5mph (585km/h) at 15,400ft (4,700m), and it reached 16,400ft (5,000m) in 5.85 minutes.

Analysing the results, Tarakanovsky noted that the I-301's service ceiling was 330ft (100m) less than that of the Yakovlev fighter prototype tested shortly before. It transpired that the area of the I-301's inlet pipe opening was too small, and Lavochkin agreed to enlarge it. In addition, the exhaust pipes were reworked, the flaps were locked (for one flight), and the radiator shutters were closed completely. As a result the aircraft attained a speed of 375.9mph (605km/h) at 16,250ft (4,950m), making the I-301 the fastest Soviet aircraft powered by the Klimov M-105.

The flight tests of the I-301 prototype lasted only ten flying days, during which 42 flights were made. Many defects and problems were eliminated, but many others were left as they were owing to a lack of time. The fighter's spinning and diving characteristics were

not examined, and despite the efforts of armament engineer V Berezin its weapons system was not improved. It was decided to proceed with updating and developing the I-301 while simultaneously building a small batch of 25 to 30 aircraft for operational trials. The prototype's test report concluded:

'In terms of design, the problem of creating an aircraft utilising re-inforced wood has been mainly solved in the I-301. People's Commissariat of the Aircraft Industry Alexey Shakhurin is requested to ask the Commissariat to devote more attention to the problem of refining, testing and building the I-301.'

Although the new fighter was obviously of interest to the Red Army Air Force, 115 defects and deficiencies, not including the armament, were detected, 14 of them being eliminated during the tests. Among the main faults mentioned in report were:

• the cockpit was hot,
• the canopy transparency was substandard,
• the stick forces when operating the ailerons and elevators were too great,
• longitudinal stability was inadequate,
• at the aircraft's flying weight the wheel loads were limited, preventing normal operation of the undercarriage.

Development work continued. An accident occurred on 11th August 1940, when the low sun dazzled Nikashin during a landing and the aircraft was seriously damaged. It was decided to speed up construction of the second example while the first prototype was repaired. On 2nd October 1940, as both aircraft were about to be rolled out, the government issued an edict that all new fighters should have a range of 621 miles (1,000km). One of the bureau's leading designers, Semyon Alexeyev, remembered how this decree shocked the personnel. Reworking the aircraft might delay the work by several months and give their competitors an unassailable lead. It was not easy to modify the fuel system on the aircraft already built, but, led by Yuly Sturtsel, the team resolved the problem in the best possible way. Two torsion boxes accommodating additional fuel tanks were incorporated in the detachable outer wing panels.

Although this modification was prepared for production aircraft, it was impossible to incorporate it in the prototype because static tests of the reworked wing were required. This would have taken about two months, but the time could not be spared. An additional tank of about 3.29 gallons (15 litres) capacity was therefore positioned behind the pilot's cockpit on the second prototype, the fuel from this tank flowing into the three tank fuel system by gravity. In accordance with the wishes of the designers, the Air Force officials took into account the results of a flight made on 29th October 1940, and believed that the aircraft's range met the Government requirements.

Things now moved extremely rapidly. The fighter designers were summoned, together with the test pilots, by G Malenkov, the People's Commissar for Foreign Affairs, who immediately reported the main results of their work to Stalin. It was at once decided to start production of the I-301. Since all aircraft were given new designations at that time, the I-301 was redesignated LaGG-1, using the first letters of the chief designers' names. The improved version with increased fuel capacity was designated LaGG-3. Not a single LaGG-1 was built, as all of the plants began producing the upgraded version from the outset.

LaGG-3

The design triumvirate was now broken up. Semyon Lavochkin was moved, together with the majority of the bureau personnel, to the Gorkii plant (No.21), which became the major LaGG-3 production centre. Vladimir Gorbunov became chief designer at Plant No.31 in Tbilisi, where production of the aircraft was also planned. Mikhail Gudkov was supposed to stay in Moscow and become chief designer for OKB-301, initially being

tasked with designing a 37mm cannon for installation on the LaGG-3.

The decision to put the LaGG-3 into quantity production dictated an acceleration of the development work associated with the prototypes. Using the first I-301 prototype, Nikashin investigated the aircraft's behaviour in a dive and began testing the armament and a new navigation instrument, a recently installed radio compass. But on 4th January 1941 an in-flight failure of the engine's main bearings forced the pilot to make an emergency landing away from the airfield, as a result of which the aircraft was badly damaged. It was decided not to repair it.

For some time development proceeded with the second prototype, but further work using this machine was then deemed inexpedient because it had a single-spar wing, while series-production aircraft were being given a two-spar wing similar to that installed on the first prototype. It was therefore decided to use the first production aircraft for further development work.

The first production fighter was produced by Leningrad Plant No.23, which had previously manufactured Alexander Yakovlev's light aircraft. To organise the manufacture of production aircraft some of the design bureau workers, led by S Umansky, were sent to Leningrad. People worked very hard, and in

December 1940 Nikashin took the first production aircraft into the air. As soon as series-built aircraft made by Plant No.23 began to be used operationally they suffered from engine overheating, radiator and hydraulic system leakages and breakage of connecting rods. However, because only a small batch of LaGGs was produced there, the aerodynamics and standard of surface finish were higher than at the major plant in Gorkii.

Great help in eliminating defects and improving the production process was given to Plant No.23 by specialists of the aeronautical engineering service of the Leningrad Military District, under the leadership of the chief engineer of the 7th Air Defence Corps, M Plakhov, and by S Muratov, the senior engineer for the maintenance of fighter aircraft on the Northern Front. The faults were gradually eliminated, and deliveries of the new aircraft to fighter air regiments began.

The 19th Fighter Air Regiment, at Gorelovo, was the first to receive the 'Leningrad' fighters, and LaGG-3s were then delivered to the 157th Fighter Air Regiment assigned to Leningrad Air Defence. These aircraft, led by Regiment Commander Major V Shtoff, protected the Baltic Fleet from German air raids on 24th September 1941.

Load testing a LaGG-3 at TsAGI.

A LaGG-3 undergoing static testing at TsAGI.

The LaGGs managed to break up the enemy formations and thus prevent pinpoint bombing. During the combat Shtoff's aircraft was hit, and he was unable able to fly his crippled aircraft back to Soviet territory. Being an ethnic German, Shtoff was quickly accused of espionage in those suspicious times, and only after the war did it become known that he had been executed by the fascists after refusing a tempting offer to collaborate.

Production of the LaGG-3 in Leningrad did not last long. The sweep of the enemy towards the city on the Neva River made it an urgent necessity to evacuate the plant to Novosibirsk, where LaGG production was not reinstated. A total of 54 were built by Plant No.23, the backlog of aircraft in the factory were used to repair LaGGs in besieged Leningrad. Besides the plants already mentioned, one began setting up the manufacture of LaGG-3s in Novosibirsk, Tallinn and Dnepropetrovsk. It was planned to build 2,960 LaGGs by the end of 1941, more than twice the number of Yaks scheduled to be produced in the same period, and more than half of them were to be produced in Gorkii.

Semyon Lavochkin and his colleagues were not received very cordially at Gorkii Plant No.21. The workers there had hoped to built the I-21 fighter designed under the supervision of Nikolay Polikarpov's Deputy at this plant, Mikhail Pashinin, who had tried to incorporate in his aircraft most of the components of the Polikarpov I-16, which had been produced at Gorkii for the last six years.

Within the first month the Lavochkin OKB personnel had gained the workers' favour and made them enthusiastic about the new aircraft, to the great credit of Semyon Lavochkin, who seemed unaccustomed to the role of chief designer. 'Semyon Lavochkin, being a man of rare self-control, never raised his voice to anyone; nor did he use sharp words to anybody,' wrote People's Commissar of the Aircraft Industry Alexey Shakhurin. 'He did not lose his temper in the most critical situations, and considerable culture and good breeding were seen in everything. His appearance demanded respect'.

The problems entailed in mastering production of the new type were great, requiring radical changes in the production process, which had been geared to manufacturing the I-16. Woodworking processes had to be increased from the 10% of the total work required for 'Donkey' production to 36% for the LaGG-3s, and processes using duralumin decreased from 32% to 12%. Demand for bench carpenters increased at least threefold.

The principal task was the successful retraining of the skilled workers to make them familiar with the new and strange technology involved in the use of phenol-impregnated modified wood, an insufficiently known material. In addition, new shops with suitable equipment and tools had to be set up.

In January 1941 the main LaGG-3 assembly line occupied only half of Plant No.21. The last I-16 Type 29 was being completed in the other half, where a second line was under preparation for assembly of the LaGGs that were to succeed the I-16s, under the manufacturer's designation Type 31.

The first Gorkii-built LaGG-3 made its maiden flight on 23rd January 1941. After short flight test programme, the pre-production fighter was sent to complete the delayed acceptance flight tests, and from February to April the test team of Tarakanovsky, Nikashin and Berezin, mentioned previously, determined the aircraft's diving and spinning characteristics, tested its armament and special equipment, and also studied engine temperatures. Improvements in the handling qualities could not offset a weight increase of about 880lb (400kg), and engine overheating was worse for production aircraft in winter than for the prototype in summer, which made normal operation of the aircraft impossible.

There were also quite a number of problems with the armament. The MP-6 cannon mounted on the I-301 prototype and developed under the leadership of Ya Taubin and M Baburin was promising, but its recoil force proved to be 2.5 times greater than that guar-

anteed by the designers. All of the attachment fittings for the cannon failed, and it could not be installed in the 'vee' of the engine cylinders as intended. It was replaced by Berezin's 12.7mm large calibre machine gun in the first production batches.

Just before the war, several LaGG-3s were subjected to flight tests at the NII VVS, but these were interrupted by serious defects. First a landing gear breakage caused an accident, then the cockpit hood tore off. Fortunately the skill of the test pilots prevented disaster. Only the pre-production aircraft flown by Peotr Stefanovsky completed the flight tests. It transpired that the aircraft's maximum speed had fallen to 357mph (575 km/h) at 16,400ft (5,000m), and it took 6.8 minutes to reach that altitude. Even more unfortunately, degradation of engine performance and the hydraulic system had greatly reduced the fighter's combat capability. The test team also noted inadequate surface finishing on the production aircraft.

As already mentioned, neither the personnel nor the chief designer had any experience in the production of combat aircraft. Shortly after the LaGG-3 was put into production, revision of the drawings began. In February 1941 2,228 changes were introduced, most pertaining to the structure. Justifiable comments and claims snowballed. Meanwhile, operational units of the Soviet Air Force started mastering the new and 'raw' fighter.

This was preceded by a visit of Inspector General of People's Commissariat of Defence, I Lakeyev to the Gorkii aircraft factory. The General had been the first to become familiar with the LaGG-3, and was preparing to convert pilots of the 24th Fighter Air Corps to the aircraft.

Next morning, the aircraft assembled and sent to the regiment were lying on the hangar floor with their undercarriages retracted. The spontaneous collapsing of the landing gear concerned flight and maintenance personnel, for such a defect could have caused serious accidents if it had manifested itself during take-off or landing instead of in the hangar. It was found that the hydraulic locks were unfit for use, and the components were reworked at Lavochkin's request.

During the type's first month of operation many manufacturing and design defects were revealed. More than a few problems were caused by spontaneous folding of the tailwheel leg during landing, accompanied by breakage of the entire tailwheel-to-frame attachment fitting.

Gross negligence during manufacture occurred on more than one occasion, aircraft being delivered with rags in pipelines and rods, nuts, bolts, etc left loose in the structure. Development was difficult because it had to be carried out using dozens of aircraft that

Above and below: **Two views of LaGG-3 No.3121715, produced at Plant No.21, undergoing tests at NII VSS during August-September 1941. Note the mass balance on the top of the rudder.**

had been serving with VVS units, all of the machines being of different operational status.

Twenty-four pilots were drilled and trained at the 24th Fighter Air Regiment at Lyubertsy, a small site near Moscow, within a month. Flying solo, they were able to take-off, land, circle and perform elementary flying. There was no time for more advanced training.

Putting the LaGG-3 into production at Taganrog (GAZ-31) involved great difficulties. When he arrived there, Vladimir Gorbunov observed a bias towards a wide use of duralumin which he attributed to the previous manufacture of the Amtorg GST (licence-built Consolidated Catalina), Chyetverikov MDR-6, Beriev KOR-1 flying-boats and other aircraft. Gorbunov encountered the same problems as Lavochkin. Initially, thousands of changes to drawings and manufacturing processes were arriving at Plant No.31 from the major, Gorkii plant. There were no raw materials and, therefore, no finished articles. The plant delivered its first fighter in March, and was able to deliver one aircraft per day two months later. All of Gorbunov's attempts to introduce his changes into the aircraft's structure were vigorously opposed at that time by the leaders of the State Commissariat, who thought it would not be possible to unify assemblies and parts, even in the future.

The production rate was increased in May, and in August the plant delivered 130 combat aircraft, almost as many as in the whole of the previous period. At that time Colonel E Kondrat, a senior Soviet Air Force check pilot in North Caucasia, was tasked with forming a regiment of Taganrog LaGGs to conduct service tests of the aircraft and convert pilots who had previously flown other fighter types. While defending the skies over Rostov-on-Don, Kondrat had become the first to shoot down a Luftwaffe Junkers Ju88 reconnaissance aircraft.

As chief designer at Plant No.31, Gorbunov visited the regiment almost daily. He suggested that the pilots should test the first lightened LaGG-3s designed by him, but the trials ended in tragedy when test pilot V Guzin was unable to escape from his aircraft when its fuselage broke in two while he was pulling out of a dive and into a climb. Despite this fatal accident, Gorbunov persisted in his attempts to continue the production of LaGGs.

The mastering of LaGG-3 production in Novosibirsk was delayed. By the time the war with Germany broke out, GAZ No.153, named after Chkalov, had not built a single aircraft, and when deliveries to operational units finally began, the aircraft proved to be of the worst quality. Early in November Soviet Army Air Force Commander Pavel Zhigarev was informed by the 19th Reserve Fighter Air Regiment, where the Novosibirsk LaGGs were being introduced, that the fighters 'could only circle, and not a single one could be cleared to fly to the combat area'. At that period LaGG-3s produced by the other plants were quite well constructed.

The Novosibirsk plant was to become a giant aircraft factory. Its equipment, especially for woodworking, was continually built up, mainly because other plants were moved there from Kiev, Dnepropetrovsk, Leningrad and Moscow to be merged and put into operation as new buildings were completed. The factory soon became the largest within the Commissariat of the Aircraft Industry.

Meanwhile, production of LaGGs accelerated. By 1st April 1941 43 (all produced by the main manufacturer, the Gorkii Aircraft Plant, except for five from Leningrad and one from Taganrog) had entered service, and by 1st May 124 had been delivered. But the bulk of the aircraft were still in the factories, having defects remedied. Production was also impeded because the major Gorkii plant did not always have time to send revised drawings to the subcontractors so that production could be standardised.

In addition to the 24th Fighter Air Regiment, the 19th Fighter Air Regiment at Gorelovo also began converting to the LaGG-3.

The poorly finished external surfaces, non-retractable tailwheels and external radio masts of series-produced aircraft had a detrimental effect on maximum speed, which was at least 31mph (50km/h) less than the prototype I-301, while the take-off run was at least 1,640ft (500m), compared with 1,164ft (355m) for the prototype. The climb rate was reduced by 50%. Another deficiency was severe vibration at diving speeds greater than 372.8mph (600km/h), a result of poor workmanship, inadequate standards of assembly and a change in the wing centre section contours to take larger wheels. The diving speed had to be limited as a consequence. Then numerous defects were discovered in the bonding points of the load-carrying elements of the wing, requiring alteration of the manufacturing process and repair of the aircraft already completed.

A summary of the LaGG's initial introduction into service was given by the Soviet Air Force Commander-in-Chief, Lieutenant General Pavel Zhigarev, in a letter sent to Stalin on

Top: **A LaGG-3 built by Plant No.31 following a crash-landing in August 1941.**

Above left: **Another No.31-built LaGG-3, the worse for wear in September 1941.**

Above right: **LaGG-3 from the fourth batch of Plant No.21 during tests in the late summer of 1941 with eight RS-82 rockets underwing .**

24th May 1941. He said that, although 593 fighters had been scheduled for delivery to re-equip 14 regiments, only 158 had actually been delivered, and only 39 of these had reached the regiments, the rest needing modifications. A total of 66 pilots were flying LaGGs. The fighter was not difficult for service pilots to master, and they considered it more tractable than the Mikoyan-Gurevich MiG-3. However, the outstanding major defects and constant failures of LaGG-3s led Zhigarev to suggest that a series of regiments should be equipped with MiG-3s instead. It can be confidently stated that no other aircraft type has ever been so greatly affected by problems with the initiation of production as the creation of Lavochkin, Gorbunov and Gudkov. It is no wonder that, by the beginning of the war, these fighters were still not on the inventory of the Air Command of the five western frontier districts of the USSR.

In the early war period no other combat aircraft had problems as serious as those of the LaGG-3. Neither of the air regiments converting to the fighter was combat capable before July 1941, and as soon as it entered service a major and dangerous handling deficiency became apparent; namely a tendency to stall unexpectedly. According to pilots the fighter behaved like a restive horse. All of a sudden, against its pilot's will, the aircraft would abruptly adopt a high angle of attack, the wing would immediately lose its lift, and stability would be lost. In July, four fatal accidents and seven incidents occurred with LaGGs in Soviet Air Force operational units. There were many accidents at Seima airfield, where a recently formed reserve air regiment was converting to the type.

The urgent intervention of Letno-Issledovatel'skii Institut (LII - Ministry of Aviation Inudstry Flight Research Institute) specialists allowed the cause of the trouble to be determined and eliminated. A small counterbalance on one of the control system levers proved sufficient to save pilots from the aircraft's dangerous tendencies. After test pilot Viktor Rastorguev had flight tested the device, scientists recommended that it be introduced on production aircraft.

From the very first days of operation of a test batch of LaGG-3s the designers faced the problem of collapsing undercarriage legs. But this trouble was not easily eliminated, mainly owing to the impossibility of preventing leakage in the pneumatic system. This also made LaGG-3's rather powerful armament unreliable, as the system was used for reloading as well. The initial batch of aircraft had three Berezin 12.7mm machine guns, two of which were synchronised, and two synchronised ShKAS 7.62mm machine guns. Starting with the fourth batch, production of which began in July 1941, the large calibre engine mounted machine gun was replaced by a ShVAK 20mm cannon and the starboard Berezin machine gun was removed. Most of the LaGG-3s built in 1941 were so armed.

Tests of these fighters carried out by NII VVS in the summer of 1941 revealed a drastic degradation in performance. Speeds for prototype, pre-production and production contemporaries were as follows:

Aircraft	Prototype	Pre-Production	Production
I-200 / MiG-3	390mph	397.6mph	382mph
	628km/h	640km/h	615km/h
I-26 / Yak-1	363.8mph	358.5mph	347.9mph
	585.5km/h	577km/h	560km/h
I-301 / LaGG-3	375.9mph	357mph	341mph
	605km/h	575km/h	549km/h

Even then, the above speeds for the LaGG-3 were achieved with the radiator bath shutter fully closed. Semyon Lavochkin tried to prove that the fighter had to be operated in a specific manner to attain maximum speed, but he failed to persuade either the NII VVS specialists or service pilots. The engine overheated quickly. When maximum level flight speed was measured with the radiator bath shutter open, the increased drag reduced the speed to 332.4mph (535km/h) at 16,400ft (5,000m), and to 283.9mph (457km/h) at ground level.

The same was true for the other important fighter parameter, climb rate. While the I-301 prototype climbed to 16,400ft (5,000m) in 5.85 minutes, the production LaGG-3 took 8.6 minutes to climb to this altitude. In terms of vertical manoeuvrability, the LaGG-3 was close to German twin-engine fighters and completely inferior to single-engine types.

One reason was that the aircraft was too heavy for the Klimov M-105P engine, which gave 1,050hp (783.3kW) at 13,000ft (4,000m), and it was intended to reduce the fighter's weight after the initial batches. The fuel capacity was reduced from 903.8 to 749.5lb (410 to 340kg); the designers believed that a range of 438 miles (705km) would be adequate at 0.9 of maximum speed), and the maximum

payload was reduced by more than 220lb (100kg). But owing to poor manufacturing standards the fighter's structure grew increasingly heavy, and the flying weight was reduced by only 123.4lb (56kg).

Unfavourable results were achieved during LaGG-3 diving tests. The framework of the movable portion of the canopy and the undercarriage door attachment fittings were found to have insufficient strength at high speeds. The propeller speed governor of production aircraft did not permit the engine to accelerate to more than 2,350 to 2,400rpm, instead of the nominal 2,700rpm, and this was one of the main causes, along with the impossibility of using split flaps for take-off, of a great increase in the take-off run. LaGG-3's required a strip 1,788ft (545m) long, while the I-301's take-off run was only 1,164ft (355m).

To understand what is meant by 'poor manufacturing standards', it is necessary to cite the report prepared by leading engineer M Tarakanovsky following his inspection of aircraft No.3121715, which arrived at the NII VVS in August. Defects listed were:

- the fuselage skin fabric was burnt in the area of the exhaust collector;
- the cockpit windshield was splashed with oil from the propeller, which made it impossible to use the gunsight and obscured forward view;
- the canopy attachment lock failed to keep the canopy in the open position;
- the undercarriage and door extension and retraction buttons were stiff, and there were other defects.

In all, nine serious faults were discovered. Tarakanovsky concluded that the fighter could not be approved for combat operation unless these defects were corrected.

One can imagine what Semyon Lavochkin, then chief designer of Plant No.21 in Gorkii, felt when he received this information about his fighter. Moreover, he felt the unfavourable comments even more keenly because the

Close-up of RS-82 rockets and launchers under the wing of an LaGG-3.

A LaGG-3 forced down and captured by the Finns. It and several others were repaired and used operationally.

LaGG-3 serial number LG-3 of the Finnish unit LeLv 32, based at Nurmoila in early 1943. *Ken Ellis collection*

Yak-1, which had come into existence almost simultaneously with the LaGG, achieved much better test results. True, like the LaGG, the pilot's view was not quite adequate, its survivability left much to be desired and it had many flaws, but on the whole it attracted much less criticism.

Lavochkin searched hard for a solution. He realised that the war effort required thousands of aircraft, and that to sustain output the design should not be changed. Changes could have serious consequences that might affect others besides those engaged in production. They could make maintenance conditions in the field much more difficult, and those were already severe enough, especially when damaged aircraft needed to be restored to combat readiness within a few hours. The situation was aggravated for Lavochkin by the fact that three other plants were entirely dependent on the Gorkii plant workers, and were unable to eliminate the defects themselves without drawings from the Gorkii plant. As before, however, attention was concentrated on the LaGGs produced at Gorkii, the first to have encountered enemy aircraft in combat.

Pilots of the 33rd Fighter Air Regiment received LaGG-3s at Gorkii in August 1941. Led by their commanding officer, Major N Akulin, they saw action within the 43rd Air Division near Vyazma. The regiment was involved in strike missions more often than other regiments, attacking enemy tank and troop columns advancing on Moscow. The fighters' powerful armament enabled them to destroy at least 120 tanks and motor vehicles moving along the Dukhovschina-Yartsevo road in several days.

At about the same time an unconventional mission was being flown by the pilots of the 160th Fighter Air Corps. One of the squadrons was accompanying a transport aircraft carrying Georgy Zhukov, who had been sent by the Supreme Commander Headquarters to assume command of the Leningrad Front. In spite of the opposition mounted by Messerschmitts, Zhukov landed in the city on the Neva uneventfully. The officer commanding

the flight, First Lieutenant Alexander Silantiev (a future Hero of the Soviet Union and Marshal of Air Command) shot down a Bf109.

Their great battle experience enabled the pilots of the 21st Fighter Air Regiment, right at the Front, to master the LaGG-3 very quickly, in just 23 days, without being sent to the rear. The regiment engaged in combat at once, and one of its first pleasant surprises was the high survivability of the LaGGs. One returned from a combat with 75 bullet and shell holes. Both the windshield and instrument panel were smashed, but the aircraft was returned to service only a day later.

Within six days in October 1941 the pilots of the 21st Regiment shot down 23 enemy aircraft for the loss of only seven. The LaGGs had shown their excellent combat capabilities not only during ground attacks, but also while attacking enemy bombers. At the same time, pilots observed that it was very difficult to engage enemy fighters successfully. Firstly, manoeuvrability and a climb rate were very low, which was why the 33rd Fighter Air Regiment, previously mentioned, lost almost half of its strength near Vyazma on 23rd September 1941. To be fair, it should be noted that the LaGGs fought with the latest Messerschmitt Bf109Fs, which were superior in all-round performance when compared with the Soviet fighters in the autumn of 1941.

When P Piterin, a representative of the Lavochkin Design Bureau, visited the north eastern front, he had to hear not only favourable opinions but also unpalatable comments. It was claimed that the aircraft was overweight, and that its already low speed decreased by 12.4mph (20km/h) every 20 to 30 flying hours. (It should be pointed out that many problems had been resolved by October.) Piterin received many requests; the flight and maintenance personnel asked him to lighten the aircraft without reducing fuel capacity, and to retain its powerful armament.

Much earlier, Lavochkin had understood very clearly that weight had to be reduced, and on 13th September 1941 he reported the service personnel's suggestions to the State Commissariat of the Aircraft Industry. In the chief designer's opinion, a weight saving of at least 165 to 220lb (75 to 100kg) could be achieved by stripping out unused equipment, and this would also facilitate manufacture. Lavochkin thought that the primary armament should comprise a single 20mm ShVAK cannon and two UBS large calibre (12.7mm) machine guns, and that the 7.62mm ShKAS machine guns should be removed.

Unlike Mikoyan, Lavochkin flatly opposed the installation of leading edge slats, rejecting this means of improving stability at high angles of attack. No changes were introduced into the wing design until the end of the initial stage of the war.

However, various armament installations were intensively developed in the autumn of 1941. A small batch of LaGG-3s had VYa (23mm) engine-mounted cannon, and Lavochkin followed Mikhail Gudkov in having a 37mm cannon designed by B Shpitalny, A Nudelman and A Suranov mounted in the cylinder 'vee' of the M-105P engine.

Lavochkin paid equally detailed attention to equipment. He was the first Soviet fighter designer to equip production aircraft with radio compasses. The first six LaGGs passed their Service tests with the 24th Fighter Air Regiment while turning away German air raids on the capital. Efforts aimed at improving the radio equipment were not very successful at the time. Although all of the LaGGs carried at least a receiver, the quality of communication was low, with much interference and noise.

Mass-produced LaGG-3s began to take shape on the Gorkii assembly line. From Batch 11, manufactured from October 1941 onwards, armament was reduced to a ShVAK cannon and one UBS machine gun; six RS-82 82mm rockets carried under the wings became standard equipment. Internal fuel capacity was reduced to 573lb (260kg), and provision was made for suspending drop tanks under the wings to offset the decrease in range. The flying weight was reduced to 6,790lb (3,080kg), but efforts to reduce it further persisted. In the autumn of 1941 the LaGG-3 held a prominent place among tactical fighters.

By the time Germany launched its 'decisive' offensive against Moscow there were 170 LaGGs in the inventory of active aircraft (18% of the total), and when the Soviet counteroffensive was mounted there were 263 (26%). One reason for this was the fact that the Gorkii plant had not been evacuated in late autumn 1941, and, whereas production of all the other combat aircraft almost ceased, the output of LaGGs continued. More than half of all the combat aircraft built in the hardest month, November, were Lavochkins. Up to the end of 1941, 1,659 LaGGs were built in Gorkii, 474 in Taganrog, 265 in Novosibirsk and 65 in Leningrad. This amounted to 2,463 aircraft, 83% of the total scheduled for production before the war.

The Lavochkin Bureau's hopes that the Novosibirsk plant would become a large production centre for the LaGG-3 were not to be realised. On 30th October 1941 Alexander Yakovlev and his staff arrived there. This is how he described the situation at the plant in his book *The Aim of Life*:

A LaGG-3 issued by the Novosibirsk Plant No.153 was fitted with retractable skis and tested during the winter of 1941-42. Results of the tests appear to be unsatisfactory as this version was not put into production.

'The Siberian plant had been tasked for about a year with manufacturing LaGG-3 aircraft, but the status of these machines was rather sad. At the time of our arrival the plant was full of unfinished aircraft. Not only the assembly shop, but also almost all the other shops had turned into a 'bog'. In the last months no combat-capable aircraft had been commissioned.

Yakovlev goes on to describe how, as he became familiar with the situation at the plant, he came to the conclusion that the main cause of its plight was an extremely low level of manufacturing planning. At that time moving production lines did not exist in most aircraft factories. Consequently all the operations, from first to last, were carried out in the final assembly shop at one and the same place, by one team or several teams moving from one aircraft to another. Because the aircraft were not moved, the assembly shop gradually filled with incomplete airframes. A similar situation prevailed in the wing and fuselage assembly shops, and in other shops.

Ultimately, the slightest delays and problems on each separate assembly jig greatly hampered general progress, sometimes even stopping it. The lack of a radiator bath for one aircraft, a propeller for a second and an undercarriage for a third prevented their being put into service.

The situation increased in gravity because of the very severe winter. Fighters arrayed outside in disorderly fashion were covered by

a 3ft (0.9m) layer of snow. Tails, spinners and aerial masts projected through snowdrifts, and teams were busy excavating them. And this was at the time when as many combat aircraft as possible were needed at the Front.

Alexander Yakovlev continued:

'Before the October festivities we received a visit from the Secretary of the regional committee of the VKP(b), to whom the plant's administration had promised a month earlier that 30 LaGG-3 aircraft would be delivered by the anniversary of the October revolution. Owing to the situation described above, not a single aircraft had been handed over'.

The author takes issue with this statement. In October numerous hindrances were overcome and 63 LaGG-3s were built, 3½ times more than had been produced a month earlier. They were followed by 54 in November and 97 in December. Romanov, director of Plant No.153, and General Leshukov, the plant's representative of the Commissariat for Defence, who had reported that regular production would be achieved and output would increase, were accused of incompetence by Yakovlev, who telephoned Stalin repeatedly, asking that they be replaced.

A topical documentary film made with some urgency played an important part in the story. Yakovlev sent cameramen from the Moscow documentary film studio to Novosibirsk. The film portrayed poorly organised work and cluttered, dirty shops in LaGG-3 production and, in comparison, immaculate order and personnel wearing white overalls during Yak-7 assembly. This film was shown to the government. It had to persuade the country's leaders once and for all that the parallel production of LaGG-3s and Yak-7s complicated the work and made it impossible to increase fighter production. To return to Yakovlev's book:

'Stalin telephoned me again in the first half of January 1942. After making inquiries about the work, he said that the State Committee for Defence had decided to convert the Siberian plant completely to Yaks and move the production of LaGG-3s to another venue. The factory was to cancel all work associated with LaGG production immediately, and set up a moving production line for the Yak-7'.

'He said that Yaks and LaGGs were similar in performance, but that pilots preferred Yaks. Yaks were more manoeuvrable and did not have certain defects manifested by LaGGs on the battlefield. He said I would shortly receive the material relating to this, and that I was to proceed immediately with reorientation of production'.

Thus Yakovlev, the Deputy Commissar of the Aircraft Industry, forced the decision to withdraw the Lavochkin aircraft from production and promoted his own fighter.

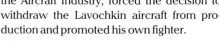

Engine replacement in very basic field conditions.

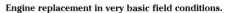

Production LaGG-3 with redesigned exhaust and cowling with separate vents for each exhaust pipe.

To consolidate his achievements he sent his 'emissaries' to Gorkii, preparatory to taking over the production line of one of the USSR's largest aircraft factories.

Extensive efforts were being made at the plant to improve the LaGG-3's performance and combat capabilities. The tests carried out there gave hope; the fighter's speed was increased to 304.4mph (490km/h) at ground level and 360mph (580km/h) at service ceiling, and its vertical manoeuvrability was enhanced. However, these results were not validated by the NII VVS, the state inspection agency authorised to conduct tests.

The LaGG-3 tested by the agency in March and April 1942 at a flying weight of 6,834lb (3,100kg), including rocket projectiles together with their carriers and guides, developed a maximum speed of only 277mph (446km/h) at ground level and 321.8mph (518km/h) at 16,700ft (5,100m), and took 7.1 minutes to climb to 16,400ft (5,000m). Without the rocket rails, the maximum speed rose by 12.4mph (20km/h). However, the movable portion of the canopy was removed to improve the view and the radiator shutters were kept open to prevent engine overheating, because this was the configuration in which operational pilots flew the aircraft at the time. It could therefore be concluded that the LaGG-3's maximum speed in 'clean' configuration was about 310mph (500km/h).

In addition to high noise level, high control column forces and short range, it was claimed that manoeuvrability was poor and that radio communication range was insufficient. The LaGG-3's range could be increased very quickly; it was delivered for its flight tests complete with two external drop tanks.

While no great contribution had been made to the aircraft's performance, the production rate had increased. Between 200 and 270 fighters went from Gorkii to the battlefield every month in the winter and spring of 1942.

To avoid a production stoppage the Gorkii plant personnel had to be very resourceful. The evacuation of industrial enterprises to the east suspended the supply of AMT weldable aluminium alloy used to make fuel tanks. The design department of Plant No.21 therefore devised wooden tanks made of birch and using VIAM-63 tar adhesive. A special shop headed by A Shibaev was set up, where the new product was successfully developed.

At about the same time an attempt was made to substitute wooden propeller blades for metal ones. Parallel tests of conventional VISh-61P metal blades and VISh-105PD wooden units showed that, using the latter, the aircraft's maximum speed fell by 14.9mph (24km/h), but the change was necessary to prevent a drop in the production rate. A batch of LaGGs with wooden propeller blades was manufactured.

Top: **Late production Tbilisi LaGG-3 carrying a pair of 220lb (100kg) FAB-100 bombs.**

Centre: **One of the last production LaGG-3s from the Tbilisi plant in March 1943, and tested in May.**

Bottom: **Repairs underway to LaGG-3s in beleaguered Leningrad.**

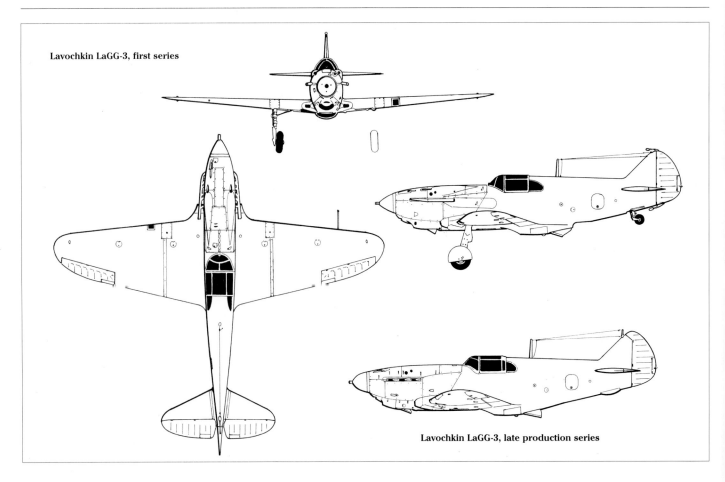

Lavochkin LaGG-3, first series

Lavochkin LaGG-3, late production series

Late production Tbilisi LaGG-3 carrying napalm-like dispensers.

LaGG-3 with Klimov M-107

Semyon Lavochkin realised that decisive steps had been taken to save his fighter, and he believed that the main task was to uprate its engine. In his opinion the most promising powerplant was the M-107 development engine designed by Klimov. Initial versions developed 1,400hp (1,044kW) at take-off and 1,300hp (969.8kW) at the service ceiling of 16,400ft (5,000m), making them 25% more powerful, and were rated at a higher service ceiling than the M-105P.

The LaGG-3 M-107 was built very quickly and began flight testing, but the pilot, G Mischenko, stated with regret that the desired result had not been achieved. The fighter made 33 emergency landings in 33 flights, mainly due to overheating of the new engine. When revs were decreased and supercharging reduced for normal flight, the M-107's power decayed and all of its advantages vanished. As a precaution, a LaGG-3 with an Shvetsov M-82 had been prepared, but Lavochkin could scarcely believe that this installation of the powerful radial would bring favourable results, especially in the short time available. To his great surprise, these efforts proved successful, resulting in the famous La-5 which is described later.

In early May 1942 the LaGG-3 was the most widely used fighter, comprising a third of the total number of fighters in use. At least ten aircraft of this type were in service with the air command at each front, from the Karelian to the Crimean. There were a great many LaGGs within the air command of the General Headquarters Reserve and in the Air Force of strike formations, and the navy began operating the type on a large scale.

The Nazi advance in the summer of 1942 was a terrible ordeal for the Red Army, and its pilot losses were considerable. Pilots became aware of the vulnerability of the LaGG-3's cooling system, the fighter being rendered *hors de combat* if it suffered the slightest damage. The aircraft also proved unsuitable for protecting strike aircraft owing to its poor acceleration, and LaGGs escorting Ilyushins often fell prey themselves to Messerschmitts, which attacked at high speed. The pilots of the 31st Fighter Air Regiment concluded that it would be better to engage Bf109Fs at medium altitudes and to maintain height, since performing dives and half-rolls in LaGGs at altitudes of 2,300 to 2,600ft (700m to 800m) or lower was simply dangerous. The 9th Guards Fighter Air Regiment involved in the operations on the south flank was outstanding, but even that unit, which began flying combat missions on LaGG-3s in June, quickly lost six aircraft, Hero of the Soviet Union A Elokhin being among those killed. Faith in the new fighter was shaken.

Major L Shestakov, the regiment's commanding officer, analysed the causes of the losses. Being a thoughtful teacher as well as an excellent pilot, he devised a 'battle formula' to counter Luftwaffe aces. This entailed breaking up the combat formation and then flying at different altitudes to deprive the Bf109F of its main advantage, vertical manoeuvre. Victory was not long in coming.

A selfless act was performed by a pilot of the 792nd Fighter Air Regiment, First Sergeant M Tvelenev. When attacking an enemy aircraft near Kharkov one of the Yaks was hit and forced down, and Tvelenev landed alongside and helped the pilot to get aboard his LaGG through a fuselage hatch. The aircraft took off under the noses of the approaching enemy.

Many dramatic incidents were experienced by Pavel Golovachev when flying combat missions on LaGG-3s in the summer of 1942. By the end of the war he had scored 31 victories, and he was twice decorated with the state's highest award. In one air combat the lieutenant was shot up by a Messerschmitt. The enemy pilot's fire tore off his canopy and broke the instrument panel, Golovachev being saved from injury by the armoured backrest. He managed to reach his base, but the undercarriage had apparently been damaged, as it refused to come down. With great difficulty he lowered the undercarriage using the emergency extension winch and landed safely.

In another combat Golovachev shot down a Junkers Ju88, but return fire from the bomber's gunner hit the LaGG-3, wounding the Russian. Recovering consciousness over the Don, he pulled the fighter out of a spin. Although the aircraft's tail came off and it plunged into the water, Golovachev survived.

In the Kletskoy region in August 1942 a flight of four LaGGs of the 440th Air Fighter Regiment was attacked by German fighters. Finding himself surrounded by Bf109s, Captain T Voitanik rammed one of his adversaries and was thrown out of his cockpit. His action caused turmoil in the German formation and three of the Nazi fighters were shot down.

Neither the courage of Soviet pilots nor the LaGG-3's high survivability could conceal the fact that the aircraft was inferior to the Bf109F and 'G. Its only advantage lay in its horizontal manoeuvrability. Many pilots tended to engage threats only when turning, and the Lavochkin, being quite heavy, usually lost speed. This made it difficult to regain energy, precluding effective vertical manoeuvring and further aggravating the combat situation.

The 440th and 9th Guard Air Fighter Regiments of the 268th Air Fighter Division lost 58 of the 69 LaGGs available. The 273rd and 515th Air Fighter Regiments of the same Division, flying Yak-1s, also suffered high attrition rates, losing 41 of the 71 aircraft in their inventories. Cases were reported of LaGG-3 pilots, alarmed by high death rates in their units, refusing to fly their fighters and being court-martialled. Late in August 1942 Soviet High Command ruled that the LaGG-3 was not to be used in the most important operations.

In July 1945 the first La-5s were rolled out of Aircraft Plant No.21, but the last LaGG-3s were still being assembled at the end of 1942. Some of these were modified for use as day bombers in the 297th Air Fighter Regiment from June 1942.

LaGG-3-37

A LaGG-3 fitted with Boris Shpitalny's 37mm gun was tested at the NII VVS. At a gross take-off weight of 7,414lb (3,363kg) the fighter's maximum speed reduced by 3.1 to 4.3mph (5 to 7km/h), and its climb rate and ceiling were also lower. Automatic slats gave manoeuvrability similar to the previous types. Evaluations showed that the gun provided high kill probability against lightly armoured targets at a range of 984 to 1,312ft (300 to 400m).

As early as July 1941 People's Commissar of Weapons Dmitry Ustinov had signed an order authorising the construction of a batch of Sh-37 guns for operational trials. Early in 1942 20 Sh-37-armed LaGGs arrived at the 42nd Air Fighter Regiment, commanded by Col F Shinkarenko, for operational evaluation on the Bryansky Front. The very first combat proved a success, three enemy aircraft being shot down, though it was noted that the 20 round ammunition supply was insufficient.

The next combat experience with the LaGG-3-37 was gained in September 1942, near Stalingrad. In spite of the fact that Luftwaffe pilots in this region were especially skilled, the results of LaGG-3-37 missions flown by pilots of the 291st Fighter Air Regiment (FAR) were even more impressive. In a report dated 31st October 1942, A Utkin, commander of the 220th Fighter Air Division (to which the 291st FAR was assigned), stated: 'The LaGG-3-37 fighter is a powerful and effective means of destroying enemy bombers'. During operational trials, pilots of the 291st FAR shot down 13 German bombers for the loss of seven of their own aircraft. This relatively low LaGG attrition rate was due to cover provided by faster Yak fighters.

The lighter and more reliable Nudelman NS-37 cannon was accepted as standard for the LaGG-3, and the first batch of these weapons was built in December 1942. Some of the fighters so equipped went to the Normandie Fighter Air Regiment.

The troubled production initiation programme at Taganrog Aircraft Plant No.31 was

April 1943. Production fighters were improving too, maximum speed reaching 354mph (570km/h) at altitude and 329.3mph (530 km/h) at sea level.

Most of the LaGG-3s manufactured in 1943 went to the Air Force of the North Caucasus District and the 4th Air Army. Pilots of the 979th Air Fighter Regiment, led by V Fedorenko, gained fame during the battle of Kuban. Aware of the LaGG-3's poor vertical manoeuvrability, Bf109G pilots tried to take advantage of the weakness. However, it transpired that the light Gorbunov version was not inferior to the German aircraft. Three Bf109Gs were shot down by Fedorenko's pilots without loss to the Soviet side. Fedorenko was awarded the Gold Star of a Hero of the Soviet Union. While the LaGG-3 was generally inferior to the Bf109G, Soviet pilots who had gained sufficient combat experience fought successfully against the German fighter.

Type '105'

Led by Gorbunov, the Design Bureau proceeded with the development of fighter prototypes. In May 1943 an in-depth modification of the LaGG-3, the Type '105' fighter, was built, with gross take-off weight reduced to 6,060lb (2,749kg). Its wing had no slats, and its aerodynamics were improved by streamlining the fuselage surface, fitting fairings and removing excrescences.

The manufacturer's development test flights, made by S Pligunov, revealed a speed increase of 15.5mph (25km/h) compared with production fighters of 1943. The fighter's performance was close to the highest recorded to date in the Soviet Union: a turning time of 16 seconds, a time to 16,400ft (5,000m) of 4.7 minutes, and an altitude gain of 4,429ft (1,350m) during a combat turn. Shevelev, a 4th Air Army pilot who flew evaluation tests, reported that the '105' was superior to all Messerschmitt variants in terms of trouble-free handling and manoeuvrability.

By that time assembly of the second and improved '105-2', was under way at Aircraft Plant No.31. This machine differed from its predecessor in having a two-stage supercharged Klimov M-105PF-2 engine with a rated take-off power of 1,300hp (969.8kW), compared with the 1,210hp (902.6kW) of the '105'. It also featured enhanced armament consisting of a 23mm VYa gun and a 12.7mm UBS machine gun.

The programme suffered delays, and the '105-2' was not rolled out until February 1944. It underwent its state flight tests at the NII VVS from May to June, and the high performance claimed by the manufacturer was not confirmed by the test results.

aggravated by the plant's evacuation to Tbilisi in Georgia, in the inner regions of the Soviet Union. The unification of two aircraft plants proved to be very difficult. By April 1942 LaGG production at Gorkii, Plant No.21, the primary manufacturer, had ceased. The Novosibirsk Aircraft Plant was converted to Yak-7A production and LaGG-3 manufacture was not resumed at Leningrad Plant No.23, which had also been evacuated into inner Russia, as it was planned to produce the MiG-3 there. The Tbilisi plant was therefore the sole manufacturer of the LaGG-3. The production programme faced problems of the simultaneous introduction of modifications into designs at different plants.

Meanwhile, a new LaGG-3 modification offering lower gross take-off weight and better controllability was developed at the prototype production plant. The aircraft's fin was reduced in weight, a very important feature of the LaGG-3 being a main integral structural element in the aircraft's tail section. Initially, the fin manufacturing process resulted in a structure that was seriously overweight. Sometimes more than 30kg of adhesive could be stripped away without any negative effect on structural strength.

Gorbunov sent the first lightened LaGG-3, No.2444, for flight testing. Its gross take-off

Prototype LaGG-3-37 prototype armed with a 37mm Sh-37 cannon. Note the muzzle projects well forward from the nose of the spinner. This machine dispensed with undercarriage fairings and the rudder balance weight for weight reduction.

Production LaGG-3-37 being tested at the NII VVS in September 1942.

weight was only 6,316lb (2,865kg), 440lb (200kg) less than that of a standard aircraft manufactured at Plant No.21. The lightweight LaGG displayed an increased rate of climb and improved manoeuvrability in the vertical plane without any increase in speed, which remained 350.4mph (564km/h) at 12,800ft (3,900m).

The next prototype built at Plant No.31 featured even more innovations, especially with regard to aerodynamics: a retractable tailwheel, an internal aerial housed in the fuselage, removal of the provision to carry bombs, the deletion of additional flaps in favour of main flaps of increased area, and removal of the aileron balances. Nicknamed 'G', this aircraft reached 341.7mph (550km/h) at sea level and 375.9mph (605km/h) at 12,500ft (3,800m), climbed to 16,400ft (5,000m) in 5.1 minutes, and its turning time was reduced to 16 to 18 seconds. This data was gathered in

Right: **The first Type '105' designed by Vladimir Gorbunov.**

Below: **Two views of the second Type '105' during tests. (Apart from the large '02' on the rudder, the stencilling '105-2' can be just discerned underneath the red star on the fin.) The second aircraft featured a lowered rear fuselage decking and a more 'bubble'-like canopy.**

Above left: **Other features of the second Type '105' were the more truncated cannon muzzle and the absence of oil cooler intake on the nose.**

Above right: **A lightened LaGG-3 with mainwheel undercarriage fairings removed.**

At a gross take-off weight of 6,338lb (2,875kg) the fighter attained 344mph (554km/h) at sea level and 384mph (618km/h) at 11,200ft (3,400m), and climbed to 16,400ft (5,000m) in 4.8 minutes. The NII VVS test pilot who flew the '105-2' during its trials, I Dzyuba, noted: 'In terms of maximum speed and climb rate the "105-2" is inferior to the Yak-1M tested at the NII in October 1943 ... because of oil and water overheating, flight at maximum speed can be sustained for only three or four minutes'.

The aircraft failed its state tests and the LaGG-3 modernisation programme was cancelled, Tbilisi Aircraft Plant No.31 being converted to production of the Yak-3. In some respects the fates of the LaGG-3 and Yak-1 were similar; both were built in series before the Second World War and up to 1944, when their programmes were cancelled in favour of Yak-3 production.

During three years of production 6,528 LaGG-3s were built, including 2,550 manufactured at Plant No.31. During 1943 and 1944 LaGG fighters were used intensively by the 4th Air Army and the air arm of the Black Sea Navy.

According to service pilots the aircraft was easy to handle and maintain, though combat reports noted its low survivability on ground-attack missions, and low firepower.

Centre left: **To overcome the LaGG-3's lack of range, drop tanks could be fitted.**

Left: **Yury Shilov, pilot with the 9th Fighter Regiment, assigned to the Baltic Sea Fleet, seated in his LaGG-3. Eight victory stars and a lion's head in a heart adorn the fuselage side.**

LaGG-3 with Shvetsov M-82 (and Gu-82)

Semyon Lavochkin initiated work on conversion of his fighter to take the powerful M-82 air-cooled radial engine later than other Soviet designers. Mikhail Gudkov's Gu-82, the Mikoyan-Gurevich MiG-3 M-82 (MiG-9) and Alexander Yakovlev's Yak-7 M-82 were already flying. However, all of this work had not resulted in any radical improvements, and none of these fighters had been put into series-production.

Arkady Shvetsov, chief designer of Perm Engine Plant No.19, where the M-82 was built, was concerned at the lack of demand for the engine. Hundreds were in store, only a small batch had been mounted on Sukhoi Su-2 short range bombers.

Lavochkin's affairs were no better in early 1942. A decision regarding withdrawal of the LaGG-3 from series-production was about to be taken. Their troubles brought the two designers together when they met at a People's Commissariat of the Aircraft Industry conference in Moscow. As a result, Shvetsov sent his engine mock-up and highly-qualified specialists, headed by E Valedinsky, to the Gorkii plant in haste.

A task force was formed at Plant No.21 to design the new fighter. This decision raised an objection from Semyon Alexeyev, the chief of the design bureau, who believed that the removal of the LaGG-3 from production would occur before the combined team could design, build and test the new aircraft. To his mind, therefore, it seemed that all effort and attention should be concentrated on installing the M-82 in the airframe of the series-production aircraft. Many thought this suggestion impracticable, as the diameter of the M-82 was 18in (460mm) greater than the maximum cross-section of the LaGG-3's fuselage. Besides, the M-82 was 551lb (250kg) heavier than the Klimov M-105P, which meant that the aircraft's centre of gravity would change. Last, but not least, there was the problem of armament. The series-production LaGG-3 had a 20mm ShVAK cannon and a 12.7mm Berezin synchronised machine gun. It was impossible to retain this ordnance on the new aircraft because the M-82's gearbox shaft was not hollow, and there was no space for the engine-mounted cannon.

The task was extremely complicated, which is why it was necessary to focus the attention of the design bureau team on this work. Alexeyev's proposal was supported by the administration of the production plant and its director, Gostintsev. Among the firm advocates of the idea was the chief of the engine group, K Slepnev. Almost the whole weight of the work had fallen on him and his subordinates.

The peculiar features of the arrangement thus created were as follows:

- Because the M-82's mid-section was considerably wider than the fuselage of the series-built aircraft, a skirting was bonded to both sides of the fuselage's load-carrying skin.
- The engine mount was reworked to take the new engine.
- Two ShVAK 20mm synchronised cannon were mounted above the engine.
- Engine cooling was effected by two variable cooling flaps on the fuselage sides, and the engine's cooling-air baffles were slightly changed to provide uniform thermal conditions for the upper and lower cylinders.

This arrangement caused keen discussion in the bureau, chiefly in connection with the engine cooling system, as radial engines were usually cooled by means of a 'skirt' fitting uniformly round their circumference. Gudkov, the first designer to fit an M-82 engine into a LaGG-3, did just that. In this case the powerplant was taken bodily from a Sukhoi Su-2. OKB-301 in Moscow started working on this design in March 1941, but Gudkov was then distracted by the need to arm the LaGG-3 with a 37mm cannon. Nevertheless, work on development of a new engine and propeller system continued. In September 1941 the fighter, called the Gu-82, was flying, and flying rather well. When industrial enterprises were evacuated from Moscow to the eastern regions, Gudkov, together with his creation, was directed to Novosibirsk.

By 12th October 1941 the People's Commissariat of the Aircraft Industry was already showing interest in the Gu-82. A go-ahead for series-production of the fighter at Gorkii, instead of the LaGG-3, was even planned before any tests had commenced.

However, the movement of the aircraft from Moscow to Novosibirsk and then to Gorkii took too long, and there was no news from Gudkov.

Two views of the production LaGG-3 airframe fitted with the M-82 radial becoming briefly the LaG-5, then the famous La-5. It was in this form that the aircraft was tested by NII VVS during April 1942.

Meanwhile, the administration of Plant No. 21, not wishing to disturb the LaGG-3 programme, defended their own fighter in every possible way and did not hurry to obtain the drawings from Gudkov. Alexander Yakovlev then intervened, securing the Government's decision to have the Yak-7 manufactured in Gorkii. Had this decision been put into effect, Yakovlev would have monopolised fighter design and production in the Soviet Union.

In contrast to Gudkov, Yakovlev was resolute and energetic in his actions. A group of designers was sent, and all the necessary drawings of the improved fighter, the Yak-7B, were handed over. Slowly but surely, Yaks began to oust LaGG-3s from Plant No.21. LaGGs continued to roll off the assembly lines, but Yak-7B parts were already being stamped and cast in the component shops.

The State Defence Committee's decision in April 1942 to stop LaGG-3 production and transfer the Lavochkin OKB to Plant No.31 in Tbilisi determined the day when Semyon Lavochkin would be able to demonstrate the best qualities of his new aircraft. At this time working conditions grew much worse. The government required the first Yak-7B to be assembled in May, and this work could not be hampered. Lavochkin and a few remaining like-minded specialists therefore worked almost illegally.

The designer had to endure many difficulties in February 1942, when his new fighter, designated LaGG-3 M-82, was rolled off the assembly line. On 14th February Yu Stankevich, who had been appointed to undertake the development tests of the aircraft, was killed while testing a high-speed two-seat LaGG intended for urgent communications flights between Gorkii and Moscow. He was succeeded by G Mischenko, a pilot of Plant No.21, and Lavochkin listened anxiously to his first comments on the fighter: 'The aircraft is good, pleasant to control and responsive, but the cylinder heads become hot. Measures should be taken'. The first evaluations showed that, compared with the series-production LaGG, the LaGG-3 M-82's speed at ground level was a full 10% greater. The result

was brilliant, as great effort was required to gain every kilometre per hour.

Valedinsky informed Shvetsov of the first flights immediately. Hoping that at last his engines would be widely used, the latter told N Gusarov, Secretary of the Perm Regional Committee, of the LaGG-3 M-82. In turn, Gusarov, like the Secretary of the Gorkii Regional Committee, M Rodionov, reported the news to Stalin.

Information about the new fighter reached the State Defence Committee by different means. A report by pilot-engineer A Nikashin, who had flown the aircraft and backed it enthusiastically was received there. The voices of the People's Commissariat of the Aircraft Industry and Air Force Command were heard in defence of the aircraft. This support came at exactly the right time; Lavochkin needed it more than ever before.

A joint commission was urgently formed, and visited the Gorkii plant at the end of April 1942. It included A Frolov of the NII VVS and V Sabinov of the LII, and pilots A Kubyshkin of the NII VVS and A Yakimov of the LII to carry out evaluation tests, for which only six flying days were allocated. The first flight was made by A Yakimov on 21st April 1942. He concluded that: 'The aircraft is a promising one', but he observed that it was very hot in the cockpit. Compared with the flights performed by Mischenko in the winter, the oil temperature rose appreciably, the oil tank beneath the pilot's feet becoming especially hot. Urgent development work on engine cooling was carried out.

Evaluation tests of the LaGG-3 M-82, also called 'Aircraft 37' or Type '37', were carried out from 9th to 14th May 1942, a total of eleven flights being made. They changed the fate of Lavochkin aircraft dramatically. On the basis of the test results the fighter was deemed a success, and it was recommended that it be put into series-production. Performance of the LaGG-3 M-82 was higher than that of all the aircraft in service with the VVS. Its maximum speed ranged from 320mph (515km/h) at sea level to 372.8mph (600km/h) at the service ceiling of 21,000ft (6,450m). A speed of

347.9mph (560km/h) at 2,000ft (600m) at the engine's take-off power of 1,700hp (1,268kW) was achieved. A climb to 16,400ft (5,000m) took six minutes at normal power rating and 5.2 minutes augmented. In the important manoeuvre of a climb to 3,600ft (1,100m) during a combat turn the aircraft outperformed not only indigenous but also enemy aircraft used at the Front. Its range was normal for a tactical single-engine fighter.

The tests also revealed quite a number of problems. Controllability proved to be even more difficult than that of the LaGG-3 M-105P. Transition from a banked turn in one direction to a banked turn in the other caused stick forces requiring great physical efforts by the pilot. It took 25 seconds to make a banked turn; too long for a single-engined aircraft. One reason for this was that the LaGG-3 M-82 was overweight, weighing 7,451lb (3,380kg).

During the tests the powerplant behaved well, but the lack of forward gills on the engine led it to super-cool even in cruising flight. This made the planning, calculation and execution of a landing difficult. Splashing of the windshield with oil, which hampered gun aiming, could not be eliminated, . The armament, comprising two synchronised cannon with 170 rounds each, was found to be good, the guns operating satisfactorily both on the ground and in the air .

These shortcomings could not overshadow the fact that the flights made by Yakimov and Kubyshkin showed the aircraft to be excellent with regard to performance and acceptable in terms of engine heating. Lavochkin was summoned to Moscow to report to Stalin. He described the LaGG-3 M-82 briefly and in a businesslike manner, and the new aircraft was backed by People's Commissar of the Aircraft Industry Alexey Shakhurin. As a result, the State Defence Committee immediately ordered that Semyon Lavochkin should return to Plant No.21.

The LaGG-3 M-82 (La-5 prototype) with cowlings open.

The La-5 prototype had gained an intake on the top of the M-82's cowling by late April 1942.

La-5 (LaG-5)

Full-scale development of the LaG-5, as the aircraft was now designated, began, and simultaneously problems arose concerning the initiation of the production process. Especially difficult to build were the first ten aircraft, assembled early in June 1942, which were manufactured in dreadful haste, with numerous errors. While it is normal practice to make parts from drawings, this time, on the contrary, final drawings were sometimes made from the parts. At the same time the tooling was being prepared and the process of producing new components was being mastered.

Aircraft Plant No.21 handled the task well. The transition to the modified fighter was effected almost without any reduction in the delivery rate to the air force. Following delivery of the first fully operational LaG-5 on 20th June 1942, the Gorkii workers turned out 37 more by the end of the month. In August the plant surpassed the production rate of all the previous months, 148 LaGG-3s being added to 145 new LaG-5s.

Series produced aircraft were considerably inferior to the prototype in speed, being some 24.8 to 31mph (40 to 50km/h) slower. On the one hand this is understandable, as the LaGG-3 M-82 prototype lacked the radio antenna, bomb carriers and leading edge slats fitted to production aircraft. But there were other contributory causes, particularly insufficiently tight cowlings. Work carried out by Professor V Polinovsky with the workers of the design bureau of Plant No.21 enabled the openings to be found and eliminated.

Series built aircraft were sent to war, and the LaG-5's combat performance was proved in the 49th Red Banner Fighter Air Regiment of the 1st Air Army. In the unit's first 17 battles 16 enemy aircraft were shot down at a cost of ten of its own, five pilots being lost. Command believed that the heavy losses occurred because the new aircraft had not been fully mastered and, as a consequence, its operational qualities were not used to full advantage. Pilots noted that, owing to the machine's high weight and insufficient control surface balance, it made more demands upon flying technique than the LaGG-3 and Yak-1. At the same time, however, the LaG-5 had an advantage over fighters with liquid-cooled engines, as its double-row radial protected its pilot from frontal attacks. Aircraft survivability increased noticeably as a consequence. Three fighters returned to their airfield despite pierced inlet nozzles, exhaust pipes and rocker box covers.

The involvement of LaG-5s of the 287th Fighter Air Division, commanded by Colonel S Danilov, Hero of the Soviet Union, in the Battle of Stalingrad was a severe test for the

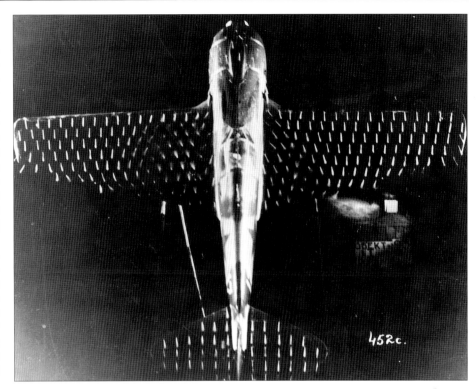

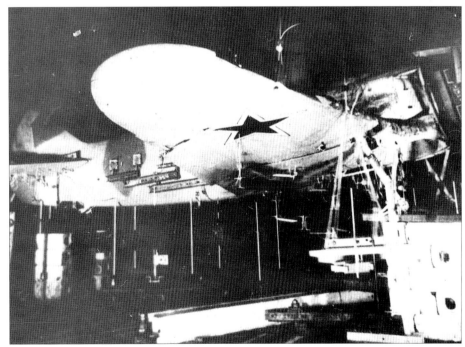

A tufted La-5 undergoing wind tunnel testing at TsAGI.

Static load tests on an La-5 at TsAGI.

aircraft. Fierce fighting took place over the Volga, and the Luftwaffe was stronger than ever before. The division experienced its first combats on 20th August 1942 with 57 LaG-5s, of which two-thirds were combat capable. Four regiments of the division were to have 80 fighters on strength, but a great many deficiencies prevented this. Serious accidents occurred; one fighter crashed during take-off,

and two more collided while taxying owing to the pilots' poor view. During the first three flying days the LaGs shot down eight German fighters and three bombers. Seven were lost, including three to 'friendly' anti-aircraft fire.

Subsequently, the division pilots were more successful. There were repeated observations of attacks against enemy bombers, of which 57 were destroyed within a month, but the division's own losses were severe.

Based on experience gained during combat, the pilots of the 27th Fighter Air Regiment, 287th Fighter Air Division, concluded that their fighters were inferior to Bf109F-4s

and, especially, 'G-2s in speed and vertical manoeuvrability. They reported: 'We have to engage only in defensive combat actions. The enemy is superior in altitude and, therefore, has a more favourable position from which to attack.'

Hitherto, it has often been stated in Soviet and other historical accounts that the La-5 (the designation assigned to the fighter in early September 1942) had passed its service tests during the Stalingrad battle in splendid fashion. In reality, this advanced fighter still had to overcome some 'growing pains'.

This was proved by state tests of the La-5 Series 4 at the NII VVS during September and October 1942. At a flying weight of 7,407lb (3,360kg) the aircraft attained a maximum

speed at ground level of 316mph (509km/h) at its normal power rating, 332.4mph (535 km/h) at its augmented rating and 360.4mph (580km/h) at the service ceiling of 20,500ft (6,250m) The Soviet-made M-82 family of engines – derived from the US-designed Wright R-1820 Cyclone – had an augmented power rating only at the first supercharger speed). The aircraft climbed to 16,400ft (5,000m) in 6.0 minutes at normal power rating and in 5.7 minutes with augmentation. Its armament was similar to that of the prototype. Horizontal manoeuvrability was slightly improved, but in the vertical plane it was decreased. Many defects in design and manufacture had not been corrected.

In combat Soviet pilots flew the La-5 with

Top left: **La-5 assembly line at Plant No.21, Gorkii.**

Top right: **Initial La-5 production utilised LaGG-3 airframes.**

Above: **An early production La-5 in service with the Valery Chkalov squadron of the 159th Fighter Regiment. Yakovlev Yak-6 twin-engined transport in the background.**

the canopy open, the cowling side flaps fully open and the tailwheel down, and this reduced its speed by another 18.6 to 24.8mph (30 to 40km/h). As a result, on 25th September 1942 the State Defence Committee issued an edict requiring that the La-5 be lightened, and that its performance and operational characteristics be improved.

The industry produced 1,129 La-5s during the second half of 1942, and these saw use during the counter attack by Soviet troops near Stalingrad. Of 289 La-5s in service with fighter aviation, the majority, 180 aircraft, were assigned to the forces of the Supreme Command Headquarters Reserve. The Soviet Command was preparing for a general winter offensive, and was building up reserves to place in support. One of these strong formations became the 2nd Mixed Air Corps under Hero of the Soviet Union Major-General I Yeryomenko, the two fighter divisions of which had five regiments (the 13th, 181st, 239th, 437th and 3rd Guards) equipped with the improved La-5. The new aircraft proved to be 11 to 12.4mph (18 to 20km/h) faster than the fighter which had passed the state tests at the NII VVS in September and October 1942.

When the 2nd Mixed Air Corps, with more than 300 first class combat aircraft, was used to reinforce the 8th Air Army, the latter had only 160 serviceable aircraft. The 2nd Mixed Air Corps, reliably protecting and supporting the counter offensive by troops along the lines of advance, flew over 8,000 missions and shot down 353 enemy aircraft from 19th November 1942 to 2nd February 1943.

Progress made in combat activities by the Air Corps aviators in co-operation with joint forces during offensive operations on the Stalingrad and Southern fronts were noted by the ground forces Command. General Rodion Malinovsky, Commander of the 2nd Guards Army (later Defence Minister), wrote:

'The active warfare of the fighter units of the 2nd Mixed Air Corps [of which 80% of its aircraft were La-5s], by covering and supporting combat formations of Army troops, actually helped to protect the army from enemy air attacks. Pilots displayed courage, heroism and valour in the battlefield. With appearance of the Air Corps fighters the hostile aircraft avoided battle.

La-5F

Service tests of the La-5 revealed a many defects. In combat it was inferior to the Messerschmitt Bf109, but it had great development potential. This was appreciated by Semyon Lavochkin, who constantly thought about his new creation. Aerodynamic improvements, engine updating, better cockpit view, control enhancement and weight reduction were the main aims of the work carried out during late 1942 and early 1943. A government decree issued on 9th December 1942 authorised development work on the fighter.

To increase maximum level speeds, extensive research using four series-produced aircraft was made jointly by the Tsentral'nyi

Top: **La-5 taxying on a typical improvised airstrip.**

Centre: **Publicity photograph showing naval pilots in front of a naval air arm La-5.**

Above: **With its wide track undercarriage, the La-5 could be operated off snow without the need for skis.**

Aerogidrodynamichesky Institut (TsAGI – Central Aerodynamic and Hydrodynamic Institute), the LII and the Tsentral'nyi Institut Aviatsionnogo Motorostoeniya (TsIAM – Central Institute of Aviation Motors).

The principal modifications resulting from this work were:

- the engine cowling joints were sealed;
- the shape of the oil cooler ducts was improved;
- a new inlet pipe was fitted;
- the area of the exhaust pipe cross-section was increased;
- the tailwheel doors were stiffened.

The test results showed that speeds equal to those of the LaGG-3 M-82 prototype, which the series-built aircraft had failed to match, could be attained. Together with engine designer and builder Arkady Shvetsov, Lavochkin's workers sought to eliminate the M-82's main deficiencies, namely spark plug failures after five to ten hours' use, unsatisfactory oil pump capacity and a tendency for the

exhaust pipes to burn through. As a result of the measures taken, engine service life increased from 100 to 150 hours, and the operating time at augmented power was not limited, allowing pilots to build up supercharger pressure without fear of the consequences. Thus the M-82F engine was created, and from January 1943 its series-production and installation in the Lavochkin fighter (consequently designated La-5F – Forsirovanny, enhanced, or literally 'boosted') began.

Work on the installation of an M-82FNV, augmented by direct fuel injection into the cylinder heads, in place of the carburettor-equipped M-82 and M-82F, proved promising. Development tests of the La-5FNV showed that speed increased to 340.5mph (548km/h) at sea level and 384.6mph (619km/h) at 18,400ft (5,600m) at normal power rating, and the engine later went into series-production as the M-82FN. This boost allowed an increase in take-off power of 1,700 to 1,850hp (1,268 to 1,380kW), and in normal power

Above: **Starting with the ninth batch, the La-5 fuselage decking was lowered to improve rearward vision. Fitted with the boosted M-82F engine, this was the La-5F.**

Bottom: **Semyon Lavochkin against a background of La-5Fs.**

from 1,300hp (969.8kW) at 17,700ft (5,400m) to 1,460hp (1,089kW) at 15,250ft (4,650m) without ram-air.

To improve the pilot's view, from the ninth batch (November 1942) the fighter was given a lower dorsal rear fuselage fairing and a teardrop canopy with armoured glass; in spite of pilots' wishes the windshield was not armoured. This work was similar to that carried out on the Yak-1.

At about the same time, in November 1942, the control column to control surface and aileron gain was changed in accordance with the chief designer's instructions. The shape of the trim tabs was repeatedly altered, the control surfaces were reduced in in area, and flap area was increased. These alterations gave a more favourable combination of controllability and manoeuvrability.

In attacking the problem of reducing the fighter's excessive weight, the designers did not leave a single component unaltered. The wing centre section, the canopy, the landing gear and the powerplant were revised and lightened without detriment to structural strength. The attachment fitting of the landing gear shock struts was welded directly to the front spar, and the shock strut stroke was increased to soften shock absorption. Changes in the structure of the main spars made it possible to reduce the total weight of the wing. The fuel system was altered to use three fuel tanks instead of five, reducing fuel capacity

from 118.5 to 102 gallons (539 to 464 litres) and eliminating the wingtip tanks which hampered manoeuvrability.

The first aircraft incorporating all of these changes was sent to the NII VVS and LII, where it was tested during December 1942 and January 1943. The results of the tests of a full-scale aircraft in the TsAGI wind tunnel were also taken into account.

In accordance with the development process at Plant No.21, the prototype was designated Type 39 (the previous La-5 had been designated Type 37). Its weight was reduced to 7,054lb (3,200kg), the dorsal fairing was lower, the cockpit gave a better rearward view and fuel tankage was reduced. One of the synchronised cannon was replaced by a large calibre synchronised machine gun.

The test results were outstanding. The aircraft reached 321.8mph (518km/h) at sea level at normal power rating, and 345.4mph (556km/h) with augmented power (a speed not previously attained by Soviet fighters), 361.6mph (582km/h) at 11,800ft (3,600m) and 372.8mph (600km/h) at 20,500ft (6,300m). Manoeuvrability was good; a banked turn was performed in 18 to 19 seconds, and the aircraft climbed 3,200ft (1,000m) within a combat turn at normal power rating. During the tests the M-82F was augmented at the second supercharger speed for the first time, and this increased the maximum speed to 380 mph (612km/h) at 19,000ft (5,800m). Tests could not be completed owing to failure of the transmission system for the supercharger's second speed. Additionally, pilot A Kubyshkin found the structural strength of the lightened La-5 inadequate during diving tests.

The new La-5 resembled the first series-built aircraft only superficially. Tests carried out by Plant No.21 in January and February

1943 confirmed that the speed increment was 18.6mph (30km/h), and that all the other performance figures had improved. Even range was not greatly diminished, because the saving of 330lb (150kg) in weight gave the fighter greater endurance despite its reduced fuel tankage. The La-5F began to be widely used on all fronts during the Soviet winter counter offensive of 1942 and 1943.

The 215th Fighter Air Division commanded by Lieutenant General G Kravchenko, twice declared a Hero of the Soviet Union, gained complete familiarity with the La-5 before running the Leningrad blockade. From 6th January to 26th February 1943 the 215th flew 1,761 missions, during which it shot down 103 enemy aircraft, the 2nd Guards Fighter Air Corps under Col E Kondrat giving a particular-

Top: **La-5F of the 21st Fighter Regiment, 1944.**

Below: **A winter camouflaged La-5F on display in the New Technology Hall at TsAGI.**

ly good account of itself. However, 26 pilots were lost, Division Commander G Kravchenko and Major Kuznetsov, Commander of the 233rd Fighter Air Corps, being among the officers killed.

The fate of First Lt P Grazhdaninov was unusual. After arriving at the 169th Fighter Air Corps with other ferry pilots he remained there. An outstanding fighter pilot, he completely mastered the La-5 but did not survive long, being killed in battle on 5th March 1943, by which time he had scored 13 victories.

The 4th Guards Fighter Air Corps of the Baltic Fleet was converting from the Polikarpov I-16 to the La-5 in April 1943. Although the pilots and their commander, Major V Golubev, considered the La-5 a modern aircraft not inferior to the Bf109F and Fw190A in speed, they became aware of its disadvantages: a tendency to turn sharply to the right during take-off, difficult to taxy on soft ground and a propensity for the engine to overheat during ground running.

These and other defects were observed at the other fronts as well. When large numbers of La-5s began to enter service in early 1943, the failure rate was three times as great as those of other fighters. Urgent measures were required to improve reliability. Specifically, Viktor Rastorguev and Alexey Grinchik conducted inverted spinning tests in early 1943, and as a result recommended piloting techniques for the La-5 were passed to operational units. Previously, pilots in these units had abandoned their aircraft if they entered an inverted spin.

Some comment is required regarding the La-5's survivability. The use of self-sealing fuel tanks and an inert gas system in two areas, and, of course, the use of a highly-survivable air-cooled engine, placed the aircraft in a good light compared with LaGG-3s and Yaks. However, only in early 1943 were radical improvements achieved. The adoption of central fuel tanks of greater capacity, relieving the wings their hazardous fuel load, and the drastic shortening of the fuel and oil lines resulted in a reduction in combat losses, especially during ground-attack sorties.

In the spring of 1943 the La-5 was not inferior to its opponents with regard to combined flying qualities. At that time Plant No.21 was sending 350 to 400 La-5s to the lines monthly, and Plant No.99 in Ulan-Ude and Plant No.381 in Moscow also started assembling the type.

This allowed certain reserves to be accumulated by the summer. On 1st July the forces in the field had 978 La-5s and La-5Fs, more than a quarter of all the fighters available. Only 85 needed repair; the rest were combat-ready on the eve of the great battle of the Kursk Bulge.

Among those keeping watch in La-5 cockpits was Ivan Kozhedub of the 240th Fighter Air Corps, unknown at the time but destined to become the greatest Soviet ace. By early June 1943 about 200 aircraft powered by M-82FNs had been assembled; they were delivered unfinished to service units.

Top: **Air-to-air study of an La-5F. Soviet fighter pilots habitually flew with the canopy open.**

Second and third from top: **Two views of the first of four La-5s (No.37210514) with improvements following joint TsAGI, LII and TsIAM recommendations. Note the redesigned air intake on top of the engine cowling.**

Bottom: **Thorough aerodynamic researches resulted in a revised cowling for this La-5 (No.37210850). These modifications were taken up in the La-5FN.**

Right: **Another La-5 (No:37210853) from the development batch of four. While retaining the former cowling shape, much sealing and reshaping has taken place.**

Below and bottom: **Two views of the first production La-5 (No.39210101) of the Type 39 that benefited from numerous changes.**

Second La-5 Type 39 (No.39210102), designated La-5FNV with the direct injection M-82FNV engine.

Moscow Plant No.381 test flew La-5F '03' with direct fuel injection to the Shvetsov engine; these trials were unsuccessful.

The fourth La-5 Type 39 (No.39210104) was fitted with the M-82FN and a new air intake previously tested on two La-5s.

La-5FN

A delay in the testing of the La-5 Type 39 did not stop Semyon Lavochkin's work. During March 1943 the bureau completed the second prototype Type 39, a duplicate powered by the already tested M-82FN engine. Unlike other La-5s it had metal main spars, like those of the Yak-9. Like the series aircraft, however, it was armed with two synchronised ShVAK cannon, and its finish and aerodynamics were even more improved. Pilot A Nikashin managed to attain a speed of 369.7mph (595 km/h) at sea level at augmented power, and 402.6mph (648km/h) at 20,000ft (6,300m). The time to 16,400ft (5,000m) was 4.7 minutes at normal power rating. Reduction of the aircraft's weight to 6,984lb (3,168kg) enabled it to perform a banked turn at low altitude in 18.5 seconds. Just after these flights the Government issued a decree ordering the aircraft into series-production, and requiring that the performance of the second prototype be matched in the production machines.

This was the last occasion that Semyon Lavochkin and A Nikashin worked together. A skilled pilot and gifted engineer, Nikashin devoted much effort to improving the LaGG and La fighters, and his outstanding role in testing the I-301 and starting its series-production must be acknowledged. In June 1943 he was killed while testing the Gu-1 fighter designed by Mikhail Gudkov.

Unfortunately, not all of the innovations could be incorporated in series aircraft in the spring of 1943. They had a wing, centre section and other components similar to those of series-built La-5s and a flying weight of 7,286lb (3,305kg).

Performance proved to be rather worse than that of the prototype Type 39. Speed fell to 329.3mph (530km/h) at sea level and 379mph (610km/h) at 19,000ft (5,800m), and time to 16,400ft (5,000m) was about five minutes (a figure typical of all subsequent La-5FNs). Tearing of the fabric covering from the surface prevented tests with augmented power. During the trials, manufacturing defects were noticed.

Top: **Semyon Lavochkin (fourth from left) among pilots and co-designers, with an La-5FN in the background.**

Centre: **La-5FNs in post-war service with the Czechoslovakian Air Force.** *Philip Jarrett collection*

Bottom: **A production La-5FN that underwent operational testing with the 32nd Guards Fighter Regiment, operating over the Bryansk Sector of the Front, July-August 1943.**

This did not impede the service tests of the La-5FN. The first series-produced aircraft became operational with one of the best Soviet Air Force regiments of the time, the 32nd Guards Air Corps, commanded by Hero of the Soviet Union Colonel V Davidkov. During the battle of Kursk the regiment's pilots flew 25 combat missions on La-5FNs, bringing down 33 enemy aircraft (including 21 Fw 190As) for the loss of six, four being shot down and two crashing during forced-landings. Soviet aces greatly appreciated the new fighter. Hero of the Soviet Union Captain V Garanin noted:

'Combats were fought at altitudes up to [13,000ft] 4,000m with obvious advantages over the Fw 190 and Bf 109, both in speed and in horizontal and vertical manoeuvring. The La-5FN with an open canopy [as Soviet pilots used to fly it] overtakes hostile fighters, albeit slowly, gets on their tails during banked turns, and in a vertical air combat always turns to get above the enemy'.

Shortcomings were also reported. Gun aiming was made more difficult by the presence of the top air intake cowling, which could obscure the target, and by the high position of the sight, which precluded the possibility of flying with the canopy closed. It was claimed that the cockpit was very hot and that exhaust gases entered it, and also that radio communication was inadequate. When assessing the results of the service tests it should be borne in mind that they took place when the opposing forces were very strong. The Soviet pilots faced the Fw 190A-4s of the Luftwaffe's Jagdgeschwader 51, assigned to Luftflotte 6, and it is worth comparing the two fighters.

The intention of Focke-Wulf chief designer Kurt Tank to provide the Fw 190 with powerful ordnance and adequate armour led to a considerable growth in payload and, consequently, to an increase in the total flying weight. The Fw 190A was at least half a ton heavier than the La-5FN. At the same time, in an effort to ensure maximum speed, Tank opted for a rather high wing loading, which degraded take-off and landing characteristics and manoeuvrability. Of no small importance was the fact that, with similar dimensions, cubic capacity, speed and boost, the power of the M-82FN engine was much greater than that of the BMW 801D-2 at altitudes up to 14,700ft (4,500m). It was at low and medium altitudes that the German fighters were most inferior in speed. Even with the MW 50 methanol-water injection system used on the Fw 190A-4 and the La-5FN being flown with its canopy open, the latter had a 9.3 to 15.5mph (15 to 25km/h) higher speed up to 10,000ft (3,000m) and could get on the enemy's tail after the first combat turn.

Kurt Tank's creation had advantages as well. Its all-metal structure had much higher survivability, and vital components were heavily armoured; the pilot's view, both in flight and on the ground, was better; a single master control operated from the central control column greatly facilitated piloting; and its armament was about three times as powerful. On the whole, however, the comparison was not in the Fw 190's favour.

German experts considered the La-5FN the most dangerous threat on the Eastern Front in the summer and autumn of 1943. When one forced-landed on enemy territory, it was repaired by the Luftwaffe and tested extensively. The resulting report was clearly intended to reassure German pilots, as the Soviet fighter was described as 'rather primitive' and 'not completely equipped', and as having 'unreliable equipment, a rudimentary sight and a very troublesome hydraulic system'.

In spite of its merits, the La-5FN was not put into quantity production immediately because M-82FN engines were not available in the numbers required. Production in sufficient quantities and delivery to Gorkii began only in the autumn of 1943, while the other plants continued building La-5Fs.

In November 1943 La-5FN No 39210495 was thoroughly tested at the air force NII by pilot A Kubyshkin and leading engineer V Alexeenko. It was stated that the improved aerodynamic elevator balance made the aircraft nicer to fly, but attention was mainly directed at performance. At a weight of 7,323lb (3,322kg) the La-5FN developed a speed of 336.7mph (542km/h) at sea level (356mph – 573km/h with augmented power), 377mph (607km/h) at 10,500ft (3,250m) and 385mph (620km/h) at 20,000ft (6,150m), maintaining excellent manoeuvrability in both the horizontal and vertical planes.

Kurt Tank's exceptional Focke-Wulf Fw 190 ('A-3s illustrated) and Semyon Lavochkin's La-5 have much in common, in terms of performance and development history. *Ken Ellis collection*

Close-up of a taxying La-5FN.

An La-5 M-71 inside the TsAGI wind tunnel.

The La-5 M-71 that was used in the TsAGI tunnel
tests was refurbished and entered flight test.

Aware of the La-5FN's high performance,
German pilots refused to engage with them at
medium altitudes, trying either to draw them
higher or attack them during a final dive.

Soviet airmen gained a tactical advantage
from the close external similarity of the La-
5FN to its slower and less powerful predecessor, the La-5F, because Luftwaffe pilots could
not tell them apart.

It is acknowledged that the La-5FNs played
an important part in establishing Soviet air superiority and around 1,500 were built up to
late 1943.

La-5F with TK-3 supercharger

The Lavochkin OKB also studied high altitude
fighters, choosing to use turbosuperchargers
to increase service ceiling. Construction of
three prototypes fitted with S Treskin's TK-
3 supercharger started in early 1943. One was
intended for powerplant development, another for perfection of a pressurised cockpit.

As far as is known from OKB documents,
only one La-5F with the TK-3 was built in the
summer of 1943. No significant changes were
introduced in the airframe. The supercharger
increased service ceiling to 31,000ft (9,500m),
similar to that of the modified Yak-9PD, but at
7,341lb (3,330kg) the La-5F TK-3 was more
than half a ton heavier, and its service ceiling
was 1,600ft (500m) lower as a result. Later,
design studies of high altitude interceptors
were concentrated in the Yakovlev and
Mikoyan bureaux.

La-5 with Shvetsov M-71

Work on the installation of the more powerful
M-71 engine in the La-5 is interesting. Compared with the series-produced aircraft, the
air intake was relocated to the lower portion
of the engine cowling, and dual and triple exhaust pipes were fitted in place of the exhaust
collector ring. The oil cooler was moved rearwards to position the centre of gravity further
aft, and improvements were introduced into
the fuselage structure, landing gear and engine mounting. The M-71 delivered 2,200hp
(1,641kW) at sea level, compared with 1,850
hp (1,380kW) of the the M-82FN at take-off. It
was also shorter, reducing the aircraft's overall length by 7.8in (200mm).

The La-5 M-71 was flight tested by G Mischenko from late April to early June 1943.
Having made 20 flights he observed:

'Compared with the series-built La-5, the
La-5 with the M-71 is less stable longitudinally,
which gives it better control sensitivity, easy
and pleasant handling, and improved manoeuvrability; landing is simple to perform'.

The aircraft was extensively tested and developed by the LII in the autumn of 1943, the
evaluations of stability and controllability
being especially exhaustive. On the whole,
the comments were favourable, and the aircraft's performance was also pleasing. At a
weight of 7,773lb (3,526kg), which had increased because of the heavier engine, it
reached 380mph (612km/h) at sea level and
425.6mph (685km/h) at 18,000ft (5,500m).

The main reasons why the La-5 M-71 was
not put into production were the unavailabili-
ty of M-71 engines in sufficient numbers and a
reluctance to upset the already organised
process of La-5 production.

La-5UTI

Another La-5 variant was the La-5UTI (Uchebno-Trenirovochny Istrebitel – training fighter)
fighter trainer, which featured a second cockpit for an instructor. The starboard cannon,
armoured canopy glass, armoured backrest,
radio and oxygen equipment, the inert gas
system and the bomb racks were removed.

The La-5UTI was tested at the NII VVS by pilots A Kubyshkin and Yu Antipov and leading
engineer V Alexeenko in September 1943. It
was highly praised and recommended for
use by flying schools and reserve air regiments. Especially attractive were the insignificant differences from the series-built La-5F
with regard to handling and performance.

A small quantity of La-5UTIs was produced
at Gorkii, 28 being delivered to the Soviet Air
Force. A more modified trainer at the time
was the Yak-7V, which became the main
fighter trainer of the second half of the war.

Top left: **Major I Vishnyakov, Deputy Commander of the 171st Fighter Regiment, in his La-5FN. The legend beneath the cockpit reads 'For Oleg Koshevoy'. Koshevoy headed an underground anti-Fascist youth organisation and was posthumously awarded the title of Hero of the Soviet Union.**

Top right: **Production La-5UTI, with enclosed rear cockpit, during tests at the NII VVS.**

Above: **The prototype La-5UTI, with a second, open, cockpit inserted in what was the radio bay of the conventional single-seater.**

Left: **A specialist from the Lavochkin OKB in discussion with pilots in front of an La-5UTI.**

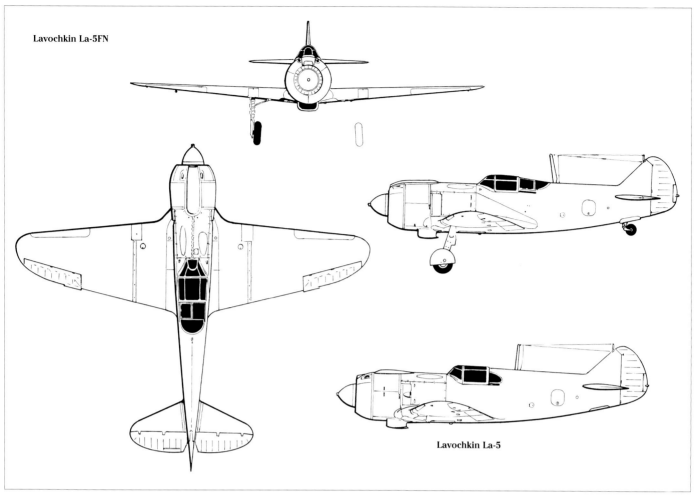

Lavochkin La-5FN

Lavochkin La-5

La-7

Series production of the La-5, and the fighter's success in combat, gave impetus to its further development. However, all of the innovations proposed by the design bureau, the LII and the TsAGI were far from being realised in quantity production at the various plants.

In the middle of 1943, TsAGI continued studies of a possible further improvement of the La-5. Based on extensive wind tunnel tests of the aircraft, a series of measures aimed at aerodynamic improvement were determined. These included complete sealing of the engine cowling, re-arrangement of the wing centre section, and changes to the oil-cooling and exhaust systems. These alterations formed the basis for the second stage of La-5 improvements (the first modification stage was mainly carried out in early 1943, when the La-5FN appeared).

To prove the effectiveness of its proposals, the TsAGI modified La-5FN No.39210206, which underwent flight tests at the LII in the hands of test pilot N Adamovich and engineer V Molochayev from December 1943 until February 1944. These tests fully validated the effectiveness of the improvements suggested by TsAGI. With an engine identical to that installed in the La-5FN and at a weight of 7,594 lb (3,445kg) the new fighter attained a speed

of 425mph (684km/h) at 20,200ft (6,150m), 39.7mph (64km/h) higher than that of the production La-5FN and 22.3mph (36km/h) higher than that of the La-5 duplicate Type 39. In terms of speed, La-5 No.39210206 was superior to its counterpart with with the more powerful Shvetsov M-71 engine up to an altitude of 14,100ft (4,300m).

Semyon Lavochkin followed the work at TsAGI closely. When the Government tasked him with creating a standard for the 1944 production aircraft, all of the TsAGI recommendations were taken into account. The aircraft built by Plant No.21 in Gorkii in January 1944, under the leadership of Semyon Alexeyev, differed in several notable respects from its forebears:

- metal wing spars replaced the wooden examples;
- improved internal and external sealing of the powerplant and airframe (as on La-5 No.39210206);
- three test B-20 synchronised cannon, based on the M Berezin 12.7mm machine gun, instead of two cannon;
- the oil cooler was moved from the bottom of the engine cowling to the rear fuselage underside, and housed in a duct of improved aerodynamic configuration;
- the location and shape of the engine inlet pipe was changed (it was provided with

two intakes brought out to the wing centre section leading edge, instead of having one intake placed on the top of the engine cowling);

The following external features distinguished the 1944 standard production aircraft from La-5 No.39210206:

- improved wing/fuselage fillets;
- individual exhaust pipes for each of the engine cylinders;
- fewer engine cowling covers;
- longer landing gear shock struts and a shorter skid;
- the use of a propeller having a flapping-resistant blade profile, as already tested on the La-5FN;
- a metal nose-over-protection frame in the fixed, aft portion of the canopy;
- an updated gunsight.

On completion the aircraft went almost immediately to the NII VVS for tests undertaken by pilot A Kubyshkin and leading engineer V Alexeenko. After a short period of trials, from February to March 1944, the flights were suspended owing to two engine failures when connecting rods were broken and the fuselage skin was torn off. Kubyshkin made only nine flights, but they were sufficient to show that the aircraft was good.

At a flying weight of 7,197lb (3,265kg) – weight was saved by using metal in the wing

Two views of La-5 No.39210206 at TsAGI. It served as the prototype for the La-7 series.

structure – the 1944-standard La-5 achieved a speed of 370mph (597km/h) at sea level and 422mph (680km/h) at 20,000ft (6,000m) at normal power rating (there was no time for further tests), while 4.45 minutes were required to climb to 16,400ft (5,000m). The test report stated that, in terms of maximum level flying speed and rate of climb, the 1944-standard modified La-5 kept pace with the best modern fighters. It was 31 to 37mph (50 to 60km/h) faster than production La-5FNs, and almost met the government's requirements for aircraft of this type. Almost all of the innovations introduced were recommended for adoption in series-built aircraft. The exception was the B-20 cannon. As its tests had been delayed it was decided to equip the production fighters, designated La-7, with ordnance similar to that of the La-5FN.

By the time the La-7 was being introduced into production, extensive work had been carried out at Gorkii to improve the processes. As a result, labour required for building production aircraft was more than halved. The People's Commissariat of the Aircraft Industry believed that this was still not enough, and demanded the final assembly line work at a fixed production rate. This required interchangeability of components, and called for the manufacture of many standard templates and special fixtures to avoid the making and reworking of individual parts *in situ*.

At the same time, the flow-line methods conflicted with the necessity to improve and modify the aircraft continually. Partial revision of the drawings enabled the chief designer to introduce new variants relatively smoothly.

Plant No.21 could organise production of the La-7 within two or three months. Pre-production was arranged so that the first production La-7 was scheduled to be built as soon as the 1944-standard La-5 completed its official flight tests. Twenty were commissioned.

La-5s were put into production even more successfully by Plant No.381 in Moscow. There, it had been planned that the first five would be completed in May 1944, but they were already assembled in March, and three had even been accepted by the military.

In both cases, the setting up of La-7 production did not cause a reduction in total output. The reason for the difference between the two factories was that the stock of wooden wings in Gorkii was so great that the plant continued assembling La-5FNs until October 1944, while the Moscow plant had turned entirely to the improved La-7s by June.

As before, performance of series-produced La-7s was inferior to that of the prototype.

Thus flight tests conducted at the LII in July 1944 showed that the maximum speed had fallen to 344mph (554km/h) at sea level and 397mph (640km/h) at 6,000m, which meant that the La-7's speed was not significantly greater than that of a production La-5FN. Although the La-7's weight had fallen to 7,131lb (3,235kg), the time to climb to 16,400ft (5,000m) was 5.1 minutes.

The reasons behind the loss of speed were analysed by a team headed by Molochayev. The main causes were as follows:

- departure of the ASh-82FN engine characteristics from the specifications owing to improper adjustment and defects;
- incomplete sealing of the engine cowling and fuselage;
- deviation of the propeller's aerofoil section from the theoretical profile.

When tested at the LII, a production La-7 with these defects remedied reached 361 mph (582km/h) at sea level and 418mph (674km/h) at 20,000ft (6,000m); figures conforming to those of the prototype. It only remained to realise this performance in the production aircraft, but, as it transpired, this was not an easy task. Both plants had built about 400 La-7s when production aircraft made by Plants No.21 and No.381 were flight tested at NII VVS in early September 1944. At a weight of 7,164lb (3,250kg) they reached a speed of 355.4 to 359mph (572 to 578km/h) at sea level (with augmented power speed increased to 380mph – 612km/h), and 407 to 408mph (655 to 658km/h) at 19,400 to 20,000ft (5,900m-6,100m), and gained 3,300 to 4,000ft (1,000 to 1,230m) in a combat turn, even at normal power rating. This last figure, defining vertical manoeuvrability, was respectable.

Only the Yakovlev Yak-3 VK-105PF2 and Yak-9U VK-107A could compete with Semyon Lavochkin's creation, which gained 4,600ft (1,400m) under augmented power. Various modifications of the Messerschmitt Bf109G which had hitherto been superior in vertical manoeuvrability could not match the La-7. This was soon discovered by Luftwaffe pilots, who had to change tactics in combat with the new Soviet fighter.

Service flight tests of the La-7 began in mid-September 1944, and were conducted by the 63rd Guards Fighter Air Corps at the First Baltic Front for one month. Thirty La-7s, mostly built by the Moscow aircraft production plant, were assigned to the tests. All of the pilots had been flying La-5s in combat from the autumn of 1942, so each needed only three to five flights to convert to the new type. Maintenance personnel did not find it difficult to become familiar with the La-7.

During the tests, the regiment made 462 sorties, during which 55 enemy aircraft were shot down for the loss of eight La-7s (half of which were non-combat) and three pilots.

All of the accidents resulted from engine failures. Unfortunately the engine, which was already giving satisfactory service on the La-5FN, exhibited numerous and serious defects when installed in the La-7. One cause was the lower position of the air intake, resulting in the ingestion of sand and dust into the cylinders.

Armament operation was also complicated, making it more difficult to prepare for a mission. Most importantly, the combat operations revealed the insufficient salvo power of the La-7's guns. A burst of fire was rarely sufficient to bring down an enemy fighter, especially a Fw190, even though Soviet pilots opened fire at 164 to 328ft (50 to 100m).

These problems could not overshadow the evident advantages of the new fighter. According to a regimental commander, Hero of the Soviet Union Colonel E Gorbatyuk:

'The La-7 exhibited unquestionable advantages over German aircraft in multiple air combats. In addition to fighter tasks, photographic reconnaissance and bombing were undertaken with success. The aircraft surpasses the La-5FN in speed, manoeuvrability and, especially, in landing characteristics. It requires changes in its armament, and urgent fixing of the engine'.

A positive assessment of the operational capabilities of Lavochkin's new production fighter cannot ignore the increased skill of Soviet pilots, particularly in guards regiments. Major A Voronko added eight more victories to his eleven, and Major A Pashkevich ten more to his seven during the month of tests. Both were made Heroes of the Soviet Union.

Following the 63rd Guards Fighter Air Corps, the 156th Fighter Air Corps of the 4th Air Army began operating the La-7. During October 1944 no fewer than 14 aircraft went out of commission simultaneously as a result of ASh-82FN engine failures. This was even more disappointing because the flight personnel thought rather highly of the new fighter's operational capabilities.

During October and November 1944 La-7s began to be used widely on all fronts. Along with Yak-3 VK-105PF2s and Yak-9U VK-107As, they played an important part in air combats in the closing period of the war. More than 2,000 La-7s, mainly built by major Plant No.21, were sent to the front up to the war's end.

These aircraft proved troublesome during late October 1944. Owing to failure of the wings in flight, six accidents, four of them fatal, occurred in operational units within a short time, and Soviet Army Air Force Commander Marshal A Novikov was obliged to ground the La-7 until the cause was determined. The accident board, consisting of air force and industry representatives, quickly found a reduced density of the spar material, and the defect was remedied.

By early 1945 there were 398 La-7s in front line air force units, and 291 were combat ready. This was equivalent to about 6% of all serviceable fighters. By the end of the war this had increased to 15%.

An especially notable part was played by the La-7s of the 2nd, 3rd and 4th Air Armies, which were among the best in terms of survivability. A total of 115 La-7s were lost in combat, half the number of Yak-3s, though the intensity of air combats was similar for both aircraft at the end of the war.

The La-7's high performance became fully apparent in the change of Luftwaffe tactics at the end of the war. German fighter units re-equipped with the multi-purpose Fw190A, 'F and 'G used the tactic of 'surprise pirate raids' on a large scale. They would attack advancing Soviet vehicle columns, the forward edge of the front line and close rear positions, then escape at full speed using augmented power. Yak-3s and Yak-9Us had an insufficient margin of speed to intercept the Fw190s at low altitude, but the task could be performed by the La-7, though not without difficulty.

This was confirmed again during the air battle over Herasdorf on 10th April 1944. Captain N Skomorokhov, a squadron commander in the 31st Fighter Air Regiment, downed two Fw190s in the combat, and when the enemy aircraft retreated he gave chase and brought down another that was making off at full speed. The excellent qualities of the La-7 enabled Skomorokhov to score 46 personal victories and eight shared ones by the end of the war. For these successes he was awarded his second Hero's Gold Star.

Ivan Kozhedub, declared Hero of the Soviet Union three times, flew an La-7 until the end of the war. His 17 victories gained on this aircraft included a Messerschmitt Me262 twin-jet fighter flown by Luftwaffe ace Colonel Walter Schuck (206 confirmed victories). Kozhedub's La-7 is now exhibited in the Air Force Museum at Monino.

A Gorkii-built La-5, defined as the '1944 standard' was modified further from the status of La-5 '206 and became the base-line for the La-7.

This aircraft differed from the previous La-5 series in having metal wing spars, the oil cooler installed in the centre section and three 20mm cannon as armament.

Photographs on the opposite page:

Top: During the winter of 1944 two plants (No.381 in Moscow and No.21 in Gorkii) launched into production of the definitive La-7.

Centre: La-7 No.45210139, used by NII VVS to evaluate manufacturing quality.

Bottom: La-7 No.45210150, Gorkii-built and also used by NII VVS to evaluate manufacturing quality.

Photographs on this page:

Top: From the autumn of 1944 La-7s began to reach all sectors of the front line. The type was received with immediate enthusiasm by both pilots and mechanics and was destined to become one of the best fighters of the war.

Above: Posed shot showing pilots in front of an La-7 under camouflage netting.

A total of 5,753 La-7s was built by the three plants (No.21 in Gorkii, No.99 in Ulan-Ude and No.381 in Moscow) up to the war's end. The last of them were fitted, like the 1944 standard fighter, with three fully developed synchronised B-20 cannon. With this armament the weight of the La-7's volley increased to 7.5lb (3.4kg) per second, which met battlefield requirements in full. Production of the three-cannon La-7 began in January 1945, when 74 were built.

As with previous Lavochkin types, the La-7 formed the basis of a great number of variants. Like the La-5, prototypes of the La-7 TK (equipped with a turbosupercharger) and the La-7 M-71 (with a more powerful engine that did not go into production) were created.

La-7UTI

Compared with the La-5UTI, a more fortunate fate awaited the La-7UTI because it was mass produced at Gorkii. The La-7UTI differed little from its predecessors in design and equipment, but the report issued following its official tests at the NII VVS in August 1945 claimed that the aircraft could not be used as a trainer, mainly because it was insufficiently equipped for the adequate training of cadets and flying personnel, the requirements for aircraft of this type having become much more stringent since the war's end.

The La-7UTI underwent prolonged development, the oil cooler alone being relocated several times. It was equipped with a radio compass and a camera, and as a result its flying weight reached 7,716lb (3,500kg), considerably greater than that of the La-7. However, the La-7UTI's handling qualities differed little from those of the single-seat fighter. Production of the La-7UTI totalled 584 aircraft, the last two being completed in 1947.

La-7PVRD and La-7R

The La-7 served as a test-bed for experiments with the first jet engines, the work being similar to that carried out by the Yakovlev Design Bureau. With two PVRD-430 ramjet motors under its wings, the La-7 was expected to attain a speed of 497mph (800km/h) at 19,600ft (6,000m). However, the high drag of the underslung ramjet units prevented it exceeding 416mph (670km/h), which lessened interest in this work.

The La-7R (Reaktivny – literally, 'reaction' meaning rocket or jet) was more promising. This experimental aircraft, which emerged in late 1944, was fitted with an additional liquid-propellant rocket engine designed by Valentin Glushko, giving 661lb (300kg) of additional thrust. The engine was housed in the rear fuselage, beneath the fin and rudder, as on the Yak-3RD, the tailplane being slightly raised. The fuel reserve for the 'R was 19.8 gallons (90 litres) of kerosene and 39.5 gallons (180 litres) of acid. To save weight, the fuel load was reduced to 474lb (215kg), but the aircraft still weighed some 7,716lb (3,500kg).

Compared with the La-7, speed increased by 49.7mph (80km/h) with the rocket engine operating for 3 to 3.5 minutes, but the fighter's other flying qualities, such as controllability and manoeuvrability, deteriorated. During the first three months of 1945 pilots G Shiyanov and A Davydov made 15 test flights, but not without accident. On 12th May 1945 the rocket engine exploded on the ground; fortunately nobody was killed. Then there was an in-flight explosion, but Shiyanov managed to land the damaged aircraft. Despite all the difficulties, the La-7R was displayed in a parade at Tushino on 18th August 1946 with its rocket engine ignited.

The completion of work on the La-7 signified a great milestone in the history of the Lavochkin OKB. It had achieved a considerable

improvement in production fighters by installing more and more powerful engines (Klimov M-105P and M-105PF, Shvetsov M-82 and M-82FN), consistently lightening the structure and enhancing the aerodynamics. While many claims were made regarding the LaGG-3, which does not rank with the best fighters of the initial period of the war, Luftwaffe pilots considered the La-7 one of the most dangerous threats on the Eastern front.

Flying weight rose from the 7,297lb (3,310kg) typical of a LaGG-3 in the autumn of 1941 to 7,429lb (3,370kg) for the La-7 in March 1946 – an insignificant increase. Maximum speed rose from 287mph (462km/h) to 396 mph (638km/h); an increase of 109.3mph (176km/h) at sea level and 62mph (100km/h) at 16,400ft (5,000m). The time to climb to 16,400ft (5,000m) fell from from 8.6 to 4.6 minutes, and climb within a combat turn increased from 1,640 to 1,968ft (500 to 600m) to 4,593 to 4,921ft (1,400 to 1,500m) – at augmented power rating. Manoeuvrability did not suffer, as the time required for a banked turn was 20 to 21 seconds. Such results were impressive.

The Lavochkin Design Bureau completed the first stage of its history with the La-7 fighter. Although they looked similar, the Types '126', '130' and La-9 production aircraft were neither a modification nor a follow-on of the La-7 design. They were entirely new aircraft of all-metal construction, with a very different single spar wing (instead of the two-spar wing of the earlier modifications) using a TsAGI laminar flow section and lacking leading edge slats. The La-9, which also had other distinctive features, was built in series after the war. These aircraft played their part before jet aircraft entered into Soviet Air Force service.

For technical data, see Table A, page 174.

Above: **Semyon Lavochkin (second from right) amid pilots of the Naval Air Force with an La-7 in the background.**

Photographs on opposite page:

Top and centre: **Quality control testing of production aircraft was always being undertaken at the NII VVS. Two views of a production La-7 under assessment. Note the La-7 logo immediately above the red star on the tail.**

Bottom: **La-7 No.45214468 at the LII during tests of a moulded windscreen and hydraulic booster.**

Lavochkin La-7 series production standard

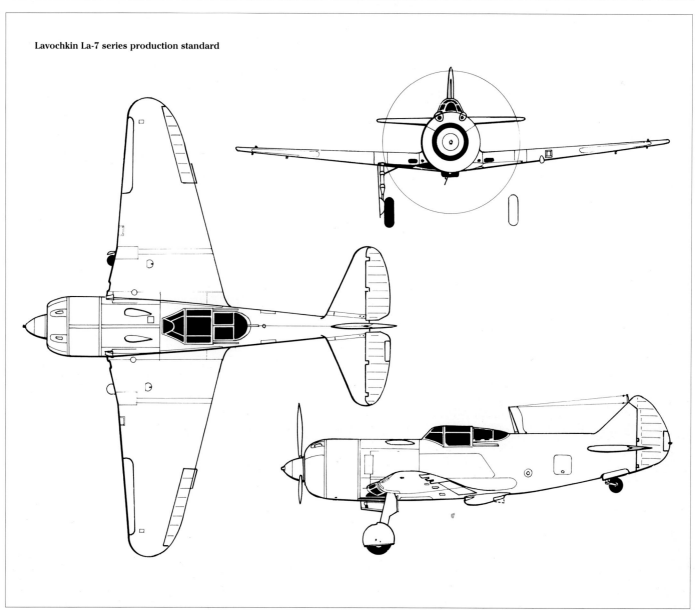

Photograph on opposite page:

Another La-7 with moulded canopy. Note the double pitot head mounted under the starboard wing.

Photographs on this page:

Top: The La-7TK prototype, fitted with a pair of superchargers to improve high altitude performance.

Right: Port turbosupercharger installation, La-7TK.

Bottom: La-7UTI No.46210117 undergoing trials, October 1945.

Top: **Much work was carried out on refining the La-7UTI. No.46210315 under test, March 1946.**

Above right: **The cowling removed from the nozzle of the RD-1KhZ liquid rocket in the extreme tail of the La-7R.**

Centre left: **The ramjet-equipped La-7PVRD proved to have a disappointing performance.**

Above left and bottom left: **Two views of the La-7R rocket-augmented fighter, with the booster located in the lower rear venting underneath the modified rudder.**

Above: Only known photograph of the M-71-powered prototype La-7 with enlarged diameter engine cowling. The deletion of the detail on the horizon is presumably the work of a wartime censor.

Below: The Monino Museum's La-7 was put on display in the static at Domodedovo Airport, Moscow, in the summer of 1967. The fighter had been flown by Soviet ace Ivan Kozhedub with a total of 62 'kills'.

Mikoyan-Gurevich

For more than 50 years MiG aircraft have been famous not only in the USSR but worldwide. It is therefore interesting to know what the first MiG fighter, combining the initial letters of the surnames of Artyom Mikoyan and Mikhail Gurevich, looked like.

Designated I-200 (I - istrebitel, fighter, or 'destroyer') before full scale production, the MiG-1 was designed in the Polikarpov Opytno Konstruktorskoye Byuro (OKB – experimental design bureau). Nikolay Polikarpov, being very gifted, was the instigator of a great many projects. In 1939 he was chief designer of Aviahim Plant No.1, the unquestioned leader in the Soviet aircraft industry.

At that time production of the I-15*bis* (literally from the French or Latin 'again' or encore, more practically, a rethought version, or even Mk.2) and I-153 Chaika (Seagull) was the main task of the plant. Polikarpov himself considered that, in addition to high speed monoplanes, it was necessary to produce manoeuvrable biplanes of the Chaika type, so in late 1939 he proposed the preliminary design of a new version of the Chaika, retrofitted with a Klimov M-105P water-cooled engine, to a group of engineers headed by Nikolay Matyuk. Estimated speed of a new aircraft was 316mph (510km/h), and its armament was to comprise a 20mm ShVAK gun mount-

ed between the engine cylinders and two synchronised 7.62mm ShKAS machine guns.

Taking into consideration the latest experience of combat operations in Spain and Europe, the chief designer tasked N Andrianov with the preparation of a preliminary design for a high speed fighter with the new water-cooled AM-37 rated at 1,400hp (1,044kW), which at that time was being designed by the Alexander Mikulin Design Bureau.

Estimated performance of the new fighter included a maximum speed of 416mph (670 km/h) at 23,000ft (7,000m); time to 16,400ft (5,000m) of not more than 4.6 minutes and a service ceiling of 42,600ft (13,000m).

Two turbosuperchargers would increase the speed to 445mph (717km/h) at 38,000ft (11,600m). Work on this project proceeded slowly, because it was considered to be insufficiently advanced. Polikarpov himself was busy introducing the I-180 fighter into production.

It is now difficult to determine the process, but late in November 1939 the I-153 was phased out owing to its dated structure. This was reasonable, because an up-to-date plant could manufacture a more advanced aircraft, but nobody knew exactly what kind of aircraft this might be. Personnel at the plant did not want to waste time waiting for their fate to be decided by those in power, so they organised a commission headed by the chief of production, Y Karpov, to become acquainted with the new generation of combat aircraft.

After investigations, the commission chose the I-26. Alexander Yakovlev had promoted his aircraft, which seemed assured of success, because he appreciated the advantages of having the I-26 built in such a modern factory as Aviahim Aircraft Building Plant No.1. At this time assembly of the first prototype was under way, and its designer expected it to have a maximum speed of 360mph (580 km/h), exceeding that of the I-16 by 62mph (100km/h). However, Polikarpov Design Bureau personnel were in favour of the preliminary design of a new fighter, faster than the I-26. The conclusions of the commission were signed by Mikhail Gurevich, Nikolay Matyuk, N Andrianov and A Karev.

A final decision was quickly taken; the preliminary design of the AM-37-powered fighter should be completed as soon as possible. In early December the project was ready, and it was adopted by a director of Plant No.1, P Voronin, chief engineer Peotr Dementiev, People's Commissar of the Aircraft Industry M Kaganovich and the Voenno-vozdushniye Sily (VVS – air forces of the USSR) commander-in-chief. The decision to organise the design of a new fighter designated I-200 at Plant No.1 as a matter of urgency was adopted. In order to accomplish this task successfully the leaders of the Commissariat decided to set up a Special Design Department (OKO) under the leadership of Artyom Mikoyan.

A small digression is needed at this point.

Photographs on the opposite page:

Two views of the MiG-1 prototype, the I-200, which completed development testing by the end of May 1940.

Photographs on this page:

The third I-200 prototype during flight tests. Compare the nose contours with the first I-200.

The year 1939 had been very busy for young military engineer Artyom Mikoyan. Early in the year he had been merely a military acceptance official at Plant No.1, but in March he was appointed head of the Manoeuvrable Fighters Design Group of the Aircraft Industry. In May Mikoyan deputised for Polikarpov with regard to full scale production of the Chaika, and in November he became a chief designer, acting on behalf of the 'king of the fighters', who had been sent to Germany on business. Although Mikoyan had been a good engineer during his two years at the plant, this was not the main reason for his headlong advancement. His elder brother, Anastas, was a National Commissar of Foreign Trade and a Vice-Chairman of the Council of National Commissars of the USSR, and was in favour with Joseph Stalin.

M Gurevich and V Romodin, who had great experience and vast academic qualifications, became deputies of Mikoyan. The OKO staff comprised engineers and designers from the Polikarpov Design Bureau, and though this was not ethical with respect to Nikolay Polikarpov, he made light of the situation upon his return from Germany. During his absence

his project had been slightly altered. The length of the fuselage was increased to improve longitudinal stability, wing centre section fuel tanks were installed in addition to the fuselage fuel tanks, and the airframe became a mixed structure instead of all-metal. Nevertheless, it was still undoubtedly Polikarpov's aerodynamic configuration.

Polikarpov was more concerned about the division of his design bureau into two parts. With one half he at once began work on another project, the I-185 fighter. Although the design and mock-up construction of the I-185 proceeded faster than the I-200 project, the OKO team had a great advantage owing to the powerful industrial base of Plant No.1.

The young personnel of the OKO managed to exploit that advantage by means of innovations in the organisation of the design process. Release of a drawing was combined with the development of detailed production technology, and little time was consumed. Designers and technologists were working in close contact, and this allowed machine-tool attachments to be produced without delay. During the production process the I-200 was termed Izdelie (product, or item) No.61.

I-200 (MiG-1)

The I-200 differed from the preliminary design only in having the Mikulin AM-35A engine, which had the same dimensions as the AM-37 (the design of which had now been abandoned), but produced 200hp less. By late January 1940 the design was complete, and the first prototype was finished two months later. The whole task had been accomplished in three months, while it took the Yakovlev team eight months to do the same thing, not to mention the other bureaux. Tests in the TsAGI's T-101 full scale wind tunnel had also accelerated the process. When the first prototype was rolled out on 31st March 1940, it looked so streamlined that it seemed likely to fly away immediately.

Structure of the I-200 was mixed. The forward fuselage, including the engine mounting, comprised a welded tube truss covered by duralumin panels and cowling panels with Dzus-type locks. Powerplant was an AM-35A

delivering 1,350hp (1,007kW) at sea level and 1,200hp (895kW) at 19,700ft (6,000m). Two water radiators were installed in tunnels along the fuselage sides, and the oil radiator was located beneath the cockpit, which had a removable floor. The cockpit's primary structure was a welded tube truss fastened to the fuselage frame by three bolts, so the floor was a separate unit. The tail section, integral with the fin, was a wooden monocoque structure with pine spars and Bakelite plywood composite skinning.

The single spar wing with Clark 'YH' aerofoil section had a rigid skin, as distinct from previous fighters such as the I-15 and I-153, which were fabric covered. The wing centre section was all-metal, while the detachable outer wing panels were wood. This simplified production and provided work for the plant's woodworking shop. The spars were glued with resin cement, while the plywood skin was was fixed with casein glue. The outer wing panels could be disassembled in three

parts and were easily attached to the centre section, and the underside wing skin panels could be quickly removed, allowing easy access to the fuel tanks.

The designers had managed to develop a technologically efficient aircraft suitable for mass production. The equipment fit was conventional for Soviet fighters, allowing daytime missions to be flown. An ⅛in (8mm) armour plate backrest was installed for pilot protection. The engine's design did not permit the installation of a gun firing through the propeller boss, and so the armament comprised synchronised 12.7mm Berezin machine gun and two 7.62mm ShKAS guns.

The plant's oldest pilot, A Ekatov, made the I-200's maiden flight on 5th April 1940. During his 25-year career he performed a number of successful flight tests. A Brunov, who had actively participated in building the prototype, was appointed leading engineer for the tests. After the first flight a number of test flights were carried out, not all of which were successful. During the third test flight an engine backfire caused a fire in the inlet pipe, but Ekatov managed to land and extinguished the flames. A maximum speed of 402mph (648.5 km/h) at 22,600ft (6,900m) was reached on 24th May. In a combat turn the aircraft climbed 2,788ft (850m), and time to 16,400ft (5,000m) was 5.1 minutes. While these figures were promising, the tests revealed a problem with the canopy, which was sideways-hinged and proved impossible to open in flight. The wheelbrake system was also underdeveloped.

Engine overheating dogged the first stage of I-200 production testing. Water and oil temperatures were constantly higher than the specified limits, and it was impossible to use the AM-35A's full power. Engineers changed the structure and rearranged the water and oil radiators dozens of times, but without positive results. Finally, the installation of a new and more powerful water radiator and an additional oil cooler brought the temperatures within specified limits.

On 1st May 1940 Ekatov flew the I-200 over Moscow's Red Square, and on 25th May, before completion of the production tests and before state trials had even begun, the fighter was placed in production in accordance with a Government resolution. On 31st May an inspection of new aircraft structural techniques took place at the Central Airfield in Moscow. It was organised for military leaders and headed by Klim Voroshilov, who wished Artyom

The side hinged canopy of the I-200 was disliked by pilots used to flying either with an open cockpit, or with the canopy slid back.

Overhead view of the MiG-1 prototype.

Mikoyan success in the future. By that time Mikoyan was a chief designer at Plant No.1, while the Polikarpov Design Bureau had been transferred to Plant No.51, based in the development shop.

The production tests were carried out during July and August, and the second and the third I-200 prototypes went for state trials on 28th August. The second prototype was to be used for flight performance tests and the third for armament tests. The trials were successfully conducted by pilots S Suprun and A Kubyshkin, and leading engineer P Nikitchenko. At a flying weight of 6,832lb (3,099kg) the I-200 was capable of a maximum sea level speed of 301mph (486km/h), while with brief supercharging it reached 323mph (520km/h) at sea level and 390mph (628km/h) at 23,600ft (7,200m). A climb to 16,400ft (5,000m) took 5.3 minutes, turning time at 3,300ft (1,000m) was 20 to 22 seconds and service ceiling was 39,000ft (12,000m).

These results proved that the I-200 was the best of the Soviet fighter prototypes. It was decided to conduct service trials as soon as possible in order to deliver these modern aircraft to Soviet Air Force combat units.

The only anxiety was that the AM-35A engine was underdeveloped, as it did not pass its 50 hour flight tests and caused many problems for pilots and engineers. On the last day of testing, 12th September 1940, A Kochetkov suffered an engine failure in an I-200. Only his coolness and skill enabled him to complete a turn and land the aircraft safely. Kochetkov later recalled that the extended undercarriage locked down just as the wheels made contact with the runway.

Highly skilled test pilots noted that the I-200 was demanding to fly. It appeared to be longitudinally unstable and to have neutral stability laterally, a distinguishing feature of Polikarpov aircraft. Its handling was similar to that of the I-16 with an aft centre of gravity position.

As a result of the state trials a list of 112 defects was drawn up. The main requirements concerned the updating of the fighter, and structure came next:

• improve longitudinal and lateral stability;
• protect the centre section fuel tanks;
• fit slats and new wheels to correspond to the increase in mass;
• install two removable 7.62mm and 12.7mm machine guns;
• increase fuel tank capacity to meet the required range of 621 miles (1,000km) in long range cruise conditions.

These requirements determined the modification programme. The most difficult task was to increase range. With 88.8 gallons (404 litres) of fuel the I-200 had a range of 360 miles (580km). Engineer Yakov Seletsky suggested moving a radiator forward and replacing it with an additional 54.9 gallon (250 litre)

fuel tank, nicknamed Karakatitsa (Cuttlefish) because of its shape. In addition, cooling was improved owing to the changes made to the radiator's shape and intake design. The canopy was moved rearwards and the wing sweep angle was changed.

In October 1940, during the updating of the I-200, a pre-production batch of 25 was built. Because of bad weather conditions the aircraft were sent to the 146th Fighter Air Regiment at Evpatoria, commanded by Major Orlov, for operational trials. The Nauchno Issledovatelyskii Institut (NII – scientific and research institute) VVS's leading pilot, Suprun, and engineers Nikitchenko and A Karev from Plant No.1 participated in these trials, which proved the high performance of the fighter, designated MiG-1 in December 1940. The winter trials with the regiment were marred by two accidents and one fatality.

MiG-3

In February 1941 MiGs were turned over to the Kachinsk Military Pilot School, where future military pilots began their training. Also delivered to the school was an updated version, designated MiG-3, which was tested by A Ekatov. On 13th March 1941, when the test programme had almost been completed, disaster struck. Evidently the supercharger impeller was damaged at high altitude and killed the pilot, because he did not attempt to escape from the aircraft.

In April two more MiG-3s underwent state testing. A weight increase of 564lb (256kg) compared with the I-200 reduced the rate of climb, take-off and landing performance and manoeuvrability. Maximum level speed was even higher than the forerunners; 307mph (495km/h) at sea level and 397mph (640 km/h) at the service ceiling 25,500ft (7,800m). Evaluation of the MiG-3's range showed that one aircraft had managed 509 miles (820km) and the other 532 miles (857km), instead of the anticipated 621 miles (1,000km), the results having been influenced by the absence of a mixture control on the underdeveloped engine.

Artyom Mikoyan was not satisfied with the results, and reached an agreement with the engine's chief designer, Alexander Mikulin, that the ban on the use of the mixture control should be lifted for one flight. He sent two of the plant's pilots on a flight from Moscow to Leningrad, and upon completion of the flight and the necessary recalculations the estimated range of 621 miles (1,000km) was found to have been achieved. This had far-reaching consequences. In May 1941 it became evident that a programme for converting the air force to a new generation of combat aircraft

had failed. The machines delivered to the combat units were unfinished and had many shortcomings. Troubleshooting was undertaken at the airfields by 'brigades' (working parties) from the plant, who discovered that the armament of the new aircraft had not been harmonised.

It was necessary to find scapegoats, and they were found in the persons in charge of the NII VVS, who were said to have committed serious errors during the testing of the new aircraft. It was noted in the orders of the People's Commissar of Defence dated 31st May 1941 that the NII VVS tests were faulty and incomplete. Consequently the government received misleading conclusions regarding the results of the tests; for example, the MiG-3 was attributed with shorter range than it was capable of. Leading NII VVS specialists, including A Voyevodin, P Nikitchenko and N Maksimov, were immediately dismissed, and the Director of NII VVS, Alexander Filin, was arrested shortly before the war and killed in the State Commissariat for Internal Affairs (NKVD).

Filin had been a distinguished figure in the history of Soviet aviation. He was the first to receive the pilot-engineer qualification and took part in flight tests of all new aircraft at NII VVS, and could emphasise their principal features and describe their defects. Filin was one of the leading investigators of spinning, both in theory and practice. Together with Mikhail Gromov and I Spirin, he had established a new flight endurance record of 75 hours on an Tupolev ANT-25RD. He had been head of the NII VVS for only three years.

These tragic events for Soviet aviation brought the process of designing new aircraft, especially those of the MiG family, to an end, because the number of MiG aircraft in combat units exceeded 50% of the total just before the war.

Up to January 1941 Plant No.1 had produced 150 MiG-3s, compared with 100 MiG-1s and 20 MiG-3s produced in the last quarter of 1940. (Production aircraft, beginning from No.101, were designated MiG-3; although the first 'improved' fighters were similar to the MiG-1, the structure was changing all the time.) By 28th March 1941 military officials had accepted 473 MiG-3s. Of these, 270 were sent to VVS combat units, 200 were at the plant, and three were damaged. Ekatov was not the only pilot killed while testing a MiG. On 12th January 1941 another very skilled test pilot, V Kuleshov, failed to recover from a spin, although he fought until the last second to save the new aircraft. The centre of gravity position on production aircraft was further aft, at 27.7% of mean aerodynamic chord, compared with 26.3% on the I-200 prototype, and this made the MiG-3's handling even more difficult.

Another factory test pilot, N Baulin, suggested that piloting techniques applicable to biplanes were not suitable for the high speed MiGs, and that over-correction of the control column during loops resulted in a spin. This was found to be true. A few days later test pilot V Gursky wrote: 'During four days of flights I made seven emergency landings, and in two of them I was close to disaster'. As this was said by a skilled test pilot, one can imagine how difficult it was for ordinary pilots in combat units to master the aircraft. Spring 1941 was probably the peak accident period in the history of Soviet aviation, and most of the disasters involved Mikoyan fighters. Defects appeared one after another, but the MiG-3 was gradually mastered.

By tradition, the honour of 'possessing' a new MiG-3 was granted to the most skilled pilots of the Moscow region Air Defence. In February 1941 some MiG-3s were delivered to the 16th Fighter Air Regiment of this command. Technician Varenik recalled:

'The MiG aircraft were standing menacing, long-nosed. The pilots, mechanics and air fitters surrounded them on all sides, touching wings, looking into the cockpits, searching to find where the armament was installed, examining the undercarriage. The new aircraft were interesting to everyone'.

Captain Bondarenko, remembered: 'It was difficult to master the MiG-3 after the I-16. It seemed to be less manoeuvrable, and was complex to control. This evoked doubt about the new aircraft's combat performance.'

Early in March the best pilots of the 34th Fighter Air Regiment of Air Defence visited Plant No.1. Their commander, Major L Rybkin, was the first to master the fighter, and he was followed by M Trunov, A Smirnov, V Naidenko and N Shcherbina. By 1st May, the day of the air parade, all of the unit's pilots had mastered the MiG-3. While preparing to take part in parade they flew 165 sorties in their 69 MiG-3s. Sadly, a pilot was killed in an accident three days before the event.

In April and May 1941 MiG-3s were being produced at a rate of nine per day. They were 18.6mph (30km/h) slower than the initial production series aircraft, and the weight of one a second salvo was 238lb (108kg), no better than that of the I-16.

The greatest headache was the constant stream of demands sent to Plant No.1 and the leaders of the State Commissariat for Aviation Industry by the VVS, requiring the resolution of problems. These included an unsatisfactory canopy which was impossible to open at high speed, the leakage of fuel and fuel vapour into the cockpit, and the unsatisfactory arrangement of the instrument panel.

Below, left and bottom: **Two views of the MiG-3 prototype during range determination tests by Plant No.1 and NII VVS at Kacha in February and March 1941.**

Below: **A MiG-3 during testing in the TsAGI wind tunnel.**

The main problem was the AM-35A engine. One accident, a major disaster and 30 emergency landings occurred because of unsatisfactory engine acceleration. The inadequate oil supply system caused lowering of the oil pressure while the aircraft was in a dive with a negative 'g' load.

The first attempts to make a high altitude flight showed that the fuel pump had a low service ceiling and engine operation was unstable, causing choking even at 16,400ft (5,000m). This became apparent when three pilots of the 31st Fighter Air Regiment attempted to intercept German reconnaissance aircraft trespassing on the boundaries of the USSR and flying over Kaunas. In the resulting dogfights all of the MiGs snapped into spins, and one of the pilots was killed.

Pilot-engineer A Kochetkov went to Kaunas and discovered that, in addition to the shortcomings of the aircraft, the training of the pilots was inadequate. None had sufficient flying time on the new fighter, and they had never before flown high altitude missions. Kochetkov organised special tests of the MiG-3 to define handling and spin performance within the 23,000 to 36,000ft (7,000 to 11,000m) altitude range, and it was determined that the MiG-3 could perform combat turns at up to 34,500ft (10,500m). When properly controlled it could also intercept flying targets without snapping into a spin. Requirements concerning operation at altitudes greater than 26,200ft (8,000m) were as follows:

- it was necessary to retrofit an automatic mixture control on the carburettor;
- it was necessary to maintain normal oil and fuel pressure in all flight modes and at all altitudes up to 36,000ft (11,000m);
- it was necessary to provide the pilot with reliable oxygen equipment.

The work had been done very thoroughly. The pilots of the 4th Fighter Air Regiment, based near the Romanian border, had shot down three trespassers. That regiment, together with the 55th Fighter Air Regiment, which also had MiG-3s, formed part of the 20th Mixed Air Division, with General Osipenko at its head. Having received the MiG-3 a little earlier than the others, the pilots of this division were flying the new fighter confidently as early as May. Having been sent to Kishinev, the test pilots helped to convert the pilots of the combat units to the new aircraft. Peotr Stefanovsky recalled:

'The division had two complete sets of fighters – aged I-16s and I-153s and modern MiG-3s. Nobody wanted to fly the MiG-3s, which was surprising. I decided to show them the capabilities of the MiG-3, and I squeezed all I could out of the aircraft and then a bit more. When I landed, the attitude to the new aircraft had changed sharply. The conversion was very intensive, flights being conducted from early morning until darkness'.

Among the trainees was a young pilot named Alexander Pokryshkin of the 55th Fighter Air Regiment, destined to become a leading ace and three times Hero of the Soviet Union. He recalled: 'I had encountered MiG aircraft just before the war; they left an unforgettable image in my memory and their advanced aerodynamic configuration captivated me at once. They outclassed the I-16 in vertical manoeuvres while dogfighting.'

Pokryshkin compared the MiG-3 with a highly-strung racehorse: 'Under a skilful rider it rushed along like an arrow, but when you lost control you could end up beneath its hoofs'.

In spring and early summer Plant No.1 was not only involved in troubleshooting and increasing the production rate. Sixteen versions of armament and radio equipment were developed within the year. The MiG-3 equipped with radio and two additional underwing Berezin 12.7mm machine guns with a total weight of fire of 6.1lb/sec (2.8kg/sec) became the factory's primary product. The Mikoyan Design Bureau decided to use 20-23mm underwing guns, but tests of a version armed with five machine in May 1941 showed that the additional armament reduced the maximum speed by 12.4 to 18.6mph (20 to 30 km/h) at all altitudes. Moreover, it inhibited manoeuvrability to an unacceptable degree. For this reason it was recommended that all underwing weapons be removed and that the capacity of the aft fuel tank be reduced by 176.3lb (80kg), and that of the central fuel tank by 79.3lb (36kg).

Shortly before the war, 821 MiG-3s armed with five machine guns had been manufactured, but the additional armament was removed from many of these aircraft when they joined their combat units. The performance of 'light' MiG-3 No.3262 can therefore be regarded as typical for the aircraft that went to war. At a weight of 7,242lb (3,285kg) the fighter had a maximum speed of 287mph (462 km/h) at sea level, 347mph (559km/h) at 16,400ft (5,000m) and 374mph (603km/h) at the service ceiling of 25,500ft (7,800m).

Time to climb 16,400ft (5,000m) was 6.8 minutes, the service ceiling was 35,600ft (10,850m), a turn at low altitude took 23 seconds and the take-off run was 1,049ft (320m). The maximum operational range was 447 miles (720km).

Deterioration in performance compared with the initial production series MiG-3s was due to the camouflage finish and the rough surface finish of the fuselage and cowling. Late in May 1941 five production MiG-3s were reworked; the aileron compensation was increased, the tailplane and elevator area ratio was changed, and counterbalances were installed in the rudder and the slat control system. Twelve pilots from Plant No.1, the Letno-Issledovatel'skii Institut (LII - Ministry of Aviation Industry Flight Research Institute) and the NII VVS evaluated and approved these modifications, but the outbreak of war prevented their adoption for production.

Although 17 Soviet Air Force Fighter Regiments operating a total of 917 MiGs were distributed near the Soviet border, only the pilots of the 20th Mixed Air Division, the 41st, 124th and 126th Air Regiments of the Western Special Military District and the 23rd Kiev Air Regiment mastered the aircraft. Another 64 MiGs were in the front line inventory of the Baltic and Black Sea Navy. They were expected to face severe trials.

The fate of the MiGs distributed near the border was tragic. They became the main targets of Luftwaffe aircraft during the first assault on the morning of 22nd June 1941. An especially strong blow was dealt to the Soviet Air Force units of the Western Special Military District, where the most powerful unit was undoubtedly the 9th Mixed Aviation Division, which had received 233 new MiG-3s several days earlier. This division suffered the heaviest losses on the first day of the war, losing 347 of its 409 operational aircraft. Practically all of the MiG-3s were destroyed on the ground by bombs.

Among those who did manage to take off was D Kokonev, who rammed a German aircraft as early as 0430 hours. One source says it was a Dornier Do15, while another describes it as a Messerschmitt Bf110. It was the first ram attack using this type of fighter in the Second World War.

On the whole the situation was inauspicious, and examples of individual heroism could not change it. The aircraft were positioned close to each other a few kilometres from the border, and this made things worse. Each regiment had two types of aircraft; old and new. On the 129th Fighter Air Regiment airfield at Tarnovo, 7.4 miles (12km) from German-occupied Poland, there were 57 MiG-3s and 52 I-153s, although only 40 pilots were ready for combat. Many of the MiG-3s were not airworthy or had not been mastered by the pilots, so, given the choice, the 'Stalin Falcons' flew the aged Chaikas.

In Soviet historical literature Major General S Chernykh, commander of the 9th Mixed Air Division, is reproached for his failure to take the necessary measures to save even a part of his forces from the onslaught. In response to his repeated appeal to the high command on the eve of the war: 'The tension on the border increases, what should I do?,' he received reply: 'Just don't give in to any provocation!'. A day later the general, noted for his actions in the Spanish Civil War and awarded the title of Hero of the Soviet Union, was denounced as a 'people's enemy' and shot. But such repression did nothing to save the situation.

The first aircraft provided in an effort to replenish the shattered Soviet aviation forces on the Western Front were MiG-3s. On the morning of 22nd June Soviet Army Air Force Commander General P Zhigarev ordered that 99 new fighters be sent there, but they also suffered an unfortunate fate. Soviet evacuation teams were forced to destroy many of the aircraft because, in the prevailing general chaos, there was no possibility of moving them to the rear. On 24th June there was not a single new fighter in the west, but on 25th June more than 200 new aircraft arrived, and thenceforth a new regiment arrived at the front almost daily. The MiG-3s became conspicuous again.

At the time, General Headquarters representatives Klim Voroshilov and Boris Shaposhnikov reported to the Council of the People's Commissars: 'Our aviation is not worse but better than German aviation. There are only eleven MiGs but they are active all day long, and they are a menacing weapon against the Germans. In an engagement today, 29th June, two of our MiGs have shot down three Messerschmitts.'

An important event in the new fighter's life was the establishment of five regiments staffed by test pilots. Two of these were fighter regiments, equipped with MiG-3s. These units were formed on the initiative of Hero of the Soviet Union Stepan Suprun, who convinced Stalin that the appearance of the well-trained pilots would play an important part in the struggle for air superiority, providing service pilots with good examples of how the new fighter could be operated effectively.

The 401st Special Purpose Fighter Air Regiment, commanded by Suprun, and the 402nd Special Purpose Fighter Air Regiment, led by Lieutenant Colonel Peotr Stefanovsky, were supplied with 67 MiG-3s fresh from the assembly line, and both regiments flew to the front on 30th June.

Having arrived at the airfield in Zubovo, the 401st Special Purpose Fighter Air Regiment re-inforced the Western Front Air Force. It took part at once in intense air battles, flying in conditions disadvantageous to the high altitude MiG-3s. They attacked enemy ground troops, flew reconnaissance missions and fought Messerschmitts and Junkers at low and medium altitudes. In only two days, 2nd and 3rd July, the regiment's pilots shot down eight enemy aircraft. On the next day Suprun, the 401st Special Purpose Fighter Air Regiment's commander, having shot down four German aircraft, perished in the battle. Posthumously, he was awarded the title Hero of the Soviet Union for the second time.

In the records of the 402nd Special Purpose Fighter Air Regiment Captain Proshakov is mentioned more often than other distinguished pilots. Ace Peotr Stefanovsky used to say that Proshakov was the 'boldest pilot of the regiment'. On one occasion, just after being one of the first to take off from Velikie Luki airfield, Proshakov managed to shoot down a German observation balloon in a surprise attack, and in a night combat over Idritsa he shot down a Dornier bomber and landed his fighter safely on the unprepared airfield using only his landing light. At that time the MiG-3 had yet to undergo night flying tests, and the pilot did not know how the light was adjusted, or even if it was adjusted at all.

It would be an exaggeration to say that only test pilots could master the MiG-3. The pilots of the 55th Fighter Air Regiment were among those who mastered and successfully used the new sharp-nosed beauties. Among the little-known regiment pilots at that time, Alexander Pokryshkin was notable, having shot down five Bf109Es of Jagdgeschwader 77.

Pokryshkin's achievement can be better assessed when a detailed comparison of the two fighters is made.

At altitudes below 13,100ft (4,000m), where the majority of air combats took place in the summer of 1941, the MiG-3 was slightly faster, as flight tests had shown. But the Soviet pilots knew that in critical situations they would not be able to open the canopy and escape from the aircraft, and therefore preferred to fly with the canopy removed. This reduced the MiG's speed by some 18.6mph (30km/h), so the Bf109E gained superiority in that respect. Although the Bf109E surpassed the MiG in a steep climb, the MiG-3's vertical manoeuvrability was better. The turning time of the two fighters was approximately the same, although the Messerschmitt's turning radius was 25% tighter owing to its lighter wing loading. Being lighter, the German aircraft also had more powerful armament. A comparison of the radio equipment was not in the MiG's favour. At altitudes above 16,400 to 23,000ft (5,000 to 7,000m) the MiG-3 completely outclassed the Bf109E and, at the least, was not inferior to the more advanced 'F, but combats at such altitudes were rare.

Much more than any shortcomings in performance, numerous defects manifested during operational flying prevented the MiG-3 from showing its true capabilities. Accordingly, a message from the Western Front units was sent to the People's Commissariat of the Aircraft Industry on 19th August 1941. It reported that the MiG-3's landing gear often failed to extend, forcing its pilot to make a belly-landing. Another frequent occurrence was damage to the upper undercarriage component during landing, and after an emergency landing the fighter remained un-airworthy for a long time because the replacement of damaged radiator ducts was very difficult. It was also difficult to repair fuselage structural members because the fin was integral with the fuselage.

In the Western Front units all flights were made with the canopy removed. Besides the unreliable canopy lock, pilots complained of the unsatisfactory view, the splashing of oil on the windshield and the high cockpit temperature. Flying without the canopy reduced both speed and range, and the MiG-3's inadequate endurance ruled out its use as a reconnaissance aircraft. If air combat occurred during a reconnaissance mission, which was not unusual, there was insufficient fuel was for a safe return. The aircraft did not have a fuel flow indicator. One urgent demand to the designers was for external tanks to be installed.

Left and opposite page: **Rare illustrations of MiG-3s patrolling the Moscow sky, each armed with six RS-82 rockets.**

The day after receipt of the message, when the prospects of new Soviet fighters were discussed at the NII VVS, nobody mentioned the MiG-3. Evidently its fate had been already been determined before resolutions about stopping production of the new Mikoyan and Gurevich aircraft were adopted. The MiG's weaknesses and the failure of its performance to meet combat requirements played a significant part in this decision.

Quantities of AM-38 engines, structurally similar to the AM-35A with which the MiG-3 was equipped, were required for the Ilyushin Il-2 attack aircraft, and it was decided to convert engine production to AM-38s.

One more supposition can be made. Although Aviahim Plant No.1 had provided appreciable assistance in introducing the MiG fighter into production, it also terminated its production. Had the fighter been built by a minor factory instead of the pride of the Soviet Aircraft Industry, production might have continued for some time, but it was considered inexpedient to devote the facility's resources to a rather unsuccessful aircraft.

At the end of the summer the MiG-3 underwent many changes. Aircraft delivered to the front at that time were equipped with slats, the gear ratio of their AM-35A engines was increased from 0.902 to 0.732, and they had automatic propellers instead of the VISh-22E

variable pitch propellers fitted previously. Consequently handling characteristics, stability and reliability improved. However, rate of climb and take-off performance changed for the worse. A typical fighter, No.3943, had maximum speeds of 289mph (466km/h) at sea level, 353mph (569km/h) at 16,400ft (5,000m) and 382mph (615km/h) at 25,600ft (7,800m).

It took 7.1 minutes to climb to 16,400ft (5,000m) and 22 seconds to complete a turn at 3,330ft (1,000m). Flying weight was little changed, being 7,272lb (3,299kg) without external fittings and with 738lb (335kg) of fuel.

At that time the series-production plant increased its output, producing 562 MiG-3s in August 1941. This was to be an unbeaten record for Soviet fighters during the war. If this figure is added to the 496 MiG-3s built in July and the 450 built in September it becomes apparent why this fighter was the one in the most widespread use in the Soviet Air Force at the peak of the German advance to Moscow. It was because of the MiG-3s that, of 8,278 German sorties against the capital, only 207 bombers managed to get through.

Among the regiments defending Moscow were many manned by experienced pilots who had thoroughly mastered the MiG-3.

The best were the 16th, 27th and 34th Fighter Air Regiments. The 16th, commanded by Lieutenant Colonel T Prutskov, destroyed 72

enemy aircraft during the latter half of 1941. At the beginning of October pilots of the 27th Fighter Air Regiment, commanded by Major A Pisanko, in company with pilots of the other regiments, successfully attacked a German mechanised column on its way to the town of Bely. At the same time the MiG-3 pilots of 34th Fighter Air Regiment, commanded by Major L Rybkin, distinguished themselves in defence of the Western Front troops and railway traffic, flying five or six missions per day. Even the bad weather did not prevent them taking off. On 22nd October, in spite of the autumn rain, the regiment flew 59 missions, took part in 24 air battles and shot down 12 aircraft. Before his famous night time ramming attack over Moscow, Victor Talalikhin gained five victories flying the MiG-3.

The greatest success was gained by the MiGs of the 42nd Fighter Air Regiment while escorting a dozen Il-2s. Early one morning, led by Captain G Zimin, they attacked Orel airfield. Approaching fast and unexpectedly, the Soviet aircraft destroyed four Bf109s as they took off, 57 Junkers Ju52s while they were landing and up to 60 various types of aircraft on the airfield, returning to base without loss.

Many favourable reports on the MiG fighters relate to this period of war. The MiG-3's manoeuvrability was a pleasant surprise even to the test pilots. Yu Antipov remembered that in one air battle he noticed condensation trails issuing from the wingtips during a sharp turn. He said: 'the MiG turned like an I-15!'. Another example comes from a simulated air combat in which a Yakovlev Yak-1 played the role of the 'enemy'. Flying his MiG-3 at a low altitude, I Rubtsov of the 120th Fighter Air Regiment managed to out manoeuvre his opponent. The MiG had to be written off after the flight because it was overstressed beyond repair!

Another well known test pilot, Konstantin Kokkinaki, wrote: 'It was the MiGs which played the decisive role in the air defence of the capital ... I flew the MiGs myself, and I can say that at that time it was an advanced and manoeuvrable fighter.' In this period more than 40 MiG pilots became Heroes of the Soviet Union

Several successful high altitude combat operations in the autumn of 1941 showed that the AM-35A engine had been successfully developed. On 28th September 1941, B Pirozhkov, a pilot of the 124th Fighter Air Regiment, initiated an attack on a high altitude reconnaissance aircraft at 26,250ft (8,000m), and managed to follow the enemy and shoot it down at 32,800ft (10,000m). It was the first such interception of the war, attracting the attention not only of pilots, but also of the LII.

In October, before the evacuation of Plant No.1 at that time, a new version of the MiG-3 with two 21.9 gallon (100 litre) external fuel tanks and wide-chord propeller blades was developed.

Despite their high rate of fire the 12.7mm ShKAS machine guns were not very effective, and for this reason they were replaced by 12.7mm UBS machine guns. This increased the weight of fire from 2.6 to 3.1lb/sec (1.2 to 1.44kg/sec) without affecting the aircraft's weight. At the same time the installation of rocket projectile launchers was begun (the aircraft had previously been converted to carry rockets by combat units in the field). Up to the end of October 1941 49 MiGs were equipped with launchers for six RS-82 rockets, and 180 fighters of this type were produced altogether.

The MiG-3 continued in vextremely intensive operational use after series-production was completed. Complete interchangeability of components and fittings and high main-

tainability allowed the fighter to be kept in perfect combat ready condition. On 1st May 1942 the Soviet Army Air Force had 134 MiGs in its inventory, three-quarters of which were combat capable. Contradictory reports came from the air regiments at this time. While the pilots of the 487th Fighter Air Regiment gave the MiG-3 a very low assessment owing to its poor manoeuvrability, those of the 519th Fighter Air Regiment put it in first place, considering the Yak-1 too fragile, the Lavochkin LaGG-3 too heavy and the I-16 too slow.

In the summer of 1942 the air regiments of the 201st Fighter Air Division, fighting on the Western Front, began to convert to the Yak-1, their MiG-3s being turned over to the 122nd Fighter Air Regiment commanded by Major G Bayandin. All of the MiGs coming from repair plants were also delivered to that unit, and this led to a surplus of aircraft in the regiment. When the 201st Fighter Air Division under the command of Colonel A Zhukov was deployed near Stalingrad in the autumn of 1942, the 122nd Fighter Air Regiment remained on the Western Front because the Luftwaffe's best aircraft were operational near Stalingrad and

Above left: **Having outstanding performance at high altitude, the MiG-3 often failed in low level combat.**

Left: **Many of the air defence regiments around Moscow in 1941-42 operated MiG-3s.**

Above right: **MiG-3s provided the first combat taste for many aces and Heroes of the Soviet Union**

the MiG-3 was considerably inferior to them in performance.

The pilots of this regiment continued to fly MiG-3s as late as the spring of 1943, when they encountered not only Bf109s of various marks, but also the new Focke-Wulf Fw190As of Jagdgeschwader 51. The courage and heroism of the Soviet pilots, who had great combat experience, did not change their commonly-held opinion; the Fw190A was better than the MiG-3 in all respects.

During 1942 and 1943 the MiG-3 was operated mainly by the Air Defence units, and in the summer of 1942 MiGs and I-16s were the most widespread Soviet fighters. Half of the total number, some 320 aircraft, defended the skies over Moscow. They were used successfully against German bombers and reconnaissance aircraft with service ceilings up to 36,000ft (11,000m), but they were helpless against Junkers Ju86P and 'R reconnaissance aircraft, which had a service ceiling of more than 39,000ft (12,000m). Consequently, the Mikoyan Design Bureau was the first to be engaged in the development of a special high altitude fighter.

Top: **Messerschmitt's Bf109E (example captured and evaluated by the RAF illustrated) formed the main opponent to MiG-3s during the German sweep towards Moscow. The MiG was generally inferior to the Luftwaffe fighter.**

Above: **A MiG-3 with two additional machine guns in underwing fairings.**

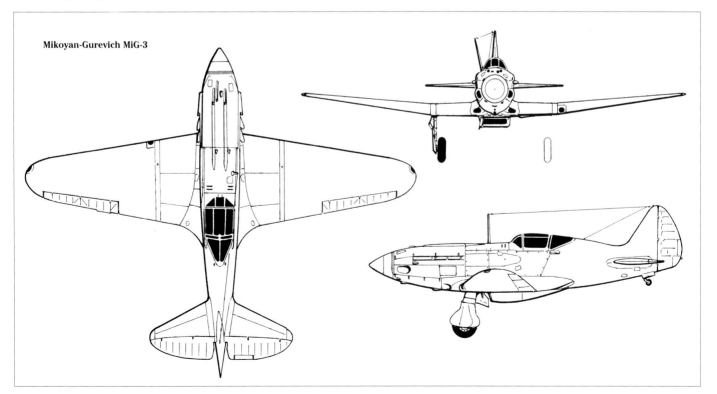

Mikoyan-Gurevich MiG-3

MiG-3 AM-38

In the autumn of 1941 the efforts of the Mikoyan OKB were mainly directed at replacing the MiG-3's engine. At the beginning of August a Klimov AM-38, which had higher power but lower altitude capability, was installed in a production fighter. The aircraft, designated MiG-3 AM-38, underwent tests at the LII at a weight of 7,330lb (3,325kg) – slightly heavier than a production MiG-3 AM-35A – and reached 319mph (514km/h) at sea level and 361mph (582km/h) at its service ceiling. At the suggestion of Artyom Mikoyan the exhaust pipe fairings were then redesigned and other modifications undertaken, and as a result the speed at service ceiling increased by 6.2mph (10km/h) and at sea level by 3.1mph (5km/h), the latter figure being 339mph (547km/h) with the AM-38 engine on short term boost. In speed at low and medium altitudes the fighter outclassed not only all Soviet production fighters, but the most up-to-date Bf109F-2 and 'F-4.

Compared with the later production series MiG-3 AM-35A, the new fighter's rate of climb was the same at low altitude and inferior at high altitude. Consequently the time taken to climb 16,400ft (5,000m) was about 8 minutes. More importantly, the installation of an engine capable of another 400hp (298.4kW) but using the same-sized oil and water radiators caused a great increase in temperatures both on the ground and in the air. After a flight by test pilot A Kochetkov on 12th August it became clear that if the demanding operational requirements were to be met, modification of the MiG-3 AM-38 was necessary. The work came to a halt.

MiG-3 M-82 (MiG-9)

The idea of producing a fighter powered by Arkady Shvetsov's advanced M-82 radial engine was treated more seriously by the Mikoyan Design Bureau, and a preliminary design, given the manufacturer's designations MiG-3 M-82 or MiG-9, was completed. The aim behind the preliminary design was to retain the maximum possible commonality with the production MiG-3, so the outer wing panels, empennage, main landing gear and tailwheel remained the same, only the wing centre section and fuselage being slightly changed. Mikoyan believed that this would simplify the aircraft's entry into production. On 23rd August 1941 the NII VVS's approval of the MiG-9 was signed. Although its estimated performance at low altitude was a little worse than that of the MiG-3 AM-38 (a sea level speed of 329mph – 530km/h was specified), the rate of climb and take-off performance were radically improved, and Artyom Mikoyan's promise to improve the MiG-9's armament by installing two synchronised 12.7mm UBS machine guns aroused great interest.

The proposal was attractive because M-82 engine assembly had started in Perm (Molotov) following the successful completion of state trials. Although the Sukhoi Su-2 short range bomber had flown successfully with this engine, its future was unclear.

Construction of the MiG-9 was carried out at Kuibyshev at the end of 1941 under difficult conditions during the bureau's evacuation. Assembly took place in the open air because the roof of the workshop had yet to be built. Although Mikoyan had started converting his fighter to take the Shvetsov radial before

Alexander Yakovlev and Semyon Lavochkin had begun similar conversions of their fighters, the work dragged on and it was clear the aircraft's development would require a lot of time.

During evacuation the plant assembled 27 MiG-3s, and the final 1941 production total was 3,100 aircraft. On 23rd December Tretiakov, the plant's director, received the order to stop production of MiGs in favour of Ilyushin Il-2 attack aircraft. Over the text of the order was written: 'Confirmed, Stalin'. It was the decisive verdict for the MiG-3.

I-211(E)

After operational tests of the MiG-3 powered by the M-82, produced in a small batch of five aircraft designated MiG-9 M-82, one more modification was built in 1943, this time with a boosted engine. The fighter was designated I-211No.211 (or Type 'E'). Its fuselage was reshaped to give a smoother transition from the cowling and controllable gills to the side panels, the cockpit was moved a little further aft, the air intakes of the oil cooler were positioned in the wing centre section leading edge near the fuselage sides, the shape of fin was changed and the tailplane was raised. Two ShVAK synchronised guns were housed in the wing centre section.

A production MiG-3 with the AM-38 engine installed as tested at LII in August 1941.

The flight test data obtained in 1943 were quite good. The maximum speed at 23,000ft (7,000m) was 416mph (670km/h), and only four minutes were required to climb to 16,400ft (5,000m). The second I-211(E) prototype, which was also undergoing production tests, was not placed into series-production. Instead, the new Lavochkin La-5FN fighter with the same ASh-82FN engine (the M-82 was redesignated in 1943 by giving it the initials of designer Arkady Shvetsov) was put into series-production, using a well developed manufacturing base, and proved itself at the front line.

I-230(D) (MiG-3U)

The MiG-3 fighter was developed in many directions simultaneously. A series of prototypes was developed to take the new engines, but the standard Mikulin AM-35A-powered aircraft also underwent modification. In 1942 the Mikoyan OKB designed and produced the I-230 fighter, given the in-house designation 'D'. The new prototype's design took into account the opinions and suggestions of the pilots and engineers of combat units equipped with the MiG-3. Its structure was similar to that of the MiG-3, allowing most of the manufacturing tools developed for that aircraft to be used in the event of full scale production.

Combat experience in the first months of the war had shown that the MiG-3's machine gun armament was inadequate. Therefore two 20mm ShVAK synchronised guns were installed in the upper part of the forward fuselage and provided with 370 rounds of ammunition. The new fuselage had no central welded truss; it was an all-wooden monocoque structure with a plywood skin of three layers of 1mm thickness in the wing centre section and two layers in the tail (not a veneer skin like that of the basic MiG-3). This simplified production and reduced. A container for the bladder-type fuel tanks, made of special flame-resistant plywood, was placed between the engine and cockpit.

The cockpit itself was also changed, taking into account the pilots' suggestions. To improve visibility the glazed area of the canopy was increased, and the standard control column was replaced by a new design incorporating the brake lever, fire control button and press-to-transmit button.

The I-230(D)'s wing and tailplane differed from those of the the MiG-3 in having metal main spars, and the tailplane was 200mm higher. The structure of the undercarriage doors was improved, a special lock protecting the central doors from suction during flight. The I-230 had only one oil radiator with

The MiG-3 M-82 (or MiG-9) was a reworked MiG-3 with the Shvetsov M-82 radial engine.

a normal intake, located under the radiator's 'tunnel' or scoop.

Owing to the cessation of AM-35A production, the new fighter was powered by an engine based on the AM-38F. This engine was 88lb (40kg) heavier than initially estimated by its designers, but was totally different from the AM-38F. Only some details of the new model were used, and it drove an AV-5L-126A propeller of 10ft 6in (3.2m) diameter. In technical documentation the engine was described as an AM-35A.

The first prototype of the I-230(D) modified fighter went for testing in July 1943. At that time it was called the 'improved' version of the MiG-3, but later it was designated MiG-3U. The tests were conducted at the NII VVS by leading test pilot V Khomyakov. The maximum sea level speed was 313mph (505 km/h), 326mph (526km/h) being reached with engine boost. At 23,000ft (7,000m) the aircraft attained 407mph (656km/h), exceeding the speed of the series-production MiG-3 by 24.8mph (40km/h). It took only 6.2 minutes to climb to 16,400ft (5,000m), compared with

7.1 minutes for the MiG-3. Service ceiling was 2,300ft (700m) higher at 39,000ft (11,900m). The I-230(D) had a range of 807 miles (1,300km).

Although the aircraft's combat features were obviously improved, pilots noted a number of shortcomings, including difficult or even dangerous landing characteristics for inexperienced pilots. After close examination of the MiG-3U's performance, the acceptance commission at the NII VVS withheld its recommendation to put the improved aircraft into series-production. (MiG-3U – usovershenstvovanny, improved.) Nevertheless, the Mikoyan Design Bureau and Aircraft Plant No.155 managed to produce another five prototypes of the fighter, and in August 1943 the first, third, fourth and sixth prototypes were delivered for operational tests to the 12th Guards Fighter Air Regiment, then defending Moscow. As a result, the MiG-3U gained some approval, although a number of defects were also noted. The type was not put into series-production, and the design bureau began to develop new high altitude fighters.

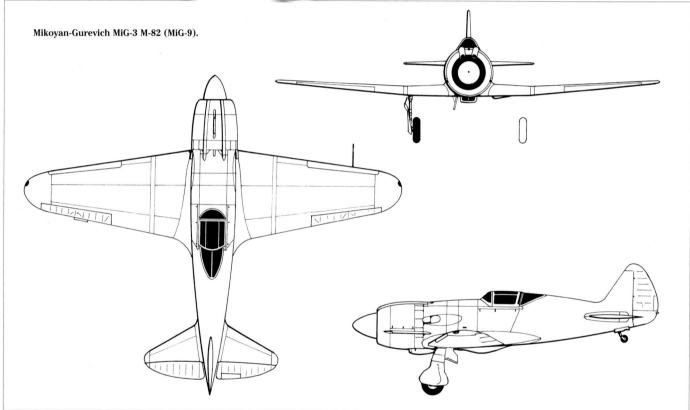

Mikoyan-Gurevich MiG-3 M-82 (MiG-9).

I-231(2D)

In 1943 the Mikoyan Design Bureau designed a further version of the MiG-3/MiG-9 fighter family, featuring an all-metal fuselage and powered by the AM-39 high altitude engine rated at 1,700hp 1,268kW). Designated I-231 (production code '2D'), the aircraft had the same armament (two synchronised ShVAK guns) and fuel capacity as the MiG-3U. It attained a maximum speed of 439mph (707 km/h) at 23,300ft (7,100m) and climbed to 16,400ft (5,000m) in 4.5 minutes. Because of continued attempts to increase the top speed and service ceiling of MiG aircraft even further, this version, too, did not go into series-production.

I-220(A)

In late 1942 the Mikoyan Design Bureau designed the I-220 fighter (production code 'A'), with its cockpit positioned on the centre of gravity, in front of the fuselage fuel tank. This reduced the 'g' loading on the pilot during manoeuvres and improved his view considerably. The fighter's wing had a swept leading edge and a straight trailing edge, compared with the MiG-3's equi-tapered wing. (Note that Alexander Silvansky also developed a fighter designated I-220, which see.) The fuselage consisted of a truss of welded chromansil tubes with a wooden tail. The bladder-type fuselage fuel tanks were housed in a container made of a special fireproof ply-

wood, covered inside and out with chlorvinyl varnish. For its installation a special hatch was provided on the lower fuselage, protected by an aluminium 'cup' which at the same time provided support for the tank. The cockpit, located between the fuselage truss and fuel container, was protected from the engine bay by an aluminium firewall with a thin layer of asbestos. The cockpit canopy had an armoured glass windscreen.

The wing comprised a centre section and two detachable wooden outer panels with metal spars. Landing flaps and leading-edge slats took up the entire span of the wing. To simplify production the all-metal fin and tailplane had a chordwise joint and were connected by means of bolts.

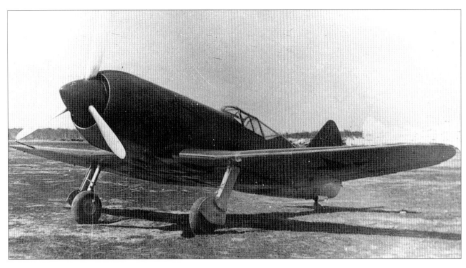

Photographs on the opposite page:

Top left: Field maintenance to a MiG-3 M-82 during operational trials.

Top right: Pilots involved in operational trials of the MiG-3 M-82 discussing their tactics.

Photographs on this page:

Further attempts to improve the performance of the MiG-3/MiG-9 family resulted in the I-211(E) with a boosted M-82 and other modifications. Note that the censor has again been at work, deleting something sensitive from the background of the photograph immediately to the right.

Combat experience had shown the necessity of increasing the armament. Four 20mm ShVAK guns with 600 rounds of ammunition were to be installed.

The designers paid great attention to improving the fighter's aerodynamics. Tunnel-type radiators in the wing centre section, with air scoops in the wing leading edges, were used instead of the under-fuselage type of the basic MiG-3 fighter. The oil cooler and air intake for the supercharger were installed in the wing centre section fillets.

The I-220(A) prototype was designed for the new 1,700hp (1,268kW) Mikulin AM-39. Pending its installation, however, the fighter was submitted for its official state flight tests in January 1944 with a production AM-38F engine with poor altitude capability. The aircraft's structure was otherwise unchanged. Thus powered, and at a flying weight of 7,879lb (3,574kg), the I-220(A) had a maxi-

mum speed of 386mph (622km/h) at 13,750ft (4,200m), service ceiling of 31,000ft (9,500m) and a range of 596 miles (960km). Two guns instead of four were installed, with 300 rounds.

By the summer of 1944 the AM-39 high altitude engine had been developed, and one had been installed in place of the AM-38F. Armament remained the same. Flight test data obtained during the production development tests in July and August 1944 showed a slight improvement. At gross take-off weight of 8,040lb (3,647kg) maximum speed at sea level was 354mph (571km/h), while at 25,600ft (7,800m) it was 433mph (697km/h). Time to climb to 16,400ft (5,000m) was 4.5 minutes.

For the official tests conducted at the NII VVS in September the I-220(A) was powered by a production AM-39 engine and carried its full complement of four ShVAK guns, but the

ammunition was slightly reduced at 400 rounds. At an increased take-off weight of 8,454lb (3,835kg) the maximum speed fell to 415mph (668km/h) at 22,300ft (6,800m), the service ceiling was 36,000ft (11,000m) and the time taken to reach 16,400ft (5,000m) was 6.3 minutes. These tests revealed a number of shortcomings, including excessive aileron and elevator loads on the control column, poor rearward view, and difficulty in achieving full undercarriage retraction without the help of pilot-induced 'g' loads.

Although the I-220(A) outperformed the operational series-production fighters, it did not go into production in 1944 because Lavochkin and Yakovlev types completely met the VVS requirements and could provide the desired air superiority in dogfights with German fighters. A family of new high altitude fighter-interceptors based on the I-220(A) was developed later.

Mikoyan-Gurevich I-211(E)

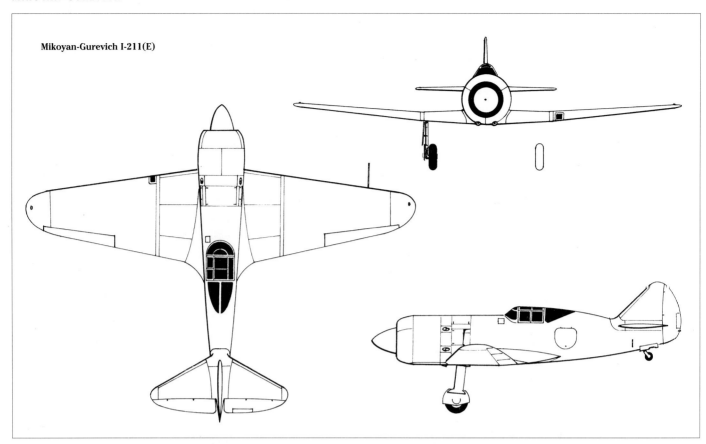

Mikoyan-Gurevich I-230(D)

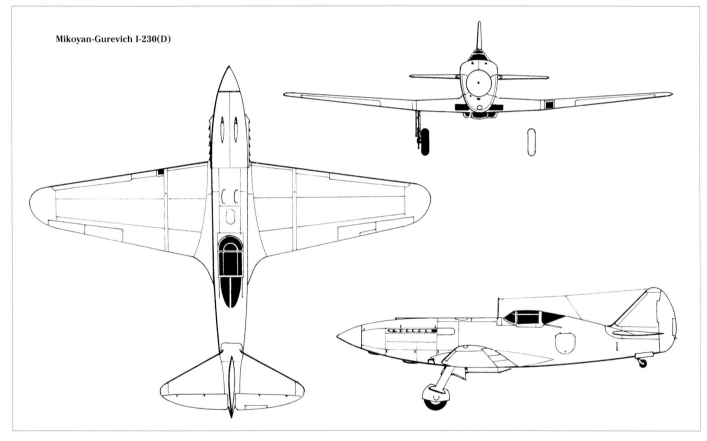

Photographs on the opposite page:

Centre: **First I-230 (or MiG-3U) high altitude fighter during manufacturer's tests.**

Bottom left and right: **Two views of the retrofitted I-230(D). Note the aerial mast ahead of the cockpit.**

Photographs on this page:

Top: **Second prototype I-230(D) which undertook operational trials with the 12th Fighter regiment, based near Moscow.**

Right: **Close-up of the I-230's centre section. Oil troubles are evident!**

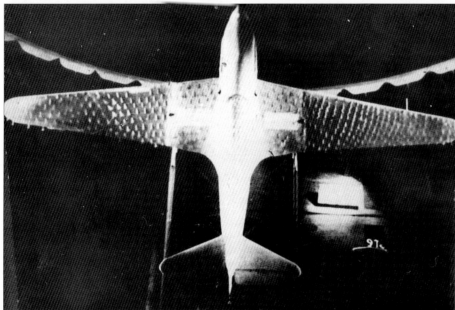

Top: **MiG's I-231 high altitude prototype possessed very clean lines.**

Above: **Wind tunnel testing of the I-220 Type 'A' high altitude fighter.**

Below: **The AM-38F-powered I-220(A).**

I-221(2A)

In the summer of 1942 a German reconnaissance aircraft crossed the sky over Moscow at high altitude. As it transpired, it was a Junkers Ju86R with a pressurised cockpit and high altitude engines, and all of its armament removed to increase its service ceiling. The crew considered themselves completely immune from attack as the aircraft climbed to 39,500ft (12,000m) because there were then no fighters in Soviet combat units capable of intercepting aircraft at such an altitude.

The Mikoyan Design Bureau received a request for a fighter with a service ceiling of 46,000ft (14,000m), and, using the I-220(A) as a basis, the bureau responded quickly. Designated I-221 (production code '2A'), the prototype was of mixed construction and, taking into consideration the requirement for high altitude, its wing was made larger than those of contemporary fighters, having a span of 42ft 7in (13m) and an area of 240ft^2 (22.38m^2). To sustain the power of its prototype Mikulin AM-39 engine up to 46,000ft (14,000m), two TK-2 turbosuperchargers, driven by engine exhaust gases, were installed.

Unfortunately the new aircraft suffered a disaster at the very beginning of its life. Instead of being performed by a highly skilled test pilot, its maiden flight was made by a young and insufficiently experienced pilot who landed with the undercarriage retracted, ruling out further flight tests.

I-222(3A)

Because of the accident with the I-221(2A) one more aircraft, the I-222 (production code '3A') prototype high altitude interceptor, was manufactured. This differed from its predecessor in having a pressurised cockpit, and for the first time in a Soviet aircraft a special cooler was provided to cool the air entering the carburettor after the first compression stage by means of the AV-9L26 four-bladed propeller. The I-222(3A) was powered by a Mikulin AM-39B-1 with a single TK-300B turbosupercharger working from the port exhaust manifold, and ejector exhaust pipes were fitted on the starboard side. Take-off power was 1,860hp (1,387kW), and at 43,300ft (13,200m) the powerplant developed 1,430hp (1,066kW).

The aircraft had two 20mm ShVAK guns, the canopy was protected front and rear by armoured glass, and pilot's seat had an armoured backrest. The airframe was of mixed construction. The machine differed from the I-221(2A) in having the radiator moved forward from below the cockpit to a position under the engine.

The new fighter was completed in April 1944 and made its maiden flight on 7th May, being tested by A Yakimov, a highly skilled test pilot. Its speed at 22,000ft (6,700m) was 423mph (682km/h), and at 41,000ft (12,500m) it was 429mph (691km/h). Its service ceiling was 47,500ft (14,500m), a record for Soviet Second World War fighters. However, the aircraft did not go into series-production because the Mikoyan bureau was working on a better aircraft of this type, the I-224(4A).

I-224(4A)

Developed shortly after the I-222(3A), this aircraft was under test in the autumn of 1944. In shape it was similar to the I-222(3A), but it had a four-blade, broad-chord propeller which was more effective at high altitude, and was armed with two ShVAK guns. Under test it achieved a speed 430mph (693km/h) and a service ceiling of 46,250ft (14,100m), but it failed to attain its estimated range of 870 miles (1,400km).

I-225(5A)

By the summer of 1944 Mikoyan had produced another prototype, designated I-225 (production code '5A'). Dimensions and wing area were the same as those of the I-220(A), but it had the new AM-42B engine rated at 2,000hp (1,492kW) and a TK-300B turbosupercharger. Armament consisted of four ShVAK synchronised guns. A Yakimov piloted it on its maiden flight, on 21st July 1944, and during tests it reached a speed of 437mph (704km/h) at 25,500ft (7,800m). However, on 9th August, during its fifteenth flight, the aircraft was damaged in an accident.

The second version, powered by the boosted AM-42FB engine with a TK-300B turbosupercharger and with pilot visibility improved, did not embark on its flight test programme until 14th March 1945, by which time the war's outcome was decided and there was no longer an urgent demand for high altitude fighters. Moreover, combat actions were now conducted outside Soviet territory. The aircraft did not achieve production.

For technical data, see Table B, page 175.

Top and second from top: **The I-220(A) prototype during undercarriage retraction tests.**

Third from top and bottom: **Later version of the I-220(A), powered by the AM-39.**

Mikoyan-Gurevich I-220(A)

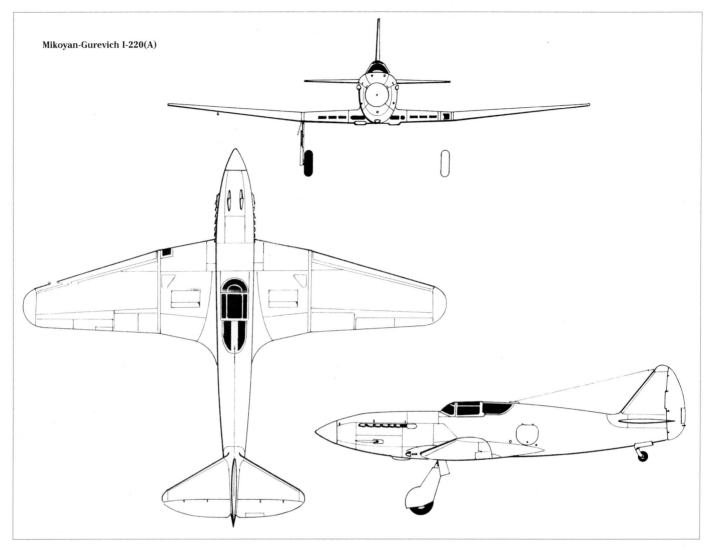

Left: **The I-222(2A) showing the single TK-300B turbosupercharger working from the port exhaust manifold.**

Below left: **Large, paddle-like blades on the I-224. This prototype was powered by a Mikunin AM-39FB.**

Photograph on opposite page:

Continuing the evolution of the I-220, the I-225(5A) was the ultimate MiG high altitude fighter prototype.

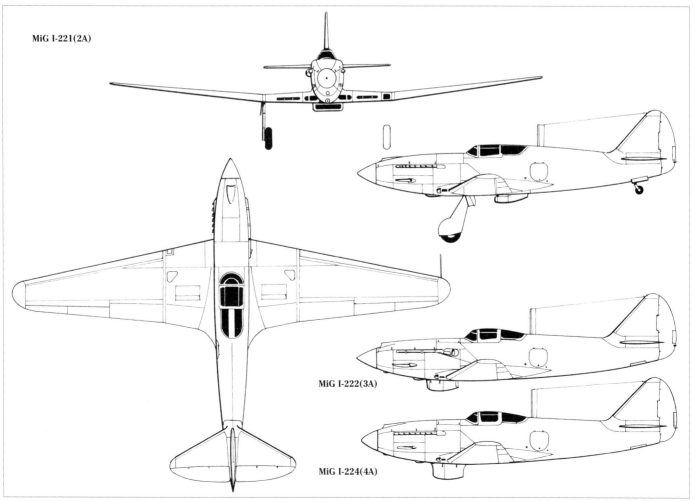

MiG I-221(2A)

MiG I-222(3A)

MiG I-224(4A)

Nikitin

IS

The struggle to increase the maximum speed of a fighter by by adopting the monoplane configuration, using more powerful engines and increasing the wing loading led to an aggravation of the take-off and landing characteristics in spite of the use of high-lift devices. The new fighters required increasingly longer runways, causing difficulties with the basing of Fighter Air Regiments in front line areas.

The problem of combining high speed with good take-off and landing performance was solved in an original way by designer Vasily Nikitin and pilot Vladimir Shevchenko, who suggested using a retractable *wing* configuration. At take-off and landing the fighter was a biplane with low wing loading, but once it was airborne, with its lower wing retracted, it became a high speed monoplane.

The team intensively set to work designing the prototype, the IS-1 (Istrebitel Skladnoy - foldable fighter), planning to power the aircraft with the 900hp (671.4kW) Shvetsov M-63. It was completed and proceeded to flight testing in 1940. The IS-1 was built of metal, the tail structure being fabric covered. With its

lower wing extended the aircraft was a sesquiplane with a Polikarpov Chaika-type wing. Each lower semi-wing consisted of two hinged parts, and in flight the inner wing sections retracted into fuselage wells by means of rigid rods, while the outer wing sections retracted into wells in upper wing.

The landing gear was conventional, with a tailwheel. The main undercarriage retracted into the inboard section of the lower semi-wing, the front part of the wheel being housed in the fuselage. Once the wheels were retracted the undercarriage wells were closed by doors, retraction of the wings and undercarriage being a simultaneous operation. During take-off and landing, when wing loading needed to be as low as possible, the IS-1 looked like conventional biplane with a fixed undercarriage, but in all other phases of flight it was a high wing monoplane.

The IS-1 was one of the lightest fighters, having a take-off weight of only 5,070lb (2,300kg) with an empty weight of 3,086lb (1,400kg). It had an open cockpit, and to improve control the rudder and elevator were fitted with trim tabs. Under test the IS-1 showed a maximum speed of 281mph (453

km/h), a service ceiling of 27,250ft (8,300m) and a range of 372 miles (600km). Its time to 16,400ft (5,000m) was 8.2 minutes. The lower wing and undercarriage extension/retraction system operated faultlessly during testing.

In 1941, using experience gained with the IS-1, the design team built a second version of folding-wing fighter, the IS-2 powered by a Tumanskii M-88 air-cooled radial. The aerodynamics were improved by giving the engine cowling a more streamlined shape and fitting a cowl shutter to regulate the flow of cooling. Instead of several holes arranged around the cowling perimeter, two exhaust pipes were fitted on the engine. In addition, the tailwheel was made retractable. Even with improved aerodynamics and powered by the 1,000hp (746kW) engine the aircraft could not match the LaGG-3, MiG-3 and Yak-1 in speed.

Further development of IS-type fighters was cancelled owing to the outbreak of war, although the designers had already embarked upon the preliminary designs for the IS-3 and IS-4 prototypes.

For technical data, see Table E, page 177.

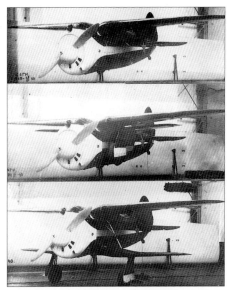

Photographs on the opposite page:

Far left and upper right: **Sequence showing the combined lowering of the undercarriage and lower wing on the IS-1.**

Bottom left and right: **Two views of the IS-2 improved version.**

Above: **With the undercarriage and wing in the 'down' position the IS-2 resembled the Polikarpov Chaika fighter – although it was appreciably heavier.**

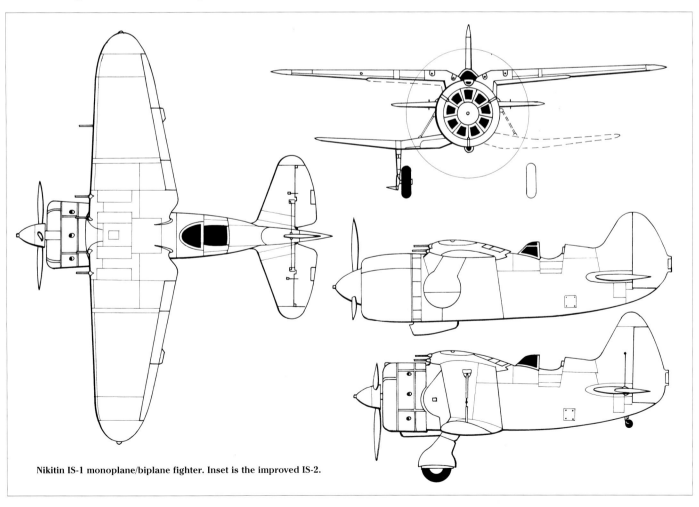

Nikitin IS-1 monoplane/biplane fighter. Inset is the improved IS-2.

Pashinin

I-21 (IP-21)

In 1939 Mikhail Pashinin, the deputy chief designer of the Polikarpov OKB, suggested that a fighter be designed with an uncambered wing profile to give the aircraft a high diving speed. Some time earlier, wings had often been damaged in dives owing to insufficient rigidity and strength. It was also suggested that the ejection effect of the exhaust gases could be exploited.

Design of the I-21, given the plant designation IP-21, began in January 1940, and by the spring it was ready. P Fokin performed its maiden flight on 11th July, but it was damaged beyond repair during production testing.

The second I-21 prototype went for state trials in December 1940. Pilot Stepan Suprun considered the aircraft difficult to fly and suitable only for highly skilled pilots. It was noted that it was unstable and had a high landing speed.

Due to the low undercarriage the conventional propeller for its Klimov M-105P almost touched the ground even when the machine was at rest. Maximum speed reached during the tests was 427mph (573km/h) at 16,400ft (5,000m).

The third and improved prototype was built in January 1941, and first flew on 5th April.

It had a revised wing structure and more powerful armament, a 23mm BT-23 cannon replacing the 20mm ShVAK. Its performance was better, though landing still remained very difficult, and further development was cancelled because the LaGG-3, MiG-1(I-200) and Yak-1 had already been introduced into production by this time.

With the cockpit position well behind the trailing edge of the wing, and sharply tapering outer wings, the Pashinin I-21 was intended to achieve the highest possible dive speed.

For technical data, see Table E, page 177.

Polikarpov

By 1940 military aviation worldwide had undergone considerable changes, and the Soviet Union remained almost the last country in which biplane fighters were still operational with the air force. These were the aircraft of famous Soviet designer Nikolay Polikarpov, the I-5, I-15, I-15*bis* and the I-153 Chaika, the successor of the earlier types, which was still on the inventory. All were single-strut, wire-braced biplanes of composite structure with Soviet-built engines. Nevertheless, they were to play a major role in the Second World War.

I-5

The I-5 was designed in 1930, mainly under the leadership of Nikolay Polikarpov, although the design was begun with the co-operation of another well known designer, Dmitry Grigorovich. The imported Bristol Jupiter VII radial which powered the first prototype was replaced by a Mk.VI in the second

prototype. Later, after completion of the pre-production batch, this in turn was replaced by the Soviet-built 480hp (358kW) M-22.

Production of the M-22-powered I-5 fighter continued for some years, and the aircraft was operational until the beginning of the Second World War. A small quantity of I-5UTI (Uchebno-Trenirovochny Istrebitel – training fighter) two-seat dual-control trainers had also been manufactured.

One I-5 was used for ground testing of underwing rocket pods, both lower outer wing panels being fitted with three launchers. The aircraft was fixed to a special base and the rockets launched at the target. It was thus possible to assess accuracy, and to conduct further development of the weapon while testing continued.

An interesting version of the I-5 had been developed at the Peotr Grokhovsky Design Bureau. Special beam-type bomb carriers were installed under the lower wing to carry two 551lb (250kg) bombs, thereby converting the aircraft into a fighter-bomber. However, the flight tests of the prototype revealed considerable deterioration in performance due to the significant increase in weight. The idea

was resurrected at the beginning of the war, when many I-5s were destroyed on the ground as well being as shot down in combat, and it seemed expedient to use the aged biplanes as single-seat light attack aircraft armed with four machine guns. Such a suggestion had been put forward earlier but rejected.

The Soviet aircraft industry built 803 I-5s, and the type was considered successful for its time. It was lighter than Britain's Bristol Bulldog, America's Curtiss P-6E and Germany's Heinkel HD-37 and therefore excelled them in climb rate and manoeuvrability, but it was inferior to them in speed. Simulated dogfights with available foreign fighters conducted by Nauchno Issledovatelyskii Institut Voenno-vozdushniye Sily (NII VVS – scientific and research institute of the air forces of the USSR) proved the superiority of the Soviet fighter. Nevertheless, the type soon became dated owing to the appearance of new powerful and lightweight air-cooled engines which offered improved fighter performance.

I-15 (TsKB-3)

Using experience gained with the I-5, a group of designers led by Nikolay Polikarpov, while being held in the so-called 'internal prison' of the NKVD (Narodny Commissariat Vnutrennikh Del – People's Commissariat of Internal Affairs), designed the new TsKB-3 (Tsentral'nyi Konstruktorskoye Byuro – central, ie state, design bureau) fighter biplane, later designated I-15. It is necessary to devote special attention to this type, as it participated in combat operations in Spain and the Far East on the eve of the Second World War. Furthermore, the I-15*bis* and I-153 versions flew operationally during the early war period.

Production flight tests of 630 to 715hp (470 to 533kW) Wright R-1820 Cyclone-powered TsKB-3 were conducted in November 1933, but were interrupted by an accident. State trials of the second prototype were completed in the ten days from 21st to 31st December. Equipped with ski landing gear, the aircraft was capable of 201mph (324km/h) at sea level, and 218mph (352.3km/h) at 6,500ft (2,000m). With wheeled undercarriage, maximum speed was 228mph (368km/h) at 10,000ft (3,000m). Turning time was eight seconds, and time to climb to 16,400ft (5,000m) was 6.2 minutes. These figures attained at a normal flying weight of 2,991lb (1,357kg).

Armament included two PV-1 machine guns provided with 1,500 rounds. In overload the aircraft could carry the same two machine guns plus four 22lb (10kg) bombs or chemical weapons on D-1 carriers under each lower wing.

In the test results the State Commission concluded that the performance of the I-15 (TsKB-3) prototype surpassed that of all USSR fighters, and its manoeuvrability and climb rate matched those of the best foreign-built fighters. Its successful combination of high manoeuvrability and horizontal speed was especially noted. Pilots stated that control was easy and the cockpit view excellent. At the same time, the designers were requested to improve to the directional stability of the aircraft, especially at speeds exceeding 155 mph (250km/h).

It is interesting to note that two months later, in February 1934, the TsKB-12 (I-16) low-wing monoplane fighter prototype was undergoing state flight tests. The chief designer of this aircraft, too, was Nikolay Polikarpov, but this M-22-powered machine proved inferior to the I-15 prototype in performance.

When the I-15 had completed its state tests it was recommended that the type be put into full scale production, preparation having been started simultaneously some months earlier at two plants, No.39 and No.1 in Moscow. The pre-production I-15 prototype,

built at plant No.39, underwent flight tests at the NII VVS in November 1934. The flight tests of initial production aircraft built at Plant No.1 were carried out in December the same year.

Early production aircraft were powered by the Wright Cyclone, but later, owing to a lack of imported engines, this was replaced by the Soviet-built M-22 rated at 480hp (358kW). Despite a consequent deterioration in performance, several hundred such aircraft were built. Maximum speed at 10,000ft (3,000m) fell to 215mph (347km/h), but manoeuvrability remained practically the same. Pilots liked the new fighter, and because of the form of the upper wing nicknamed it Chaika (seagull). Many considered it to be the best fighter in the world.

Although production of the I-15 started in late 1930 and the state trials of pre-production aircraft were successfully completed, the military disliked the Chaika's configuration. Officials at NII VVS constantly drew attention the fighter's low directional stability, which did not allow for accurate firing in the final stages of the flight tests. Nikolay Polikarpov repeatedly tried to prove that such statements were groundless by means of wind tunnel tests and demonstration flights, but owing to the absence of inertia-free flight data recorders in the USSR at the time he failed to do so. Under pressure from military officials Polikarpov was obliged to return to the normal centre section configuration.

In the spring of 1935 a new I-15 fighter prototype was manufactured at state aircraft factory (or plant) No.39. The upper wing was of the same span, but was straight, without the gulled Chaika centre section. The structure was re-inforced and new equipment was in-

Production Polikarpov I-5 powered by an M-22 radial.

stalled, but the armament remained the same; four PV-1 machine guns. The aircraft was powered with a Wright R-1820 Cyclone. The weight increased by 220lb (100kg) and wing loading reached 673.8ft^2 (62.6kg/m^2). State tests had been proceeding during the period from 21st May to 29th July. Sea level maximum speed was 193mph (312km/h) at a flying weight of 3,245lb (1,472kg), and 223 mph (360km/h) at 10,000ft (3,000m). Time to climb to 16,4000ft (5,000m) increased to 7.1 minutes. Manoeuvrability deteriorated, turning time being ten seconds; sea level rate of climb decreased to 39.5ft/sec (12.05m/sec) – pre-production I-15s were capable of 49ft/sec (15m/sec). Such performance satisfied nobody, it was decided to upgrade the fighter.

The I-15 with the M-22 engine had been under manufacture throughout 1935, but opposition by the air force officials prevented the start of full scale production. The reason lay not only in the fighter's poor directional stability, but also in the poor view from the cockpit during take-off and landing. Pilots gave contradictory opinions. A special study conducted by the Tsentral'nyi Aerogidrofynamichesky Institut (TsAGI – Central Aerodynamic and Hydrodynamic Institute) showed that the directional stability of aircraft having the Chaika-type configuration improved as speed increased. This did not change the opinion of the military officials.

At the government session in the autumn of 1935 the air force representative demanded that production of the I-15 should cease, and that the fighter should be phased out of service. In defence of his design, Polikarpov pointed to the unacceptably low production standards at No.1 and the hard service conditions in air force units, which, in his opinion, were not ready to operate such a fighter. Only after a private conversation between Polikarpov and Joseph Stalin was it decided that the I-15 should remain operational with the VVS.

Nevertheless, full scale production was interrupted and not a single fighter was produced in 1936. Work on the development of production aircraft was also suspended.

Some time earlier, licence production of the Wright R-1820 Cyclone engine, designated M-25, began at the plant headed by Arkady Shvetsov. The lightened version of the I-15 fighter (with some instruments, armament and the Townend ring removed and the pilot's seat replaced by a leather sling or trapeze) was powered by the prototype of this engine, rated at 635hp (473kW) at sea level and 700hp (522kW) at 7,500ft (2,300m).

In November 1935 this aircraft, with test pilot Vladimir Kokkinaki at the controls, reached an altitude of 47,824ft (14,577m), breaking the previous record set by Italian pilot R Donatti in April 1934, flying the special high altitude Caproni Ca 114A, by 433ft (132m).

In 1937 two more I-15 prototypes, both with Wright Cyclones, were undergoing the flight tests. The first of these, which differed in having six rockets mounted under the wing, was tested with a ski landing gear.

Owing to deterioration in performance and an increase in weight, the ceiling of the fighter decreased by 4,600ft (1,400m), time to climb to 16,400ft (5,000m) increased by 2.6 minutes, and the maximum speed at 7,900ft (2,400m) decreased by 9.3mph (15km/h). The second prototype was fitted with the 100lb (45.6kg) SK-IV high altitude pressure cabin designed by Alexey Shcherbakov.

Preliminary tests were conducted during October and November. At that time test pilot Stepan Suprun performed only three flights at 21,300ft to 31,000ft (6,500m to 9,500m). He reported favourably on the pressure cabin.

Photographs on the opposite page:

Views of the TsKB-3 fighter biplane. The side view shows the plant number, 39, set on a red star on a white circle on the rudder. The rear view in particular shows the centre section shape of the upper wing which gave the aircraft the nickname Chaika (Seagull).

On this page, right: **First production I-15.**

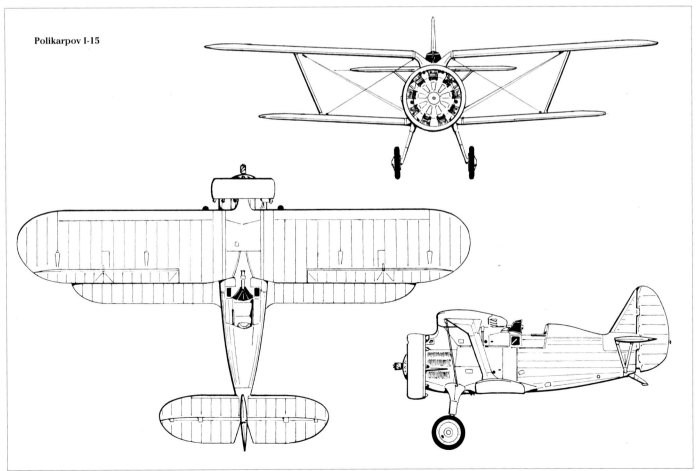

Polikarpov I-15

I-15*bis* (I-152)

As mentioned above, all production I-15 design and development was interrupted by the end of 1935, and Nikolay Polikarpov was appointed chief designer of two centres at the same time: Plant No.84 in Moscow and Plant No.21 in Gorkii. The Gorkii plant had no prototype manufacturing facilities, and the whole of 1936 was spent creating these. By this time the type had undergone significant changes. Its wing was given a new Clark 'YH' aerofoil section, the span was increased, and the more powerful M-25V was installed, driving a fixed pitch metal propeller. The Townend ring was replaced by a NACA-type cowling, the front of which was fitted with adjustable louvres. Some details were redesigned and partly strengthened in accordance with the strength requirements of 1934, and some new equipment was installed, including a power supply system with an electric generator and an RSI-type radio.

From early 1937 Moscow Aircraft Plant No.1 began development of the I-15. There were several reasons for this. On the one hand, the plant was not involved in the wide-scale production process, and the results of earlier tests of the prototype with the conventional wing centre section were not promising. On the other hand, production of the M-25, the Soviet version of the Wright R-1820 Cyclone, had begun.

Production M-25-powered I-15s outclassed M-22-powered examples, but even they did not meet the air force requirements. For that reason construction of a new fighter prototype, designated I-15*bis* (or TsKB-3*bis*), was started at Plant No.1, which had the necessary technological capability. (*bis* – literally from the French or Latin 'again' or encore, more practically, a rethought or developed version, or even Mk.2.) This aircraft also had another official designation, I-152, signifying that it was the second model of the I-15.

However, construction of the new aircraft was delayed, and the underdeveloped machine with its conventional centre-section was not transferred to the NII VVS for state tests until 2nd July 1937. These tests showed that although the maximum speed had not changed, climb rate and especially manoeuvrability had deteriorated still further. The designers tried fitting a new propeller, but this failed to improve the aircraft's performance. The main reason for the deterioration in performance was that the structure was 661lb (300kg) overweight when compared with an M-25-powered production I-15. The Commission concluded that the I-15*bis* fighter had also failed to pass the state trials.

Under pressure from the VVS, it was decided to set up a production line for the conventional upper wing centre-section fighter after modification. Production began in mid-1937 at Plant No.1. The production aircraft had its fuel capacity increased from 57 to 68 gallons (260 to 310 litres), and could also carry two 17.5 gallon (80 litre) external tanks each under the interplane struts, which could be replaced by bombs of up to 110lb (50kg). The armament remained the same; four PV-1 or VS machine guns.

Development work on the I-15*bis* never stopped. In two years several prototypes had been produced and the production fighter had also undergone development. In the middle of 1938 the production I-15*bis* had a M-25V engine and a new VISh-6A propeller underwent flight testing.

In this version service ceiling increased from 30,000 to 31,500ft (8,980m to 9,600m). The prototype I-152 M-25V was subjected to trials at the NII VVS from 3rd June to 29th July 1938. This version had stub exhausts instead of an exhaust collector ring, a Townend ring instead of a NACA cowling, a protected fuel tank, and a revised canopy windscreen with a flat front panel. The aircraft was supposed to set the standard for production in 1939. It passed its tests satisfactorily, but owing to production delays and its actual performance when compared with that of a production I-15*bis*, manufacture of this version was considered inexpedient.

Several other I-15*bis* (I-152) prototypes were test flown in 1939. One was equipped with two TK-3 turbosuperchargers to improve the type's performance at altitude, but as this increased its weight by 308lb (140kg) the experiment was a failure. Tests of the M-25V-powered I-15*bis* with a pressurised cockpit designed by Alexey Scherbakov were conducted from 29th August 29 to 4th October. The cockpit, which had a rigid riveted duralumin structure and a multi-layered semicircular rubber chamber with nine windows, was fastened to the welded fuselage truss.

This cockpit was reported to be very successful, but the consequent 147lb (67kg) increase in overall weight gave no advantages compared to a production I-15*bis*. Moreover, it was impossible to open the pressurised cockpit at high speeds. Nevertheless, the flight tests provided valuable scientific data.

The upper centre section of the I-15*bis* (prototype illustrated) was of conventional format and did away with the distinctive 'seagull' look.

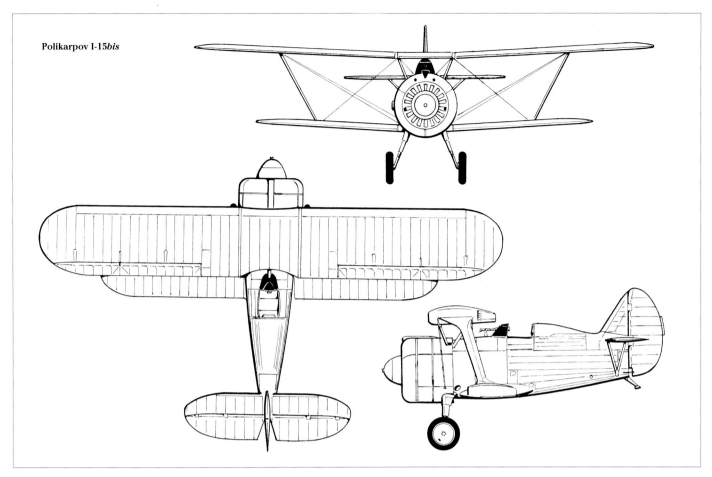

Polikarpov I-15*bis*

The result was an increase in wing loading, and hence a deterioration in rate of climb, horizontal manoeuvrability and service ceiling. Polikarpov considered that the biplane fighter still had a future. Speed could be increased by installing a more powerful engine and reducing drag, and manoeuvrability and flight safety at low altitudes were adequate. For this reason he had already asked his deputy, Dmitry Tomashevich, to design a new fighter – the third model of the I-15, the I-153.

The preliminary design was referred to the VVS and the State Commissariat for the Aviation Industry on 11th October 1937, and approved on 23rd October. The new aircraft was a further development of the I-15 and I-15*bis*. To improve speed and manoeuvrability it had a retractable undercarriage and a Chaika-type wing centre section – the 'seagull' had returned. During preliminary development five different types of undercarriage had been studied, Polikarpov choosing a rearward-retracting system in which the wheel turned into the fuselage underside.

After the project was approved, the chief designer faced difficulties. As mentioned

Photographs on the opposite page:

Top: **The I-15*bis* proved to be a robust aircraft allowing for repairs and re-entry into service.**

Bottom: **The two-seat combat trainer version of the I-15 was designated the DIT-2.**

above, all I-15*bis* fighter development was suspended for a while, and the designers lost their development facility. Appeals to different departments did not change the situation, and for that reason the preliminary design of the new Chaika made no progress for some months. Finally, the preparation of working drawings of the I-15 was assigned to the Experimental Design Bureau of Plant No.1, and the construction of two prototypes was begun there. The first prototype had an M-25V engine, and the second an 800hp (597kW) M-62. Armament comprised four 7.62mm ShKAS machine guns synchronised to fire through the propeller. The most doubtful feature was the structure of the retractable undercarriage, but testing showed this to be reliable.

The first prototype I-153, with an M-25V, was completed at the beginning of May 1938, and A Zhukov started flight tests in the middle of the month. The second prototype, with an M-62, was tested by test pilot A Davydov in the middle of June. Later, both aircraft were sent to the NII.

State trials of the first prototype began on 27th September and were completed on 5th October. They were conducted by test pilot Pavel Fedrovi. At a normal flying weight of 3,637lb (1,650kg) the maximum speed at the sea level was 223.6mph (360km/h), and at altitude it was 264mph (425km/h), outperforming the I-15*bis*. The rate of climb at sea level was 57ft/sec (17.5m/sec), and the time to

climb 16,400ft (5,000m) was 6.1 minutes. It was evident that the aircraft completely outclassed its predecessor.

The Commissariat pointed out several structural shortcomings in the I-153, and it was decided to incorporate appropriate modifications in the initial production batch. The tests of the M-62-powered I-153 were similarly successful, but because the aircraft was powered by a prototype engine it was decided not to put this version into production until production engines were delivered.

Throughout 1938 special attention was paid to production of the new fighter at Plant No.1. The initial batch of ten I-153s powered by M-25Vs was completed in October, and in November they were transferred to Baku for flight testing. One of the fighters, regarded as a second prototype I-153 M-25V, underwent state trials from 21st March to 28th April 1939. At the same time the remainder were undergoing service trials. These tests were conducted not only by NII VVS pilots, but by operational pilots as well.

The second prototype differed from the first machine in having reduced area elevators with a new control system, a strengthened undercarriage and a protected fuel tank, among other things. Flight tests were successful and the aircraft's performance was sufficiently high, but again a series of defects were noted, especially concerning the view from the cockpit.

Top left: **An I-153 during the spin tests as the NII VVS.**

Top right: **I-153 No.6566 with skis during spin tests as the NII VVS.**

Centre: **A '1940 Standard' I-153 on skis during acceptance trials.**

Bottom left: **A '1940 Standard' I-153 on skis with wingtip mounted auxiliary fuel tanks.**

Bottom right: **When the German offensive began many I-153s never got the chance to engage the enemy.**

Undercarriage retraction and extension was reliable. On 11th April one of the pre-production aircraft broke up while recovering from a dive owing to failure of its wing structure.

M-62 series-production began in 1939 and it became possible to place the I-153 thus powered into production. Delivery of service fighters started, and it was decided to eliminate all the design defects in this series and to conduct official state and operational tests of this version.

An I-153 M-62 with a fixed pitch propeller was tested at the NII VVS from 16th June to 16th August 1939. Later, another example with an AV-1 variable pitch propeller underwent service tests in combat conditions in Mongolia. The sea level speed of these two aircraft was practically equal (226.8 and 226.1mph or 365 and 364km/h respectively), but at 16,400ft (5,000m) there was a difference of almost 12.4mph (20km/h). The I-153 M-62 with a fixed pitch propeller attained a speed of 275mph (443km/h) at 15,000ft (4,600m), and its service ceiling was 32,200ft (9,800m). The AV-1 propeller gave the fighter a better rate of climb and halved its landing run, though endurance deteriorated.

The I-153's performance was rather high for a sesquiplane, yielding only a little in speed to monoplane fighters. This was taken into account by Air Force Command, and Commander-in-Chief A Loktionov announced that the initial 13 I-153s would be transferred to the eastern battle area for operational tests.

In the summer of 1939, following a series of large scale provocations by the Japanese army on the Mongolian frontier, combat operations involving troops and air units began along the Khalkhin-Gol river. Soviet I-15bis and I-16 fighters were pitted against Japanese Nakajima Ki-27s which outperformed the monoplanes in climb rate and manoeuvrability and the biplanes in speed. It was for this reason that Air Force Command decided to send the initial batch of Chaika fighters to the Khalkhin-Gol region.

The service series I-153s were delivered to Mongolia along with 45 I-15bis fighters, and entered service with the 22nd Fighter Air Regiment, flight tests lasting from 9th August to 6th September 1939. The new fighter was received with delight by the special group led by Hero of the Soviet Union Stepan Gritsevets, but their joy was premature. While the machine guns were being fired on the ground with the engines running, it was noticed that the synchronisation mechanism was broken on all of the I-153s, and one of the propellers was shot through. The new Chaika fighters were incapable of combat. Front Command held an urgent conference to solve the problem, and it was decided to rework the fire control system. The task was completed in field conditions in short order.

At last the fighters were ready for combat operations, and Stepan Gritsevets, with his group of nine aircraft, took off. On this mission Gritsevets deceived his opponents by ordering his pilots to fly with their undercarriage down until they approached to the enemy, who, it was hoped, would mistake the I-153s for I-15bis fighters. The I-153s, having made a feint, turned towards their own lines, and the Japanese fighters pursued them. At the same time the Soviet pilots were ordered to retract their undercarriages and, making a combat turn, they engaged the enemy. In spite of their numerical superiority the Japanese lost four fighters and turned tail for their lines. This tactic was used frequently, and sometimes the Japanese, seeing I-15bis fighters in the distance, mistook them for I-153 Chaikas and avoided engagement. The Western press maintained that such a manoeuvre was impossible because the landing gear could not be retracted under a high 'g' load, but the Soviet pilots retracted their undercarriages before the combat turn, thereby gaining an increase in speed.

Combat flying in Mongolia revealed structural weaknesses. It was necessary to alter the fire control system under field conditions, and on some machines the gun trigger pressure had to be reduced.

Operations in Khalkhin-Gol again proved that the high manoeuvrability of the biplane could not compensate for its low speed. It was best to use I-153s in concert with high speed I-16s, and such a combination was successfully used by Soviet pilots. This tactic had previously been adopted by I-15bis pilots.

At the same time new weapons, RS-82 rockets, were tested in combat. Five I-15bis fighters were adapted to carry the rockets, a single salvo sometimes being sufficient to disperse enemy fighters.

The Chaika's successful debut over the Khalkhin-Gol led to an increase in its production, but this could not solve the main problem; improving the aircraft's performance. Development had taken place over a two year period. On 30th December 1939 pilot A Zhukov took the new I-190 fighter into the air for its first production flight tests. The I-190 was a conversion of the I-153 powered by the Tumanskii M-88. The engine ran unevenly, however, and a month later an emergency landing was made during the seventh flight. In February testing was interrupted by an accident and the project was halted, but the prototype was repaired and tests resumed.

In the middle of April the M-88 was replaced by the M-88R geared engine with a modified cowling. Even that engine constantly overheated. Installation of the new M-88A allowed several more flights to be made, but soon all development work was stopped. During the tests a maximum speed of 279

mph (450km/h) at 23,100ft (7,050m) had been achieved (with the M-88 engine driving an AV-2L2 variable pitch propeller). The second prototype I-190 M-88 was equipped with a TK-1 turbosupercharger. Development of versions having two turbosuperchargers and a pressurised cockpit was also begun, but the People's Commissar of the Aircraft Industry ordered these projects to be abandoned.

At the same time, the development of production aircraft continued. Flight testing of an I-153 M-62 with two TK-1 turbosuperchargers was undertaken between 15th May and 28th October 1940. This version was faster than the production I-153 above 17,700ft (5,400m), but with the TK-1 inoperative it was slower at all altitudes owing to the increase in weight. In June and July 1940 an I-153 M-62 with a pressurised cockpit designed by Alexey Scherbakov successfully underwent production flight tests, designated I-153V (vysotnyi, literally height, or high altitude). The cockpit's all-welded structure was made from aluminium alloy and had a rearward-hinging transparent canopy. An airtight seal was achieved by clamping the canopy cover to the rubber moulding round the cockpit sides.

Special attention was paid to development of the fighter's armament. Following flight tests conducted in February 1940, small scale production began of the I-153P with two ShVAK cannon (sometimes the aircraft was also equipped with two ShKAS machine guns). A new version of the Chaika, with four synchronised VS machine guns, also went into production, and an attack version of the aircraft, equipped with bomb carriers, was tested. After successful combat use of RS-82 rockets over Khalkhin-Gol, the system was installed on the I-153, this version being used successfully in the Second World War.

Full scale production of an updated M-62, designated M-63, enabled this engine to be installed in production Chaikas. A new ski undercarriage was flight tested at the NII VVS from 21st January to 2nd April 1940. Although the designers failed to obtain a significant increase in speed, the sea level climb rate with short term boost was 73ft/sec (22.5m/sec), while at nominal power the rate was 55ft/sec (17m/sec) and time to 16,400ft (5,000m) was 5.1 minutes. The service ceiling of 35,000ft (10,600m) was reached in 24.5 minutes. This last figure was better than that achieved by all other production variants of the I-15, I-15bis and I-153, and the considerable increase in climb rate forced the State Commission to put the aircraft into production.

Soon, the new version replaced the I-153 M-62 in production at Plant No.1, and on 30th November 1940 the state trials of the production I-153 M-63 (the so-called '1940 Standard') were completed. The aircraft was tested in three versions: with a ski undercarriage, with a wheeled undercarriage and with external fuel tanks and a ski undercarriage.

Although the external tanks considerably increased the fighter's operational range, its take-off weight increased by 568lb (258kg), causing a deterioration in performance. The aircraft was supposed to engage in combat only after the fuel in the external tanks had been used and the tanks themselves jettisoned. The I-153 M-62 had already used such tanks during the war with Finland, but they were often not released because of the combat units lacked replacements. Finland captured several of these aircraft.

The I-153 M-63 was the last Soviet biplane fighter to enter full scale production. Production Chaika fighters were constantly under test at the NII VVS during 1939-40, with both ski and wheeled undercarriages. It was very difficult to improve performance because, on the one hand, the design was practically at the limit of its development, and on the other it was clear that high speeds could not be achieved with the biplane configuration.

To increase speed, two ramjets designed by I Merkulov were mounted on the fighter, and in September 1940 flight tests were undertaken to test the installation. During one of its last test flights the I-153DM with DM-4 ramjets attained a maximum speed of 273mph (440km/h) at 6,500ft (2,000m) – the ramjets increased top speed by 31.6mph (51km/h). In spite of their high efficiency, the mixed powerplant was not considered suitable for the biplane fighters.

The last project based on the Chaika was the I-195 fighter, designed in the summer of 1940. This was an unbraced sesquiplane with an enclosed cockpit, powered by an M-90 with a cowling that featured a ducted spinner inlet. Its estimated maximum speed was 362 mph (583km/h).

Nikolay Polikarpov's biplanes were widely used on the battlefronts from the beginning of the war. Shortly before the start of hostilities in April 1941 the air force units received the latest I-153 series fighter. All changes to their equipment and structure required by the demands of the war were carried out in the field, and often affected just a single aircraft.

The I-15bis and I-153 fighters were not among the priority targets during the Nazis' sudden attacks of Soviet airfields, but they often suffered no less than other types of combat aircraft. All of the 74th Attack Air Regiment's aircraft were destroyed, including 47 I-15bis and I-153 Chaikas. The regiment's airfield was 8.6 miles (14km) from the state border, so the losses were caused not only by bombing, but also by German artillery.

The alert signal and the order for the aircraft to take-off reached the airfield in Kurovitse, where the 164th and 66th Regiments were based, at the dawn. Unlike the 164th Fighter Air Regiment pilots, those of the 66th Regiment did not arrive at the airfield in time, and as a result the Germans burned 34 aircraft, mainly I-15bis, and the regiment was rendered hors de combat. A similar situation prevailed in the 62nd Regiment, based a little to the south and rated one of the best in the Kiev Special Military District. Almost half of its I-153 fleet was destroyed on the ground, though some aircraft were repaired by the evening.

Great losses were avoided where the aircraft were well camouflaged and dispersed, as was done by the pilots and ground personnel of the 127th Fighter Air Regiment, based at Lesitse and commanded by Lt Colonel Gordienko. Their airfield was well disguised, and not one of their 72 biplanes suffered on the ground, although the neighbouring airfield was bombed repeatedly. Exerting themselves to the full, the 127th's pilots achieved great success. Lt S Zhukovsky and Senior Political Instructor A Artemiev took off nine times in Chaikas, shooting down four and three enemy aircraft respectively.

Having recovered from the initial shock, the Soviet biplanes engaged the enemy, but the sorties were mainly isolated and individual. It was felt that the units' co-ordination had been destroyed. However, this did not concern the 43rd Aircraft Division's units, located 279 miles (450km) from the border, which did not participate in aerial combat on the first day of the war. One of its four regiments, the 160th Fighter Air Regiment, was equipped with 60 Chaikas. They defended Minsk, Bobruisk and Mogilev, destroyed enemy aircraft on their airfields, attacked the enemy on the roads, flew reconnaissance missions and supported Soviet ground-based troops. Until 2nd August 1941, the most difficult period of the war, the pilots of the regiment flew 1,683 sorties and claimed 27 enemy aircraft, but lost almost all of their own aircraft and were soon taken to the rear to reform and convert to the new LaGG fighters.

The regiment's pilots knew their aircraft well, and performed many night missions. In a night combat on 4th July the Regiment's Commander, Major A Kostromin, an excellent pilot, died. It is believed that he was shot in the head during an enemy attack, and made no attempt to bale out of his aircraft. At that time not only the biplanes, but even new Soviet aircraft did not have armoured glass.

On the north and south flanks of the Soviet-German front Polikarpov fighters operated more successfully. The pilots of the 96th Independent Squadron were the first of the Black Sea Navy Aviation pilots to open the score. The 96th had 17 combat aircraft, comprising three I-153s and 14 I-15bis, on strength. The Romanian forces that stood against them were not as active as Luftwaffe units, and it was not until the afternoon of 22nd June that they attacked Izmail. In the repulse of this assault, Lt M Maksimov became the first Black Sea pilot to gain a victory, though the unit commander, Captain A Korobitsin, also distinguished himself. They became the navy's first bearers of the Order of the Red Banner.

The I-15bis is not mentioned once in accounts of the heroic defence of Odessa. Ninth Fighter Air Regiment pilot V Greck rammed a Messerschmitt Bf109 and perished in his burning aeroplane during a combat over the city on 10th August 1941. A day later the same feat was accomplished in the north by Captain M Krasnolutsky, but in spite of serious damage his aircraft remained controllable and he managed to return to his airfield. For this and other deeds he was awarded the Gold Star on 16th January 1942.

During the first half of the year Krasnolutsky and his friends flew the I-15bis, although their regiment, led by Hero of the Soviet Union V Belousov, was designated an Attack Air Regiment. As there were not enough Ilyushin Il-2 attack aircraft at the beginning of the war, and those existing had only recently been mastered by their pilots, the I-15bis and I-153 Chaika were the main aircraft supporting the Soviet troops on the battlefield. The biplanes destroyed storehouses and even some tanks near Murmansk.

In accordance with their assigned role the 65th Regiment's aircraft were equipped with bomb carriers, and rockets were later mounted under their wings. The latter caused problems, however, because the lower wing's fabric covering could not withstand the rocket salvos and the wing structure warped. The squadrons therefore attached sheets of duralumin to the wing undersides, strengthened the spars and installed additional ribs. This turned the aged biplane into a menacing combat aircraft. A German report noted: 'although the I-153 and I-15bis were very slow, the latter with ski landing gear and bomb carriers being capable of only [149 to 167mph] 240 to 270km/h, which put them at a disadvantage, their excellent manoeuvrability compensated for this shortcoming'.

In the late autumn and winter of 1941 the number of biplanes in the first line units was reduced, but the percentage was still greater than the Soviet Command desired. Instead of 30% as at the beginning of the war, the I-15bis and I-153 Chaika at that time made up 18 to 20% of the total strength.

The participation of biplanes in Naval Aviation operations deserves special mention. By the beginning of the war Naval Aviation had 687 I-153 and I-15bis, comprising 90% of the total of 763 fighters in the force. The situation at the front dictated that the main missions should be bomb strikes on enemy infantry and materiel, and this was the case in the

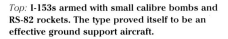

Top: **I-153s armed with small calibre bombs and RS-82 rockets. The type proved itself to be an effective ground support aircraft.**

Above: **Rare illustration of I-153s flying with Russian Naval Aviation.**

Above, right: **The I-153V prototype with pressurised cockpit. Such research helped to pave the way for the next generation of high altitude designs.**

Right: **Polikarpov I-190 prototype.**

Black, Baltic and Barents Sea regions. The bi-planes remained the principal Navy fighters until the end of 1941.

A new aspect of Polikarpov biplane operations was their use as night bombers. The document which initiated such use was an order from the Western Front Air Force Commander dated 18th November 1941. According to this document, about 30 I-15bis fighters remained for use in daytime instrument flight rules meteorological conditions to provide cover for airfields, battlefield observation and assault attacks. At night these aircraft, escorted by Polikarpov R-5 reconnaissance bi-planes, struck the first blows against ground targets, and later began to operate independently. These attacks played a significant part in halting the enemy's advance on Moscow.

Side view of a I-153 test-bed for the DM-4 ramjets. Note the miniscule clearance at the rear of the wing-mounted ramjet with the ground.

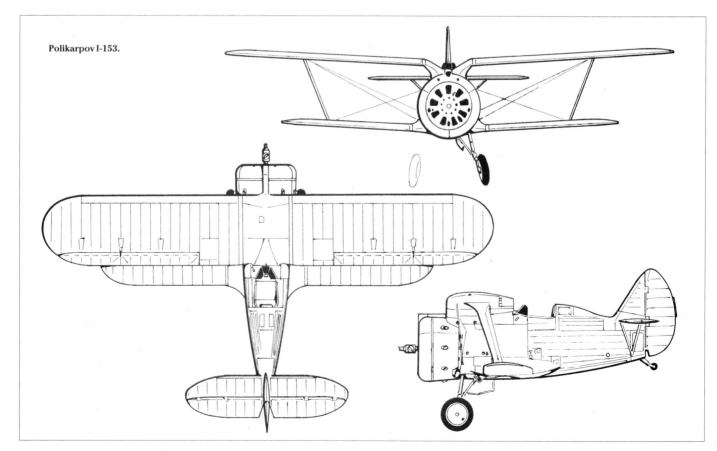

Polikarpov I-153.

I-16 (TsKB-12)

Nikolay Polikarpov developed both agile biplanes and fast monoplanes. In the latter class, the I-16 fighter represented a peak of his creative work. The aircraft opened a new era in fighter design – the era of cantilever monoplanes with retractable undercarriage.

The new fighter was publicly displayed inside the USSR for the first time on 1st May 1935, when I-16s took part in the flypast over Moscow's Red Square as part of the annual Labour Day parade. Later that year the I-16 was demonstrated at the Milan International Aviation Exhibition, where it impressed the aviation community.

To his great credit, Polikarpov correctly and opportunely saw the need for fast monoplane fighters. His concept was embodied in what became the I-16, the first fighter monoplane in the world to go into series and mass production. For an aircraft of the 1930s, when ceilings, operational ranges, climb rates and especially speeds were increasing rapidly, the I-16 had an enviably long life. The main reason for this was its high speed at its time of origin.

Preliminary design was initiated by Polikarpov in August 1933, when, as mentioned above, development of the I-15 (TsKB-3) biplane fighter was also under way. Though the I-15 was ordered by the Soviet Air Force, the I-16 was an in-house (or what would be called a private venture in the West) design.

Right: **First prototype I-16 (or TsKB-12), powered by an M-22.**

Below: **Third production I-16, at Plant No.39 in 1934.**

Such activity was not unusual for one as full of creative ideas as Polikarpov. It was not his first fighter monoplane. In 1923-24, in conjunction with I Kostkin, he had developed and successfully tested the I-1 (Il-400b) fighter, which slightly resembled its famous successor. Like the I-16, it had an aft centre of gravity position and insufficient longitudinal stability. In December 1933 the first prototype I-16 was completed, test pilot Valery Chkalov making its maiden flight.

The I-16 was of mixed construction. The fuselage was a well streamlined all-wooden monocoque. Its primary structure comprised wooden frames, longerons and stringers, and this was covered with a birch ply skin. After assembly the fuselage was primed and painted. On the prototypes and first series-production aircraft the cockpit was provided with a downwards hinged door panel on the port side to allow pilots easy access. Later a similar door was also fitted on the starboard side. In addition, the cockpits of the prototypes and first series-production aircraft had a sliding canopy, the first to be fitted on a fighter.

The wing comprised a centre section and two detachable outer panels. Primary structure consisted of two stainless trussed spars and duralumin ribs, the whole being fabric covered with the exception of the leading edges, which were covered in duralumin. The ailerons could be lowered simultaneously during landing to double as flaps. These and the tail surfaces had fabric covered metal frames.

The retractable landing gear had pyramidal struts and was equipped with an oleo-pneumatic shock absorber, but lacked automatic actuation. Retraction was accomplished by means of a winch located in the cockpit, dubbed 'sharmanka' (barrel organ) by pilots because its handle resembled the instrument's crank.

Power came from a nine-cylinder air-cooled radial. During the I-16's evolution it was fitted with progressively more powerful engines. The armament originally consisted of two wing-mounted 7.62mm ShKAS machine guns, but this was later increased. The I-16's minimal overall dimensions, barrel-like

fuselage and well developed wing fillets made it easily distinguishable from other fighters.

Originally, two I-16 prototypes were manufactured. The first, designated TsKB-12, was powered by an M-22 engine rated at 480hp (358kW), while the the second, given the same designation, had the more powerful Wright Cyclone 1820-F-2 of 600hp (447kW).

In the Crimea from 16th to 26th February 1934, test pilot Vladimir Kokkinaki carried out the first stage of the state trials of first prototype, which was fitted with ski landing gear. From 22nd March to 25th April, at the same airfield, he performed the second stage of the trials, for which the aircraft was equipped with retractable wheeled landing gear.

During the latter tests the aircraft attained a speed of 223mph (359km/h) at sea level and 201mph (325km/h) at 16,400ft (5,000m) at 2,894lb (1,312kg). At 2,916lb (1,323kg) the ski-equipped version reached 190mph (306 km/h) at sea level and 175mph (283km/h) at 16,400ft (5,000m).

In the course of the trials an unpleasant incident occurred. During an approval flight with Valery Chkalov at controls the landing gear failed to extend. The pilot therefore put the aircraft through a number of sharp manoeuvres, and under the influence of high 'g' loads the landing gear came down.

The report of the state trials recorded that: 'due to good aerodynamic shape, retractable landing gear and a high specific load factor, the I-16 aircraft, despite the disadvantage of an ageing M-22 engine, is only slightly inferior to single-seat fighters in service with foreign arms with respect to speed at [16,400ft] 5,000m, is superior to them in terms of speed at altitudes up to [6,500ft] 2,000m, and is inferior to none [of them] in terms of ceiling and climb rate'. With regard to speed at 16,400ft (5,000m), the I-16 bettered the I-15 fighter then in service with Red Army, which had the same engine, by 49mph (80km/h).

In addition to the I-16's merits, some shortcomings were revealed during trials, including insufficient strength of the landing gear retraction/extension mechanism, insecure engine cowling and looseness of the wing's fabric covering. Taking into account the results of the tests, the Air Force Administration deemed it necessary to initiate series-production of the I-16 powered by the M-22 engine once the shortcomings were rectified. Because the trials report recommended that, in terms of handling, the I-16 was suitable only for pilots of average or higher abilities, Yakov Alksnis, then head of the Air Force, ordered Air Force Staff to develop a system to select top class pilots to be trained to fly the I-16.

Military test pilots also sampled the second prototype. Fitted with ski landing gear, the 2,980lb (1,352kg) aircraft, was tested by V Stepanchyonok in February 1934, again in the Crimea. This I-16 differed from the first prototype in having a more powerful engine, though it did not affect its external appearance. The aircraft reached a speed of 215mph (346km/h) at sea level and 195mph (314 km/h) at 16,400ft (5,000m); 18.6 to 24.8mph (30 to 40km/h) faster than the M-22-powered prototype. The NII VVS report noted the aircraft had good level speed, sufficient stability in all three axes, and adequate manoeuvrability. It was recommended that the Wright Cyclone F-2 engine be replaced by a Cyclone F-3 more suited to high altitude operations, to enable the aircraft to fulfil the requirements of a modern fighter, and that the I-16 should then be put into series-production immediately.

In the meantime, the work of refining the second prototype was under way. An initial series of flights with the aircraft fitted with wheeled landing gear and piloted by A Chernavsky and A Belozerov had just begun when, on 14th April 1934, a starboard landing gear strut failed on landing and the aircraft settled on its belly, damaging the propeller. The incident prevented completion of the trials, and the armament had yet to be tested. The fighter was transferred to Moscow for a repair.

While it was under repair, personnel of Nikolay Polikarpov's design bureau made some changes to the aircraft, including:

• a Wright Cyclone 1830-F-3 of 640hp (477kW) having an operating ceiling of 10,000ft (3,000m), instead of the F-2's 4,300ft (1,300m), was installed;
• a new tunnel-type engine cowling was installed, with its trailing edge flush with the fuselage and provision for nine exhaust stacks; this cowling was later installed on all I-16 versions except the Type 4 and UTI-2 versions, and was a distinctive feature of the I-16;
• the propeller was fitted with a spinner;
• all wing upper surfaces were covered with duralumin sheet;
• landing gear strengthened and the retraction/extension mechanism changed;
• the aircraft was carefully polished.

A new batch of tests carried out by Kokkinaki at the NII VVS airfield in September-October 1934 revealed that the speed had increased to 224mph (362km/h) sea level, 271mph (437km/h) at 10,000ft (3,000m), and 256mph (413km/h) at 16,400ft (5,000m). The aircraft climbed to 16,400ft (5,000m) in 6.2 minutes, and had a service ceiling of 27,200ft (8,300m). Its landing speed of 68mph (110 km/h) was considered high at that time. The effectiveness of the series of alterations was confirmed.

Performance of the I-16 as a whole was superior to that of the best foreign production aircraft, and even to that of the prototypes.

I-16 M-22 (Type 4)

It seemed an opportune time to decide to put the I-16 into series-production, but it was pointed out that the defects had not been completely eliminated. It was still not strong enough, the undercarriage mechanism needed improvement and it was recommended that airbrakes be installed to lower the landing speed.

Taking into account the interest taken by the military and the aircraft's unconventional design, the Chief of the Main Board of the Air Force charged V Konart, head of the NII VVS, with personal control of the work to resolve the I-16's problems.

During the I-16's development many sceptics had said that it would be difficult or even impossible to recover from a spin owing to the small area its rudder and tailplane. These critics included Vladimir Pyshnov and A Zhuravchenko, who had developed spin theory and believed that the I-16 would not be recoverable. Nonetheless, Polikarpov Design Bureau chief test pilot Valery Chkalov was able to regain control of a spinning aircraft in tests. This did not eliminate all doubts, In September 1935 test pilot Peotr Stefanovsky carried out production I-16 spin trials, successfully performing and recovering from 90 spins.

By this time development of series-production was fully under way. Moscow Aircraft Plant No.39 was the first to initiate series-production, the first batch of 50 fighters appearing in 1934. The following year I-16 series-production was begun at Plant No.21 in Gorkii, and quantities began to be counted in hundreds and thousands. Having produced 527 aircraft up to 1935, the staff of the Gorkii production plant worked on Polikarpov's creation for six years.

The first series version was the I-16 Type 4, powered by the M-22 engine (there was no other engine suitable for the aircraft). The external appearance, dimensions and armament were identical to those of the first prototype but a number of improvements were implemented. In particular, a new landing gear operating mechanism was adopted, and the wing skin and some components were strengthened. Flight tests of the of the 'Gorkii fighter' conducted during October and November 1935, revealed that performance had not deteriorated even though the aircraft's weight had risen to 2,943lb (1,355kg). For the first time in a Soviet fighter, a ⅓in (8mm) thick armoured pilot's seat was installed on the I-16.

The Soviet government's policy was not to keep the aircraft secret – indeed the I-16 was displayed at the Milan International Air Show in October 1935, thereby allowing everyone an opportunity to learn about Soviet aviation and its developments.

When the new fighter entered operational service it was found to be more demanding than its predecessors, and it took some time for pilots to accept it. It should be pointed out that a many other fast Soviet fighters, such as the Tupolev I-14 and the Grigorovich IP-1, had aft centre of gravity positions. This was a common feature of Soviet fighter designs, as it was believed that such aircraft should have neutral stability.

Well known test pilot I Shelest remembered that 'the aircraft, although demanding during flight and sometimes unstable, was so smooth and beautiful, with a good response to the stick'. He wrote: 'What one likes is perfection. The eyes don't see poor visibility, no radio communication, a fretful aircraft always waiting for you to make a mistake, so that you to make a spectacle of the landing ...' The words of an experienced test pilot who made himself absolutely familiar with the aircraft. Many pilots were not as gifted as this.

Development continued. An interesting variant was the Type 4 with a fixed, faired undercarriage, tested by Pyotr Stefanovsky in 1935. The aim was to reduce the resistance of ski landing gear, but the idea was not developed, the I-16 later being fitted with retractable skis.

I-16 M-25 (Type 5)

The next series-production version of the I-16 was the Type 5. This was based on the second prototype, powered by a Wright Cyclone F-3, which was designated M-25 when manufactured by Soviet engine plants. Taking into account the results of the flight tests and service operations, elements of the structure were strengthened, a new landing gear operating mechanism was fitted and additional equipment, including a starter and an oxygen system, was installed. With all the changes incorporated the weight of the production aircraft rose from 3,350 to 3,505lb (1,520 to 1,590kg).

State trials of the I-16 Type 5 carried out by A Nikashin and E Preman in November 1936 revealed that the climb rate and the ceiling were worse than those of the second prototype. However, the speed had risen to 242 mph (390km/h) at sea level and 276mph (445km/h) at 1,900ft (3,000m). The Type 5 became one of the most prolific versions of the I-16, and gained its first combat experience in Spain in the autumn of 1936.

Nicknamed 'Mushka' (fly) by the Republicans and 'Rata' (rat) by the Nationalists, this snub-nosed fighter became the main opponent of the German Heinkel He51 and Italian Fiat CR-32 biplanes. Although it was slightly inferior to both in manoeuvrability, the I-16 proved superior in speed and climb. The I-16 was most successful in combats with biplanes, but could even cope successfully with the initial production Messerschmitt Bf109B.

To put an end to service pilots' doubts about the I-16's spin behaviour, five NII VVS test pilots conducted dedicated spin trials, successfully performing more than 3,000 aerobatic manoeuvres on the series-production aircraft.

UTI-2 and UTI-4

With the I-16 entering series-production and being delivered to the Soviet Air Force, the need for a trainer variant arose. This was even more important when the complicated handling of the aircraft was taken into account. Nikolay Polikarpov understood the situation, and two trainer variants of the fighter soon appeared. The first was UTI-2, an unarmed two-seat version of the I-16 Type 4 powered by the M-22, manufactured in 1935. Dual controls were provided, the pupil occupying the forward cockpit and instructor the rear one.

Owing to limited supplies of M-22 engines, the UTI-2 was not produced in large numbers. Fifty-seven were built during 1935-36, and about 100 in total. However, the UTI-4 development of the trainer, designated Type 15 by the Polikarpov Design Bureau, was mass produced. The overall dimensions, contours and structural design were basically the same for both the Type 5 and the Type 15. The UTI-4, like the UTI-2, lacked armament, starter and oxygen equipment. In the state trials approval document of 1937 it was recommended that, because the undercarriage retraction mechanism was not used so frequently during the training programme, a fixed undercarriage be fitted. This was incorporated in series-production aircraft only. The type was mass produced until the Second World War, 1,895 trainers of both versions being manufactured.

I-16 M-25V (Type 10)

A milestone in the I-16 fighter programme was the development, in 1937, of the Type 10, powered initially by the M-25A and later, for high altitude operations, the M-25V. The Type 10's structural design incorporated some changes. Armament was enhanced. Beside the two wing-mounted 7.62mm ShKAS machine guns, two synchronised guns of the same type were installed above the engine.

I-16 Type 5, differing in the shape of the engine cowling, while undergoing tests at NII VVS.

Two ShKAS machines guns can just be discerned at the top of the engine cowling on the I-16 Type 10.

Flaps were added to reduce landing speed and run, and a retractable ski undercarriage was introduced for the first time. Hitherto the ski gear had been fixed, significantly reducing the aircraft's speed. Valery Chkalov tested the ski landing gear retraction mechanism on an I-16 Type 4 in January 1936, with good results, but the gear was not introduced on production aircraft until the Type 10 appeared.

As a result of the changes and necessary strengthening of the airframe the weight exceeded 3,747lb (1,700kg), but the Type 10 had practically the same performance as the Type 5. It went into mass production, participating in the conflicts in Spain and China and at Khalkhin-Gol, where its main opponent was the Japanese Nakajima Ki-27 (Army Type 97). The Ki-27 was manoeuvrable and fast, and unlike the I-16 it was stable and could be flown by less experienced pilots, but the Soviet fighter had a stronger structure and was more heavily armed.

Polikarpov devoted serious attention to refining the Type 10's armament. Realising the great value of firepower, he not only doubled the number of machine guns but installed cannon as well. Although designer Dmitry Grigorovich had been the first to install cannon, fitting them to his IP-1, the I-16 was the first mass produced fighter to be so equipped.

I-16P (Type 12) and I-16 (Type 17)

The first 'gunship' version of the fighter was the Type 12 (sometimes referred to as the I-16P, pushhyechnyi being cannon), developed in 1936. Two 20mm ShVAK cannon were installed in the wing centre section, synchronised to fire through the propeller arc. This aircraft was some 220lb (100kg) heavier than the Type 5 on which it was based.

Only a limited number of Type 12s was built, but another 'gunship' version, the Type 17, was produced in greater numbers. This underwent trials in February 1939, had its wing-mounted cannon located beyond the propeller arc, but was otherwise structurally similar to the Type 10. The cannons, with their consequent increase in weight, affected climb rate and manoeuvrability and reduced maximum speed by 3.1 to 6.2mph (5 to 10km/h), but the firepower was tripled.

I-16 with RS-82s

Not only was 20th August 1939 a great day in the history of the I-16, it was also a significant date for Soviet aviation. On that day, near the Khalkhin-Gol river, five aircraft bearing red stars under the command of Captain Nikolay

Zvonarev used jet-propelled weapons (RS-82 unguided rockets) in combat for the first time, downing two Japanese Ki-27s. This and subsequent encounters revealed that, despite their wide dispersion and inaccuracy, the missiles were effective. After refinement the RS-82 was adopted by the VVS.

I-16 M-62 (Type 18)

By 1939, after five years under development, the I-16 had proved its worth in service and in combat operations. Many shortcomings had been rectified, its stability had been improved and pilots had become accustomed to the initially unfamiliar aircraft.

Polikarpov realised that, although the aircraft's performance had improved, it would be inadequate in the new decade. He knew that the I-16's potential was not exhausted, and saw two paths for development. These were a more powerful, high altitude engine, and improvement of the surface finish, which on series-production machines did not meet the higher standards required.

Another milestone was reached in October 1939, when the next version of the aircraft, the Type 18, successfully underwent trials. This was created by fitting a Type 10 airframe with the more powerful, high altitude Shvetsov M-62, which had a two-speed supercharger and drove an AV-1 variable pitch propeller (the VISh-6A propeller was also used on this type). The new engine delivered 800hp (596kW) at 13,800ft (4,200m), compared with the M-25V's 750hp (559kW) at 9,500ft (2,900m), but it was heavier.

A number of structural alterations were therefore incorporated, including a strengthened engine mounting and brackets. Additionally, the fuel tank was provided with protection.

Although the aircraft's weight increased to 4,034lb (1,830kg), performance was enhanced, speed rising to 255mph (411km/h) at sea level and 288mph (464km/h) at 14,500ft (4,400m). The fighter could climb to 16,400ft (5,000m) in only 5.2 minutes, using the M-62's 1,000hp (746kW) take-off power. While take-off performance was enhanced and take-off run reduced, the greater wing loading increased the landing speed to 80mph (130km/h), and up to 18 seconds were required to complete a full turn. The Type 18 went into series-production.

I-16 (Type 20) and I-16 (Type 27)

One aspect of performance that suffered from the installation of the more powerful

engine was operational range. With the maximum tankage of 418lb (190kg) of fuel the range at high speed was only 300 miles (484km), so the Type 20, with jettisonable fuel tanks, was developed. The M-62-powered 'gunship' version was designated Type 27, the armament being the same as in the Type 17.

I-16 M-63 (Type 24)

All of these versions increased I-16 series-production. The Gorkii production plant's annual output of I-16s in 1938 was only 718 aircraft (less than half the figure for the previous year), but it had grown to 1,147 in 1939, plus 424 trainers. Production Plant No.153 at Novosibirsk also increased its I-16 output.

The next version of the aircraft was the Type 24, powered by the M-63 rated at 900hp (671kW) at 14,800ft (4,500m), a development of the Shvetsov M-62. The prototype underwent development and state trials during August-September 1939, flown by pilot-engineer A Nikashin, and proved to have the best performance of the whole I-16 family of 'donkeys' (as they were affectionately nicknamed by Soviet pilots). Maximum speeds of 273 mph (440km/h) at sea level and 303mph (489km/h) at 15,750ft (4,800m) were recorded, and other excellent performance figures included a full-throttle climb to 16,400ft (5,000m) in 5.2 minutes and a service ceiling of 35,500ft (10,800m).

The Type 24 became the standard production I-16 variant of 1940, embodying a number of structural improvements. Plywood skinning of the upper wing surface was adopted, a radio and gun camera were installed, the tailskid was replaced by a wheel and two 154lb (70kg) fuel tanks were mounted on underwing pylons. But the most important change was the improvement in surface finish. The Type 24 entered mass production, though the innovations listed above were not incorporated in production aircraft apart from the installation of underwing fuel tanks.

I-16 M-63 (Type 29)

Strangely, the anticipated improvement in performance was not evident in production Type 24s, in spite of their uprated M-62s. The main reason lay in the wrong choice of propeller. Other shortcomings included over-cooling of the cylinder heads in a glide, exhaust pipe breakages and cracking of the engine cowling.

The improvements implemented on the standard of 1940 were incorporated only in

Top: **The first I-16 Type 17 at NII VVS with ski undercarriage.**

Centre, left: **Production I-16 Type 18 with M-62 engine.**

Centre, right: **The UTI-4 two-seat trainer was based upon the I-16 Type 5.**

Above, left: **To help overcome the shortage of operational I-16s, some UTI-4s had their rear cockpit faired over enabling them to act as fighters. Note the 'three-dimensional' red star.**

Above, right: **Captured UTI-4 pressed into service by the Finnish Air Force.**

the follow-on, final series-production version, the Type 29. But first it is necessary to describe the Type 28, which resembled the Type 27 but was powered by the M-63. Tests revealed a weapon firing weight of 6.6lb/sec (3.02kg/sec), which was heavy enough for a fighter of that period.

Although the I-16 Type 17 underwent its trials successfully and was manufactured in series from 1938, the 'gunship' was not widely used after the Khalkhin-Gol river conflict. Because the light Japanese fighters lacked armour and had unprotected tanks they were easily brought down, even by 7.62mm ShKAS machine guns, but the increase in the I-16's weight affected its manoeuvrability considerably. Only after the conflict in Finland was interest in the 'gunships' aroused.

The new version was not without its problems, but entered series-production. It was necessary to revise up to two-thirds of the drawings and alter a significant number of manufacturing tools. The transition from chromium-molybdenum to chromansil steel alloy was also difficult. Some 1,500 aircraft, including the Type 18, Type 24, Type 27 and Type 28 versions, had been built by the time Plant No.21 started production of the Type 29 in the second half of 1940. The aircraft's armament was changed. A 12.7mm UBS heavy machine gun was added to the two 7.62mm ShKAS machine guns mounted above the engine, the wing mounted guns were removed, and racks for six 82mm unguided rockets were installed under the wings. A radio mast was installed to provide communication.

103

Top and above: **Two views of the I-16 Type 24 prototype.**

Below: **I-16 Type 24s in winter camouflage.** *Philip Jarrett collection*

Above: **The I-16 Type 29 with underwing fuel tanks and six rocket projectiles. Note the angle of the radio mast.**

With it revised armament, avionics and external fuel tanks, the Type 29 was the heaviest of the family, weighing 4,662lb (2,115kg).

The increase in weight and the drag caused by the external load reduced the speed of the Type 29's to 266mph (429km/h) at 13,600ft (4,150m). Time to climb to 16,400ft (5,000m) increased to 7.25 minutes. With the guns removed and the tanks dropped the speed rose to 292mph (470km/h), approximately the same as that of the series-production Type 24. Before the outbreak of the Second World War 872 Type 29s were built.

In total, 9,450 I-16s of all types were built, a record for the time. In addition to the series-production aircraft already mentioned, some prototypes were developed. These included an attack aircraft with an armoured cockpit, armed with up to six machine guns and carrying a 220 to 440lb (100 to 200kg) bomb load; an I-16 powered by an M-25V with two TK-1 turbosuperchargers and driving an AV-1 variable pitch propeller; and the I-16PS 'gunship'.

By the end of 1941 up to 40% of all the fighter fleets of the five military districts located near the Soviet border were I-16-equipped. Unfortunately the fighter's most important battle, with Hitler's forces, came when its capacity for development was totally exhausted. Nikolay Polikarpov expected the I-180 to succeed the I-16, but this never happened.

Polikarpovs in action

During the first stages of the Second World War (known as the Great Patriotic War in the Soviet Union), the main combat burden fell on the I-16, which was considered to be the most widespread fighter from the Barents Sea to the Black Sea. Things were especially hard for I-16 pilots in the path of the main advances of German ground and air forces.

The fate of the Soviet 122nd Fighter Air Regiment was typical. The unit was closer to the border than others, and its pilots heard the sound of German aero engines at an early stage. An alert was sounded, and 53 pilots, led by the regiment's commander, managed to take-off and engage the enemy in combat. When Dornier Do17Z bombers attacked Karolin airfield their bombs fell mainly on unserviceable aircraft, and the Germans lost four bombers. Having assessed the situation objectively, the commander of the 11th Mixed Aircraft Division decided to move the aircraft to Lida airfield, in the depths of the country. Unfortunately Junkers Ju88 bombers found them there shortly after they had landed and destroyed almost all the aircraft, the regiment losing 69 I-16s. Many pilots perished, including the 11th Aircraft Division Commander, Colonel P Ganichev.

By the end of the month the main I-16 losses were occurring in air combat. The principal adversary was the Messerschmitt Bf109. Although the German fighter was at least 62mph (100km/h) faster, its pilots seemed to find it difficult to shoot down the manoeuvrable Soviet monoplane. A pilot on the staff unit of the 53rd Squadron pointed out that the most skilled Soviet pilots could determine exactly when an adversary was about to fire, and at that moment turn sharply to make a frontal attack. The effectiveness of the I-16 in skilful hands is illustrated by the fact that, on 4th June alone, pilots of the 163rd Fighter Air Regiment shot down 21 enemy aircraft in the west. General Georgy Zakharov, Commander of the 43rd Fighter Aircraft Division, to which the regiment belonged, stated that even the whole division did not always succeed in shooting down so many aircraft in the second half of the war.

Unfortunately not all pilots had the skill to use the I-16 to its best advantage. Moreover, it was an obsolete fighter, and many had short life engines. Even so, its potential was not fully exploited. The I-16s powered by M-62s and M-63s could outperform all the current Bf109 variants in horizontal manoeuvrability, and were not inferior to the widely-used Bf109E with regard to vertical manoeuvrability and rate of climb. However, the Soviet pilots did not use vertical manoeuvres in open formation. Initially the pilots flew in flight sections of three aircraft, and then turned to the swarm formation of up to 12 fighters defending each other in close rows. Luftwaffe pilots became accustomed to these tactics, and the Messerschmitts often dived on the I-16 formations, firing at them. German tactics and techniques and their greater combat experience meant that I-16s suffered much heavier losses than their opponents.

It also proved difficult to fight the German bombers. The I-16 was faster than the Heinkel He111, but could not always overtake the Ju88. Even if the Soviet pilots did manage get the bombers in their sights, the ShKAS machine guns with which most I-16s were armed were not very dangerous for the well protected German aircraft. The pilots spoke ironically about the 'humanity' of their weapons, and consequently a great many ramming attacks were made during the first months. The first of the Great Patriotic War pilots to be made Heroes of the Soviet Union were awarded the title for rammings during the defence of Leningrad.

Even less successful were the I-16s operated against enemy reconnaissance aircraft. Long range Ju88s easily escaped in the clouds or by gaining refuge at high altitudes, while short range Henschel Hs126s used their low speed and low altitude capabilities to advantage. In both cases the shortcomings of all

types of Soviet aircraft were compounded by the imperfections of the Vozdushnogo Nabludeniya, Opoveshcheniya, Sviazy (VNOS – Air Observation, Information and Communication Service) during this period of the war.

The I-16s were used not only as fighters, but also as attack aircraft and fighter-bombers. German documents record that on one occasion an I-16 attack resulted in a light artillery battery losing nearly half of its horses. I-16s also took part in air reconnaissance. Luftwaffe navigator-observer, Kapitan Reshke, noted that on his section of the front line, a month after the beginning of the war, a pair of I-16s flying at low altitude appeared daily. Later, examples were equipped with photographic equipment to improve their reconnaissance capabilities.

When 88th Fighter Air Regiment Commander Major A Markelov received information about a concentration of enemy aircraft in the region of Vinnitsa, Lt V Demenyuk made a reconnaissance flight in an I-16 and discovered about 70 German aircraft. He then immediately led an assault at the enemy which caught them completely by surprise, the anti-aircraft fire beginning only after the Soviet fighters had begun to turn back for base.

An unusual role for the I-16 was that of escorting transport aircraft, especially when the fighter's short operational range is taken into consideration. When the Germans managed to blockade Leningrad from the mainland side, a large number of Soviet transport aircraft were used to create an 'air bridge' into the besieged city. One of the units involved in this hard work was the 286th Fighter Air Regiment. Formed in June 1941, the 286th consisted mainly of young sergeants with only three months' flying experience before their first combat flights, whereas before the war pilots had undergone two to three years' preparation in service units following flying training. In spite of the difficulties the young I-16 pilots managed to repulse the Messerschmitts' attacks on the low speed transport aircraft. According to official statements, during the 14 months the 'air bridge' was in operation the 286th Fighter Air Regiment pilots, led by Major P Baranov, shot down 44 enemy aircraft, most of which were fighters.

In the south, I-16s co-operated with heavy bombers. A composite aircraft, called an 'aircraft unit' (a 'mother' craft carrying a fighter or fighters on special trapezes) was designed by Vladimir Vakhmistrov and went into combat. Each Tupolev TB-3 bomber served as as 'flying aircraft carrier', two I-16s, each carrying a pair of 551lb (250kg) bombs, being mounted under its wings. The first blow was delivered on the Romanian port of Konstantsa on 26th July 1941, under the leadership of Colonel V Kalmykov, the attackers taking off from Evpatoria airfield.

Combat operations in which the fighters were 'passengers' for a long time, being detached only 24 miles (40km) from the target, were rather unusual, and the assault upon the oil complex was unexpected. Three high explosive bombs hit the oil storage tank, one hit the oil refining plant and four hit the port. However, the I-16s encountered problems on their return flights. One aircraft crashed during a forced-landing, and the others also had insufficient fuel to return to base and had to land in Odessa to refuel. This experience was taken in account, and for the raids on the Chernavodsck railway bridge over the Danube on 10th and 13th August each I-16 was fitted with an additional 20 gallon (95 litre) fuel tank. In the last attack the bombs dropped by the fighters destroyed one of the bridge's trusses and broke the oil pipeline.

I-16 pilots and units who won glory in the first combats should be mentioned. The pilots of the 29th Red Banner Fighter Air Regiment participated in combat operations in Belorussia, flying the I-16 Type 24. During four hard months they shot down 67 enemy aircraft and performed many successful ground-attack missions, becoming the first Soviet Air Force unit to be awarded a Guard title.

Boris Safonov was not only famous in the Arctic. On 24th June 1941, as an unknown 1st Lieutenant in the 72nd Regiment, he shot down a He 111, the first enemy aircraft to be claimed in the north. Eventually his I-16, No.28213-9, had 109 missions to its credit and had destroyed 17 German aircraft. Its famous pilot then changed it for a British-built Hawker Hurricane.

The 69th Fighter Air Regiment, commanded by Major L Shestakov, played a notable part during the defence of Odessa. Their success was achieved from the development and application of new tactical methods, regiment engineering personnel being among the first to equip the I-16s with launchers for RS-82 rockets. This not only increased firepower, but permitted effective strikes against ground targets. Additionally, regiment's I-16s

also carried small calibre bombs. Their main opponents were Romanian air force units, and a special tactic was developed for combat with the Polish-built PZL-24 fighters flown by the Romanians, which had a tighter turning radius than the I-16s.

The regiment's combat record proves the success of these tactics; 94 powered aircraft and three gliders were shot down before the regiment was evacuated from Odessa. No fewer than 12 pilots were simultaneously recommended for the award of Hero of the Soviet Union, five of them posthumously. The regiment's commander was also commended, as he had shot down three aircraft personally and eight in shared claims.

At the beginning of 1942 the Soviet Air Force had a serious shortage of aircraft. The industry's evacuation to the East had caused a fall in production, and it could barely compensate for losses at the front. The VVS therefore had to take worn out aircraft, and even machines from civil aviation, training units and flying clubs, and send them to the front. Even I-5 fighters found an application, the pilots of 605th and 606th Fighter Air Regiment using them for night operations.

At the beginning of September 1941 the 2nd Attack Air Regiment was formed from the reserve of the Crimean Front Air Force. It was equipped with 32 I-5s. Until the end of January 1942 the regiment operated in the Crimea, and it was then sent to convert to the Ilyushin Il-2 attack aircraft, being redesignated 766th Attack Aircraft Regiment.

Nikolay Polikarpov's I-15*bis* and I-153 fighters were used widely. In the north at the beginning of spring 1942 the 27th Fighter Air Regiment was formed, commanded by Captain N Khryashkov. Experienced pilots joined the regiment, and combat activity took place even while the unit was forming (the beginning of March 1942). It was especially active at the time when roads became impassable and other regiments' aircraft could not take off, for the I-15*bis* required only a narrow strip cleared of snow.

The regiment provided anti-aircraft defence for naval installations in the north. The first of the regiment's pilots to gain a victory was 1st Lt I Volovodov, who shot down a Ju88 bomber near Yokanga at the beginning of April. In several days three more enemy aircraft were shot down.

Interesting attempts were made to increase the I-15's roles. In the summer of 1943 in the 5th Air Army a second cockpit was installed on the I-15 for it to be used for artillery observation. Still manoeuvrable, the two-seat Chaika could escape the attacks of enemy fighters.

But the most widely used aircraft in the middle of the war was the I-16. On 28th May 1942 all the combat-capable I-16s of the 4th Guard Fighter Air Regiment of the Baltic Navy successfully repelled enemy air attacks on the tactically important harbour of Karbona, on Lake Ladoga. More than 50 bombers, escorted by fighters, tried to attack the port from different directions and at different altitudes, but the Soviet fighters scrambled rapidly to repel the assault.

Below left: **A scene repeated on many airfields during the first days of the German advance, aircraft caught on the ground.**

Bottom right: **An I-16, equipped with four rocket rails, forced-down by the Finns.**

Photographs on the opposite page:

Top left: **Heated covers allowed I-16s to stay at readiness in the depths of winter.**

Top right: **The small dimensions of the I-16 helped when carriage to the workshops was required.**

Centre left: **Field repair under way to a battle damaged I-16.**

Centre right: **Working on an I-16 dispersed in the trees on to the edge of an airfield.**

Bottom: **Ground-running an I-16 prior to a mission over Odessa. The mechanic gives scale to this diminutive fighter.**

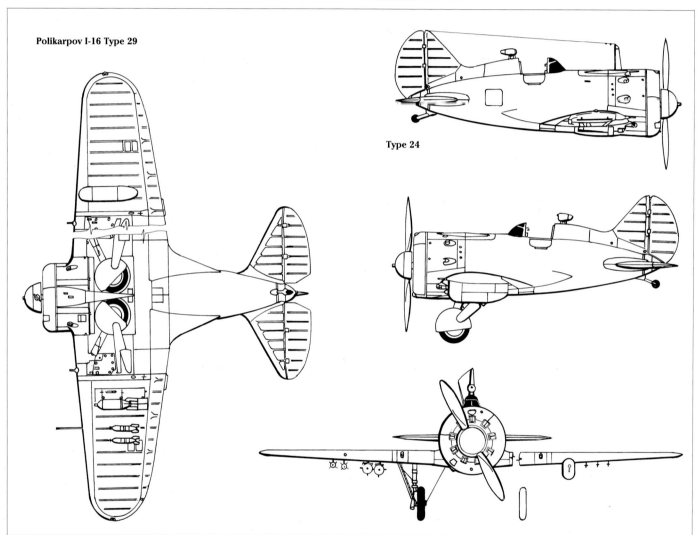

Polikarpov I-16 Type 29

Type 24

The I-16 group's commanders, Captains G Tsokolaev, V Golubov and M Vasiliev, all soon to become the Heroes of the Soviet Union, organised perfect control of the operation. By their bold interceptions the Soviet pilots disrupted the enemy's attacks and caused great losses.

A successful example of the interaction of different types of fighters in combat was demonstrated by Soviet pilots in June 1942, in the battle over the River Don. Lavochkin LaGG-3s of the 268th Fighter Aircraft Division, Hurricanes of the 235th Fighter Aircraft Division and I-16s of the 102nd Air Defence

Fighter Aircraft Division took off at different times to intercept the enemy. Having no large calibre machine guns and cannon, the I-16s protected the tails of the other aircrafts. As a result of the interaction of the different fighter types, without communication and with no understanding of the battle order, four enemy aircraft were shot down without loss to the Soviet fighters.

To repel night attacks on Leningrad the 26th Regiment, 7th Fighter Aircraft Corps, was reorganised into the Night Regiment. Command transferred the most experienced pilots from other regiments to the 26th Regiment,

Top left: **To reduce weight, UTI-4 trainers adopted fixed undercarriage.**

Top right: **I-16 Type 24 undergoing field repair.**

which was commanded by Lt Colonel V Romanov. By the summer of 1942 there were many I-16s in the regiment. First Lieutenant V Matskevitch flew the I-16 against the enemy with great success, soon being made a Hero of the Soviet Union, and the regiment was awarded a Guard title.

While the 26th Fighter Air Regiment used a single version of the I-16, in 1942 the 728th Fighter Air Regiment, led by Major Vasilyaka, operated several versions, Types 10, 18, 24 and 29, received from maintenance units and flying schools. Many of these aircraft were additionally equipped with cannon and rockets. Notable among the 728th Regiment's pilots was A Vorozheikin, who later gained 52 victories. Another of the regiment's pilots, N Ignatiev, gained 27 victories in the I-16 by March 1943. The unit then converted to the Yakovlev Yak-7B, being one of the last to do so.

At the end of its intensive combat life, the time came for the I-16 to fight the Focke-Wulf Fw 190. One such engagement took place on 23rd February 1943, when eight I-16s led by Major D Kudymov of the 3rd Independent Squadron of the Baltic Navy escorted Ilyushin Il-2s attacking enemy troops and artillery during the breaking of the Leningrad blockade. The Soviet units co-operated successfully, the Il-2s flying at extremely low altitude, excluding the possibility of enemy attacks from below. The manoeuvrable I-16s providing protecting from above. As a result the group accomplished the mission without losses, having shot down one Fw 190.

When the Soviet Air Force operation during the advance on the North Caucasian Front in March-April 1943 was analysed, the I-16's survivability in attack missions was twice as high as that of the armoured Il-2, and in air combats the losses per sortie were 1½ times less than those of modern Yak-1s, LaGG-3s and fighters obtained under the Anglo-American Lend-Lease armament and equipment supply agreement. The I-16's high manoeuvrability and survivability, and its pilots' great experience on the type, were the reasons behind the low loss rate.

Nevertheless, the Polikarpov fighters were gradually phased out of Soviet Air Force service. By 1st July 1943 only 42 Polikarpov fighters, a little more than 1% of all fighters in the Soviet fleet, remained operational. To this number must be added 143 I-16s operated by Air Defence units and 14 of the same type in Baltic Naval Aviation.

I-180

On the eve of the Second World War the I-16, which had been built in large quantities and had been operational with the Soviet Air Force since 1934, had reached the end of its development. The performance of the latest version, the Type 29, was considerably lower than that required of monoplane fighters of the pre-war period. However, convinced of the advantages of the monoplane configuration, Nikolay Polikarpov decided to continue

development of such aircraft. As early as March 1938, after the VVS had requested a proposal for development of the I-180 fighter, the Polikarpov Design Bureau began work on an 'E' variant, powered by the 950hp (708kW) air-cooled M-87A designed by A Nazarov.

In August the design was amended to take the more powerful 960hp (716kW) M-88, a double-row radial which was larger and heavier than the M-25V which powered I-16s at the time. This necessitated changes in the structure and configuration of the I-180(E) compared with the I-16. The longer fuselage was a wooden monocoque of circular cross-section, and the wing, which used the Clark 'YH' aerofoil section, had a swept-forward trailing edge and a straight leading edge to keep the centre of gravity in the same position. The tape with the fabric covering attached to it was riveted to the duralumin leading edge of the wing. The cockpit was raised 6in (155mm) to improve the pilot's view, and a new retractable undercarriage was designed. The armament included four 7.62mm ShKAS machine guns with a total of

2,320 rounds, two of the guns being mounted over the engine and two in the wing centre section. Multi-purpose beams were fitted beneath the wing to carry either four bombs with a total weight of 440lb (200kg) or two external fuel tanks.

The I-180 prototype had been completed by December 1938. It was powered by a prototype Turmanskii M-88 engine, assembled using M-87A series-production engine components. This still had to be tested, only a few ground runs having been made. The I-180 prototype had a fixed pitch propeller, owing to delayed delivery of the intended variable pitch unit. When it made its maiden flight, on 15th December, it still lacked armament and some equipment, and the undercarriage was locked down. The main shortcoming, however, was that its engine cooling system was not adjustable, for the gills in the front of the engine cowling had yet to be installed. After take-off, Valery Chkalov, the famous Soviet pilot who tested many Polikarpov aeroplanes as the design bureau's chief pilot, made several circuits of the airfield instead of the single

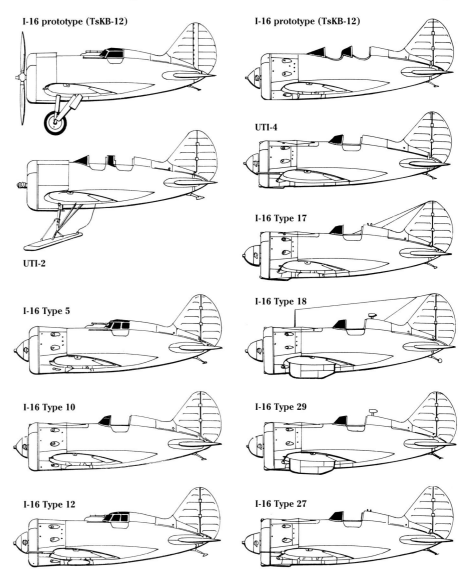

I-16 prototype (TsKB-12)

UTI-2

I-16 Type 5

I-16 Type 10

I-16 Type 12

I-16 prototype (TsKB-12)

UTI-4

I-16 Type 17

I-16 Type 18

I-16 Type 29

I-16 Type 27

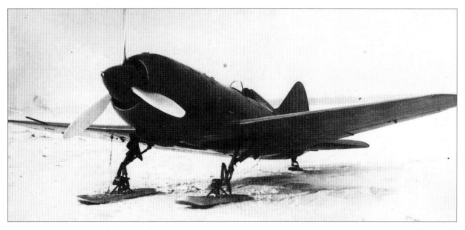

circuit required by the test programme. While the I-180 was making a low descending turn on finals the engine failed, and the fighter crashed into storage facilities on the airfield outskirts, killing Chkalov.

This was the period of widespread repressions by Stalin, and following Chkalov's death Nikolay Polikarpov's deputy, the famous Soviet designer Dmitry Tomashevich, was arrested along with some other leaders of the aircraft industry and wrongly accused of premeditated sabotage. Nikolay Polikarpov himself, who by pure chance had not given his personal permission for the I-180's maiden flight, was not arrested.

After reorganisation of the design bureau and its transfer to the new site of aircraft Plant No.1 in Moscow, Polikarpov resumed work on the I-180. On 19th April 1939 the second prototype, powered by an M 87A series production engine with a 9ft 6in (2.9m) diameter VISh-3E variable pitch propeller, made its maiden flight with new chief pilot E Ulyahin at the controls. The flight tests of this aircraft were successful, but owing to insufficient power its performance proved to be below expectations. Its maximum speed at a take-off weight of 5,224lb (2,370kg) was 253mph (408km/h) at sea level and 335mph (540 km/h) at 19,200ft (5,850m). Time to climb to 16,400ft (5,000m) was 6.25 minutes, and service ceiling was 33,600ft (10,250m).

On 1st May 1939 the I-180 took part in the mass flypast over Moscow's Red Square, but flight tests were then curtailed due to considerable wing skin deformations. In June, when the engine had logged ten hours, a new and updated 950hp (708kW) M-87B was installed, and more rigid outer wing panels were fitted. From 8th August onwards test flights were made by the famous Soviet test pilots Peotr Stefanovsky, Stepan Suprun and Tomas Suzi. The service ceiling was to be determined during the machine's 53rd flight, on 5th September, but at 29,500ft (9,000m) the spiral oil cooler was destroyed due to air pressure. Tomas Suzi, in the open cockpit, was burned and blinded by boiling oil, lost control, and the fighter entered a spin at 10,000ft (3,000m) and dived into the ground. Although the injured pilot managed to bale out, he was unable to deploy his parachute.

The loss of the second prototype and the death of another test pilot were hard blows to the Polikarpov Design Bureau. Nevertheless, a third prototype was built, taking account of the shortcomings of its predecessors. This

Top: **The second prototype I-180.**

Second from top to bottom: **The third prototype I-180 being tested on ski undercarriage.**

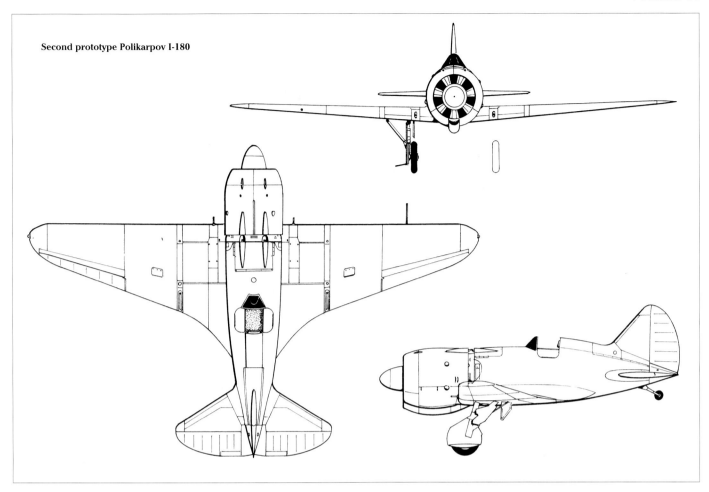

Second prototype Polikarpov I-180

machine had a more powerful M-88R engine rated at 1,000hp (746kW). Armament included two ShKAS machine guns provided with 1,000 rounds and two M Berezin 12.7mm UBS machine guns with 470 cartridges installed under the engine on a common mounting. The undercarriage was moved forward and the main legs lengthened to allow for the installation of a new VISh-23E variable pitch propeller of 9ft 9½in (3m) diameter. The oil cooler was replaced by a honeycomb type mounted in the duct under the engine.

Production flight tests of the third prototype (production code E-3) were conducted by E Ulyahin from 10th February to 18th May 1940. During this period the aircraft was temporarily fitted with a new tailplane of increased span, and an enclosed cockpit with a rearward-sliding canopy was installed.

In spite of its increased weight (5,343lb – 2,424kg), the performance of this version was higher than that of the second prototype. The maximum speed at sea level was 282mph (455km/h), and at 22,600ft (6,900m) it was 357mph (575km/h). It could climb to 16,400ft (5,000m) in 5.8 minutes and its the service ceiling was increased to 36,250ft (11,050m).

In June 1940 the I-180 third prototype was delivered to the NII for state trials, which were conducted by test pilot A Proshakov. After the enlarged tailplane exhibited signs of flutter it was replaced by the previous unit. During the

eleventh flight, on 5th July, Proshakov was forced to escape from the aircraft while performing a roll, as he could not recover it from an inverted position. It was noted in an accident report that the control system had failed while the machine was inverted.

In the repressive pre-war years, accidents to three prototypes and the death of two famous pilots would have put an end to the Polikarpov Design Bureau. Strangely, however, not only was the team able to continue its activities, but the I-180 was scheduled for large scale production at the aircraft manufacturing plant in Gorkii. Production of I-180 fighters under the constructor's designation Type 25, continuing the development of the I-16, had begun by the time the third prototype had completed the production flight tests. Delivery of ten series-production aircraft is recorded; six were delivered to the NII VVS for testing, and three others, which underwent most of the test flying, flew over Red Square during the parade on 1st May 1940.

A further accident occurred on 26th May, when the second production aircraft, with Stepan Suprun at the controls, made an emergency landing on Moscow's central airfield owing to a defective M-88P engine. During the landing run the port undercarriage leg was damaged, the wing dug into the ground and the fighter turned over.

At a meeting attended by Nikolay Polikar-

pov at the Gorkii plant on 30th July, a series of modifications for production aircraft were schemed. The aircraft were to have external fuel tanks with a capacity of 43.9 gallons (200 litres), single leg main undercarriage units, enclosed cockpits, RSI-4 radios with aerials, new M-88A engines and provision for underwing missiles. Suddenly, however, in late 1940, the People's Commissariat of the Aircraft Industry ordered the factory's administration to prepare for production of another aircraft, and the preparations for I-180 production were interrupted.

I-185

Continuing development of his I-16 and I-180 series of monoplane fighters powered by air-cooled engines, in 1939 Nikolay Polikarpov began to design a new aircraft, the I-185. He decided to give it greater wing loading to improve flying speed, and to install a new, more powerful engine to increase the power-to-weight ratio and the aircraft's rate of climb. The chosen powerplant was the 18-cylinder M-90, with a take-off rating of 2,000hp (1,492kW), designed by a bureau consecutively headed by A Nazarov, Sergey Tumanskii and E Urmin. For better engine cooling and aerodynamics an new cowling was designed,

Photographs on this page:

Top left: **Artist's impression of the I-185 with M-90 engine.**

Below: **I-185 powered by an M-71.**

Photographs on the opposite page:

Top left: **Rearward aspect of an I-185 M-71 showing the classic Polikarpov fuselage cross-section.**

Top right: **With the M-82A engine, the I-185 featured a revised nose.**

Centre: **The M-82 radial did not permit the gun to be mounted in the propeller shaft, instead, it was placed in a fairing along the forward fuselage ahead of the cockpit.**

Bottom: **Design of the I-185 was governed by the need for the highest speed attainable. The retractable tail wheel was not usual practice for the Soviet aircraft industry at the time.**

having a ducted spinner and a fan. Two versions of this cowling, with air intake inlet sections of different area, were tested in a wind tunnel, the cowling with the greater inlet section area being chosen.

On the whole the fighter looked like the third I-180 prototype, but it had slightly different overall dimensions and an enclosed cockpit. Armament comprised four synchronised machine guns, two 7.62mm ShKAS and two 12.7mm UBS, and in its overloaded version it could carry a 1,102lb (500kg) bomb load. It was estimated that the M-90-powered I-185 would have a maximum speed of 444mph (715km/h) at 24,000ft (7,300m) and a service ceiling of 33,600ft (10,250m).

By May 1940 the first prototype was ready for tests, but extensive engine bench runs and the initial taxying trials showed that the engine was not powerful enough. It was decided to install the new 1,200hp (895kW) M-81, an experimental copy of an American Curtiss produced by Arkady Shvetsov's Design Bureau. However, this low powered engine allowed only one brief take-off to be made, and

tests were delayed until the end of 1940 for the lack of a sufficiently powerful engine.

In late 1940 preliminary development of an I-185 powered by the Shvetsov M-82 14-cylinder radial engine began. Due to the M-82's high take-off power (1,700hp – 1,268kW) and small diameter (4ft 2in – 126cm), the fighter's drag was reduced. The armament was also changed. Instead of four machine guns it was proposed to install three synchronised 20mm ShVAK guns with 500 rounds. Polikarpov clearly realised that to gain air superiority it was necessary not only to increase speed and improve manoeuvrability, but to improve the armament as well. Development and construction of the fighter proceeded apace, and in May 1941 the production tests of the M-82A engined I-185 began.

In March 1941 the Polikarpov Design Bureau began to design another version of aircraft, powered by the 18-cylinder Shvetsov M-71 with a take-off power of 2,000hp (1,492 kW). The third prototype was soon built and, moreover, the first prototype was now fitted with an M-71 in place of the M-81. The M-71-

powered I-185 can be considered the most successful version of the type. It was of mixed construction, a semi-monocoque wooden fuselage coupled to an all-metal two-spar wing consisting of a centre section and two detachable outer panels. The cantilever tailplane and the elevators were made of duralumin, all of the control surfaces being fabric covered. The wooden fin was integral with the fuselage. The single leg undercarriage had air/oil shock absorption, and the castoring tailwheel could be locked before the take-off. Landing gear extension/retraction and flap operation was pneumatic.

The engine mounting comprised a frame of eight rods, the structure being integral with the gun mountings, and the engine was angled 1in (25mm) downwards relative to the aircraft's longitudinal axis. The I-185 M-82A's structure was similar to that of the M-71-powered version except for the cross-section of the forward fuselage, which was smaller owing to the smaller overall dimensions of the M-82A, and its cowling differed from that of the other variants for the same reason.

The production and state trials of the second and third prototypes were conducted following the beginning of the Second World War and the evacuation of the Polikarpov Design Bureau in 1942. While the I-185 M-71 underwent flight performance tests, the I-185 M-82A was used for the armament trials. Tests were conducted by P Loginov, a pilot of Plant No.51, and NII VVS pilots A Nikashin and Kuvshinov.

I-185 M-82A maximum sea level speed at weight 7,336lb (3,328kg) was 320mph (515 km/h) at normal rated power, and 341mph (549km/h) with boost. At 21,200ft (6,470m), the speed was 382mph (615km/h). With short

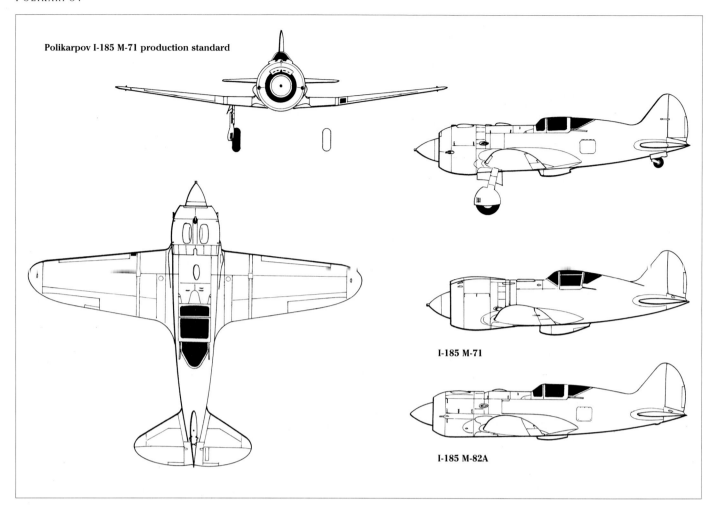

Polikarpov I-185 M-71 production standard

I-185 M-71

I-185 M-82A

term boost the aircraft could climb to 16,400ft (5,000m) in 5 minutes 48 seconds, and its sea level rate of climb was 72ft/sec (21.9m/sec). The service ceiling was 36,000ft (11,000m), and climbing ascent in a combat turn was equal to 3,200 to 3,900ft (1,000 to 1,200m).

The I-185 M-82A's flight tests promised well for the new air-cooled engines. At the the order of the People's Commissariat of the Aircraft Industry, Nikolay Polikarpov was obliged to pass the drawings of the powerplant installation and the mountings for the ShVAK synchronised guns to the design bureaux of Semyon Lavochkin, Artyom Mikoyan and Alexander Yakovlev. This accelerated development of the production La-5 fighter and the M-82-powered Yak-7 prototype in 1942.

The M-71-powered I-185 showed even better results. Its maximum sea level speed with short term boost was 345mph (556km/h), and at 20,250ft (6,170m) the speed was 391mph (630km/h). The service ceiling and turning time remained the same. The final test report issued by the NII VVS pointed out:

'The I-185 M-71 fighter armed with three ShVAK synchronised guns could be introduced into the inventory. The I-185 M-82 fighter was bettered only by the I-185 M-71 fighter, surpassing all other production aircraft, both indigenous and foreign. The piloting technique of I-185 M-82 was analogous to that of

the I-185 M-71, ie it was simple and within the capabilities of pilots of low proficiency'.

The same report had a table comparing the performance of the I-185 M-71 with the Soviet Yak-7B, LaGG-3 and MiG-3, the American Bell Airacobra, Britain's Spitfire, and Germany's Messerschmitt Bf109F and Heinkel He100, all of which had been tested at the NII VVS. The Polikarpov fighter outperformed them all, conceding a little to the He100 in speed and climb rate, but owing to its weak armament this aircraft did not enter service and was not used in the war. The Bf109F, which took part in combat operations on the Eastern Front, was 29mph (47km/h) slower than the I-185 at sea level and 12.4mph (20km/h) slower at 19,700ft (6,000m). The I-185 M-71's climb rate was also better; it reached 16,400ft (5,000m) in 5.2 minutes, while the Bf109F took 6.3 minutes to attain the same altitude.

In November 1942 all three prototypes underwent service tests with the 728th Fighter Air Regiment, where they were highly regarded by pilots. Commander Captain Vasilyaka noted: 'The I-185 outclasses both Soviet and foreign aircraft in level speed. It performs aerobatic manoeuvres easily, rapidly and vigorously. The I-185 is the best up-to-date fighter from the point of view of control simplicity, speed, manoeuvrability (especially in climb), armament and survivability.'

Even before the beginning of the operational tests, in the spring of 1942 it was decided to place the I-185 M-71 in production. A so-called standard prototype was built in April, underwent production flight tests during June-October, piloted by P Loginov, and went for state trials at the NII VVS on 18th November. This machine differed from the other prototypes in having the engine cowling external and internal aerodynamics improved, resulting in a considerable reduction in drag.

Although the fighter's weight increased by 317lb (144kg), totalling 8,000lb (3,629kg), with a take-off weight of 7,682lb (3,485kg) the state tests showed high performance. Maximum sea level speed with short term boost was 372mph (600km/h), and at 20,000ft (6,100m) was 403mph (650km/h). Climbing ascent in a combat turn was 4,900ft (1,500m), the time of turn and service ceiling being unchanged. Sufficient fuel was carried for a range of 497 miles (800km).

Test pilot Pyotr Stefanovsky gave the following assessment: 'In spite of its high wing loading, the fighter was capable of high speed and climb rate, was manoeuvrable, and was easy to fly owing to the successful combination of configuration, overall dimensions and high lift devices. Its heavy firepower allowed it to shoot down the enemy aircraft in one or two attacks'. Major-General P Losyukov, the head of the NII VVS, put it more precisely: 'The I-185 M-71 is the best up-to-date fighter. It surpasses in maximum speed, climb rate and vertical manoeuvrability both the Soviet and the latest foreign production fighters (Bf 109 and Fw 190). This fighter must be introduced into the inventory'.

From 17th December 1942 until 26th January 1943 testing was interrupted by the need to replace the engine, owing to frequent failures. Then the new engine failed after less than 24 hours of running. On 27th January the fighter crashed when its engine failed in flight. Low engine reliability was a serious obstacle to series-production of the I-185. State discussions of the I-185 project on 16th February, paid particular attention to estimated range. It was decided that additional tests should be conducted to determine the aircraft's range, in spite of the fact that its fuel capacity (1,058lb – 480kg) was greater than that of other fighters. However, on 5th April, before these tests could begin, the first prototype suffered an in-flight engine failure, and the well known test pilot V Stepanchyonok died when the aircraft crashed during an attempted deadstick landing.

In defence of his design Nikolay Polikarpov wrote a report to the Central Committee, pointing out that a number of practically idle construction plants were ready to build the aircraft, and that delivery of I-185s to the front could mark a turning point in the air war in 1943. However, it was not to happen. It was later decided to stop production of the I-185 because of its unreliable engine and the lack of production capacity. Large quantities of the M-82 engine were required to ensure production of Lavochkin La-5 fighters at the Gorkii aircraft construction plant.

It should be noted that, technologically, the I-185 was very sound. Its structure was well designed, and components could be produced at different plants for subsequent assembly at the production plant, this capability being of great importance in wartime because it enabled a significant increase in production. Another advantageous feature of the I-185 was that it could be easily modified.

In February 1943, before the project was abandoned, preliminary designs for two updated versions had been prepared. The first, designated I-187, was to have the new and more powerful 2,200hp (1,641kW) M-71F. The second, the I-188, had the M-90 engine, which had a smaller mid-section and was lighter than the M-71 and was tested in August 1942. The estimated level speed of the I-187

M-71F at 20,500ft (6,250m) was 441mph (710 km/h), its climb rate at sea level was put at 70ft/sec (21.5m/sec), and the time to climb to 16,400ft (5,000m) was 4.2 minutes. The estimated performance of the I-188 M-90 is not recorded, but apparently it was also very high. Surviving documents and drawings show that the aerodynamic configuration of these projected aircraft was exceptional.

The I-187's engine cowling featured backward-sloping intake gills between the propeller spinner and the front cowling ring, which had been moved back, thus streamlining the nose contours. The gills' movement was synchronised with that of the exit gills, thus optimizing the airflow through the cowling and the engine cooling. The ejector exhaust stubs further increased speed, and a rearward-sliding teardrop canopy reduced drag. Armament of these prototypes comprised four 20mm ShVAK guns; two in the fuselage, synchronised to fire through the propeller arc and provided with 200 rounds, and two in the wings with 120 rounds. Eight RS-82 rockets could be carried underwing.

These were the last of a series of projects for monoplane fighters with air-cooled engines from the gifted Soviet aircraft designer Nikolay Polikarpov, who died in July 1944.

ITP (M)

In late 1940, while work was proceeding on the I-185, the design section led by Nikolay Polikarpov started development of a fighter equipped with either the Klimov M-107 or the Mikulin AM-37 water-cooled engines, intended not only for dogfighting but also for bomber escort and ground attack. There were two armament configurations. The first

consisted of a single 37mm cannon firing through the propeller hub and provided with 50 rounds, plus two synchronised 20mm ShVAK cannon with 200 rounds each. The second had a 20mm cannon instead of the engine-mounted gun, with 200 rounds. There was to be provision for the carriage of bombs or rockets under the wings.

The first prototype of the ITP (Istrebitel Tyazhely Pushechny – fighter, heavy gun) was completed in October, 1941. Designated M-1, it had a 1,300hp (969kW) M-107P engine and was a single-seat, low-wing monoplane with a birch veneer wooden monocoque fuselage and metal wings. Detachable metal cowling panels ensured easy access to the engine. The oil cooler was installed in the nose, under the engine. A special hatch on the port side behind the cockpit allowed access to the radio bay. A rearward-sliding cockpit canopy followed the fuselage contours. Because it lacked a flat front panel, the curved one-piece windshield gave the pilot a rather distorted view. The fin was integral with the fuselage structure.

The wing, which consisted of a centre section and two outer panels, was provided with flaps, and automatic slats were fitted in the leading edges. Honeycomb radiators were installed in the centre section, with intakes in the leading edge, and the controllable outlet valves were in the upper surface, close to the aft spar. The landing gear, including the tailwheel, was retractable.

Following the evacuation of the design bureau to Novosibirsk, the M-1 made its maiden flight there on 23rd February 1942. The test programme was not completed, however, owing of frequent engine failures. In late 1942 the prototype returned to Moscow, where an M-107A engine was fitted and the 37mm cannon was replaced by the 20mm installation.

Three synchronised 20mm guns, one visible in this view of the engine bay of a '1942 Standard' I-185 made the type potentially the best 'bomber killer'.

Performance estimates set maximum speed at 382mph (615km/h) at 20,300ft (6,200m) and the ejector exhausts could increase this to 400mph (645km/h). Service ceiling was 34,000ft (10,400m), and the time to climb to 16,400ft (5,000m) 5.4 minutes.

Unfortunately the prototype's performance was not determined because the State Commissariat for the Aviation Industry ordered that it be used for static tests. The aircraft passed the 100% load structural testing successfully, but it was then impossible to fly it, so it was used as a wind generator at the engine testing establishment.

The second prototype ITP, designated M-2, was designed especially for the AM-37. Built at Novosibirsk in 1942, it was armed with three synchronised ShVAK guns. The AM-37

proved very unreliable and frequently failed, so when the aircraft was returned to Moscow in December 1942 an AM-39 of 1,600hp (1,193 kW) was installed.

At the same time the undercarriage structure was modified. Additionally, new wheels were fitted. The M-2 undertook its maiden flight on 23rd November 1943. The flight test programme was not carried out until as late as June 1944.

With maximum short term boost, top speed was 403mph (650km/h) at 8,200ft (2,500m), while the maximum speed at sea level was about 372mph (600km/h). The service ceiling was 37,700ft (11,500m). Although the rate of climb was not excellent, the time to climb to 16,400ft (5,000m) being six minutes, the M-2 was considered one of the best

Soviet aircraft of its type. Nevertheless, full scale production was unjustified because several aircraft with almost the same performance were already in production.

For technical data, see Tables C and D, pages 175 and 176.

Photographs on the opposite page:

Two views of the ITP (M-1) heavy gun fighter.

Photographs on this page:

Top and centre: **The ITP (M-2). Both machines bear a strong resemblance to the MiG-3.**

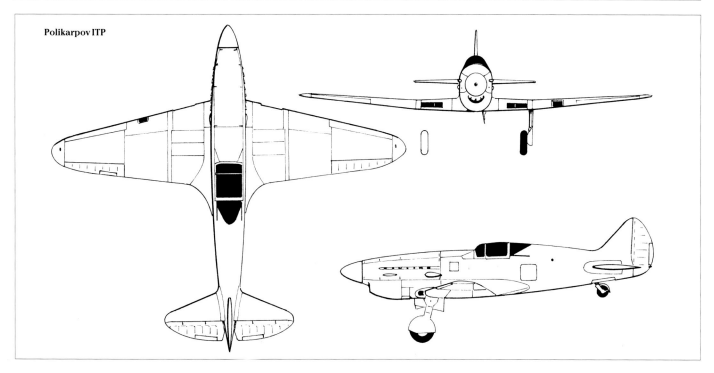

Polikarpov ITP

Silvansky

I-220

Having graduated from the institute and worked for several years at different plants, little-known Russian aircraft engineer Alexander Silvansky asked to tender to a proposal for a single-seat fighter powered by the Turmanskii M-88 engine. His design bureau was established in 1938 at one of the aircraft manufacturing plants in Siberia.

The configuration of the fighter, designated I-220 was similar to that of Nikolay Polikarpov's I-16, differing in having a longer fuselage and a shorter, single strut undercarriage. This I-220 is also referred to as the IS, for

Istrebitel Silvansky. Mikoyan-Gurevich also developed an I-220, which see.) The I-220's structure was also similar to that of I-16. By the autumn of 1939 it was complete, but owing to a delay in delivery of the intended engine, an M-87A rated at 950hp (708kW), was installed in the prototype. As a result of a design error the propeller tips had insufficient clearance, and almost touched the ground during engine runs. Silvansky proposed shortening each blade by 3.9in (10cm).

Production flight tests of the I-220 were not carried out. During ground tests from 24th September to 6th October 1939, only six taxying trials and three ground runs were per-

formed. In February 1940 the fighter was transported to the LII for testing, where it was found that the propeller thrust was considerably reduced owing to the shortened blades, and the aircraft could hardly take off and climb. The pilots and TsAGI test pilot S Korzinschikov noted that it was impossible to fly the I-220, and the development of such an unsuccessful aircraft was considered pointless.

Two views of the mock-up of the Silvansky I-220, shoe-horned into his Siberian design bureau's building.

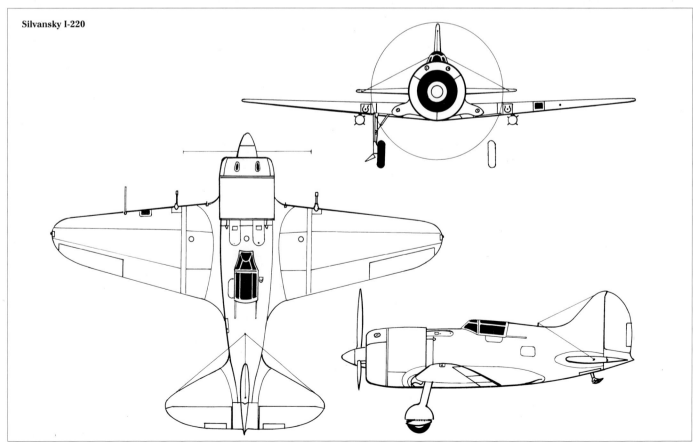

Silvansky I-220

Sukhoi

In 1939, after several meetings of representatives of the State Commissariat for the Aviation Industry, the Soviet Air Force, the aircraft industry and groups of designers, a programme was adopted for the development of the aircraft industry with regard to the designing of new fighters capable of meeting the most demanding requirements.

In July-August of that year a request for proposals for the design of a high speed, high altitude fighter was issued to several groups of designers. In addition, it was also decided to develop at the same time a manoeuvrable low and medium altitude fighter, because it was impossible to design one high performance aircraft for both high and low altitudes. The group led by Pavel Sukhoi and Artyom Mikoyan began to develop the high altitude fighter.

The Sukhoi Opytno Konstruktorskoye Byuro (OKB – experimental design bureau) began designing the new fighter in Kharkov, where the BB-1 (Blizhnii Bombardirovshchik – short range bomber, later Su-2) had already been put into production. The work was conducted under difficult conditions, because the small staff of the bureau was involved not only in BB-1 design but in series-production at the plant as well, and there were insufficient designers for the task.

Two views of the Su-1 prototype high altitude fighter. The type went no further than manufacturer's test flights.

Su-1 (I-330, I-135)

In designing the Su-1 fighter (manufacturer's designation I-330 or I-135. I - istrebitel, fighter, or literally 'destroyer'), attention was concentrated on improving aerodynamic performance and saving weight. For this reason the lighter and more compact Klimov M-105P engine was chosen in preference to the Mikulin AM-35 used in the MiG-1. The altitude capability of this engine was slightly lower, so two TK-2 exhaust-driven turbosuperchargers had to be installed to increase the M-105P's altitude capability and speed at altitude. It was believed that a lighter and aerodynamically improved aircraft would have better manoeuvrability in combat at all altitudes.

As a result of complex experimental work, a new aerodynamic configuration was born; the water radiator intake was placed under the cockpit, but the radiator itself was located inside the fuselage behind the cockpit, thereby reducing drag.

In March-April 1940 the Sukhoi OKB was given experimental Plant No.289 in Podlipki (the former plant of Vladimir Chizhevsky, Vladimir Vakhmistrov, Alexey Shcherbakov, etc), with small production factories and poor

staff. The new bureau was based on Pavel Sukhoi's designers and engineers from the Tsentral'nyi Aerogidrodynamichesky Institut (TsAGI – Central Aerodynamic and Hydrodynamic Institute) Factory for Experimental Construction (ZOK), and the factory workers were chosen from demobilised sailors of the Baltic Fleet. Under these conditions the Su-1 was prepared for its flight tests.

Following its maiden flight in August 1940, the Su-1 was transferred to TsAGI department No.8, where it underwent flight tests without its TK turbosuperchargers. Pavel Sukhoi did not want finally to dismiss TK: 'It is impossible to betray the trust of our state. We received an order to design a high altitude aircraft, and we must exactly fulfil this task'. During one flight pilot A Chernavsky made a belly-landing, and when the aircraft was repaired the state trials were continued by A Popelnyushenko.

The Su-1 was of mixed structure. Its fuselage comprised the set of wooden frames, spars and stringers. The veneer skin was covered by fabric, then impregnated and painted. The nose of the fuselage consisted of detachable metal engine cowling panels held in place by Dzus-type locks. The all-metal wing had a single spar structure with an additional rear vertical member, and the ailerons, elevators and rudder were fabric-covered

metal structures. The undercarriage was similar to that already tested on the Sukhoi ShB attack aircraft; the main legs retracted rearwards and turned through 90° to lie flat in the wing. A 20mm ShVAK gun was mounted in front of the cockpit, and a pair of 7.62mm synchronised ShKAS machine guns were installed over the engine.

At a take-off weight of 6,338lb (2,875kg) and an empty weight of 5,500lb (2,495kg) the fighter reached a maximum speed of 398mph (641km/h) at 32,800ft (10,000m) and more than 310mph (500km/h) at sea level, while its landing speed was 68mph (111km/h). The pilots who conducted the state tests spoke of the aircraft with admiration after each flight, and thought that the Su-1 should be delivered to front line units as quickly as possible, but frequent failures of the turbosuperchargers dashed the plans of designers and test pilots. The bulk of the tests were conducted without turbosuperchargers, and the results showed that the aircraft had a service ceiling of 41,000ft (12,500m) and an operational range of 447 miles (720km).

Su-3 (I-360)

In the autumn of 1941 the Sukhoi Design Bureau was evacuated to Molotov (now Perm), and during the evacuation the Su-1 was damaged and was not repaired. Instead, attention was concentrated on the Su-3 (I-360), which differed in having reduced span, a wing area of 182.9ft² (17.0m²) and advanced aerofoil sections. During flight tests at a gross take-off weight of 6,305lb (2,860kg) and an empty weight of 5,467lb (2,480kg) the Su-3 displayed a maximum speed at altitude of 396mph (638 km/h), a service ceiling of 39,000ft (11,900m) and a maximum range of 434 miles (700km). Unfortunately, the Su-3 was not put into full scale production owing to a lack of reliable turbosuperchargers.

Su-7

In 1942 Pavel Sukhoi developed a high altitude fighter around the new Shvetsov M-71F high altitude air-cooled engine with two TK-3 exhaust-driven centrifugal turbosuperchargers with controllable rpm. The supercharging gave an increase in engine altitude capability. According to calculations the aircraft would have a speed of up to 323mph (520km/h) at sea level and up to 394mph (635km/h) at altitude, a service ceiling of 41,000ft (12,500m), a range of 770 miles (1,240km) and a gross take-off weight of 9,567lb (4,340kg).

The structure of the Su-7, as it was designated, did not differ fundamentally from that of the Su-6, because it was designed using the structure of the Su-6(A) single-seat attack aircraft prototype as a basis. The armour protecting the powerplant and its accessories was omitted, as was the bomb compartment. The wooden fuselage comprised frames, spars and stringers covered by a stressed plywood skin. The low set wing was fitted with slats. While the wing centre section was all-metal, the outer wing panels were wooden structures built up on metal spars. It had a conventional tail unit with a wooden fin, and all of the control surfaces had metal frames with fabric covering. Trim tabs were fitted to the port aileron and elevator. The main landing gear legs retracted into the wing centre section, the wheels turning through 90° to lie flush in the wings. Armament included two wing-mounted 20mm ShVAK guns.

Although the new fighter was successfully undertaking production flight tests, in 1943 the engine's life was over. The ASh-71F (previously M-71F) engine was not put in full scale production, and it was replaced by a production ASh-82FH, rated at 1,800hp (1,342kW), which had several additional systems including an alcohol/water cylinder-head cooling system and a special pump drive designed by Valentin Glushko. But this engine was not sufficiently powerful for the heavy Su-7, which could manage only 305 mph (491km/h) at 7,500ft (2,300m) and 314 mph (506km/h) at 20,600ft (6,300m) under test.

In order to augment the fighter's speed when necessary, the designers decided to equip it with one of Valentin Glushko's liquid-propellant auxiliary rocket motors, including the RD-1, RD-1KhZ, RD-2 and RD-3 with nitric acid and kerosene pump supply.

The unit considered most suitable for the Su-7 was the RD-1, delivering 661lb (300kg) of thrust. In addition, metal plate on the wooden section of fuselage was lengthened to protect the structure from flames emitted by the turbosupercharger. During the flight tests, which began in late 1944, 84 RD-1 engine starts were performed on the ground and in flight. From 31st January to 15th February 1945 18 engine test starts were made on the ground using an ether/air starting system, and from 28th August to 19th December that year the investigations were continued using the RD-1KhZ rocket motor.

Frequent failures of the RD-1 prolonged the tests, but finally, in late 1945, flights conducted by test pilot Komarov showed that when the rocket was started at 20,600ft (6,300m) it increased maximum speed by 56mph (91km/h). However, the RD-1 was underdeveloped and often failed, and after five changes of the liquid-propellant booster the designers decided to abandon it altogether. Nevertheless, the development and testing of mixed-powerplant prototypes was an important stage in the development of high speed jet aircraft.

For technical data, see Table E, page 177.

The Su-3 was effectively a second, developed, prototype of the Su-1. It also did not progress far.

Tomashevich

'110'

At the end of the 1930s an unusual organisation was established in Moscow. At first called the Special Technical Department, but later known as TsKB-29 (Tsentral'nyi Konstruktorskoye Byuro – central, ie state, design bureau), it consisted of the aviation specialists who had been subjected to repressive actions by the NKVD agencies. (NKVD – State Commissariat for Internal Affairs, later to be named the equally infamous KGB.) TsKB-29 was located in the large building of the former Department of Experimental Aeroplane Construction (KOSOS) of Tsentral'nyi Aerogidrodynamichesky Institut (TsAGI – Central Aerodynamic and Hydrodynamic Institute).

Here, Andrei Tupolev, Vladimir Petlyakov, Dmitry Tomashevich and other well known designers worked there in confinement. Each led a group tasked with designing a new aircraft type. Petlyakov was involved in the design of a high altitude fighter which had received the coded identity '100', a tactical bomber designated '103' was designed under Tupolev's leadership, and the group led by Dmitry Tomashevich designed a fighter identified as '110'. (Not I-110, as in a formal fighter – Istrebitel – designation.)

The '110' prototype made its maiden flight at the end of 1942. It differed from production aircraft of that time in its engine and in the high technological effectiveness of its structure. Although Vladimir Klimov's new 1,400hp (1,044kW) VK-107 water-cooled engine was considered to be advanced, it was underdeveloped and required an improved cooling system. Mainly because of this, attempts to use the engine on production aircraft had not produced the expected results. During early design stages Tomashevich's group took the new engine's peculiarities into account, providing it with effective water and oil radiators of greater area, mounted below the engine, and thereby created the most favourable engine operating conditions.

The fighter's structure used the minimum amount of metal, which was not regarded as a conventional structural material at the time. The forward fuselage, including the engine compartment and cockpit, comprised a welded steel tube frame, while the rear fuselage was made of multi-ply beech veneer. The wing, aileron and empennage frames were of duralumin, and the wing centre section was flat. The main wheels retracted into the wells between the two wings spars, and the tailwheel retracted into the rear fuselage.

The armament of the '110' met front line requirements. A 20mm cannon was mounted between the engine cylinders, and two UBS

While the Tomashevich '110' went no further than prototype stage, it helped considerably in the development of the Klimov VK-107 engine.

large calibre machine guns and two ShKAS machine guns were installed above the engine, making the total weight of firepower almost 7.7lb/sec (3.5kg/sec). Cartridge cases were ejected through openings in the fuselage sides. Besides its gun armament, the fighter could carry 1,102lb (500kg) of bombs externally.

To ease production the designers tried to simplify assembly by making wide use of dimensions divisible by ⅖in (10mm). This enabled parts and units to be connected without adjustment. The powerplant, complete with radiators, could be mounted in the fuselage framework as a unit, using only four bolts. This attempt to simplify the structure, combined with the heavy water-cooling system, made the aircraft overweight. Empty, the fighter weighed 7,242lb (3,285kg), and its take-off weight was 8,774lb (3,980kg).

During tests conducted by pilot Peotr Stefanovsky and engineer V Bolotnikov, the '110' displayed sufficiently high performance. At sea level the '110' attained 315mph (508 km/h) and exceeded 379mph (610km/h) at 20,300ft (6,200m); service ceiling was 32,800ft (10,000m) and operational range was 652 miles (1,050km). However, its rate of climb was poor owing to its weight, it took seven minutes to reach 16,400ft (5,000m).

The '110' was not put into production because, even after the elimination of defects noted by the test pilots, it could not outperform the aircraft already in production. However, the work of Tomashevich's design group had some value. By choosing the advanced VK-107 engine, which was thoroughly tested in parallel with his fighter, he gave it the start it needed. Later the VK-107 was developed with the benefit of the experience gained from its use in the '110' and used in production fighters, giving them speeds in excess of 434mph (700km/h).

See overleaf for a three-view illustration.

For technical data, see Table E, page 177.

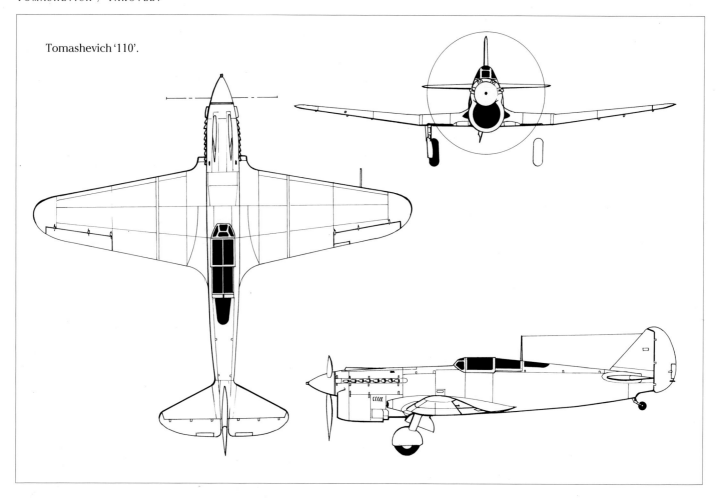

Tomashevich '110'.

Yakovlev

Alexander Yakovlev's design bureau was one of those which introduced aircraft into series-production in 1940. Yakovlev was a gifted designer and a skilled industrial policy-maker who often enjoyed Stalin's favour, to the benefit of his products. In 1974, long after the events described here, Yakovlev wrote a brilliant and very lively, but prejudiced, autobiography entitled *Life Target*. This book went to five editions in Russia, and until recently was officially considered to set the standard as an industrial history. However, the present authors will try to provide a more independent and probably more critical view of this period of Soviet aviation history.

By 1939 the Yakovlev Opytno Konstruktorskoye Byuro (OKB – experimental design bureau) had gained considerable experience having been given six years earlier an aircraft factory in Moscow where the AIR-9, -10, -12, -15, -16, -18, -14 and -20 family of monoplane trainers was built. The last two types were built in large quantities under the designations UT-1 and UT-2. The AIR-17, another Yakovlev design, was scheduled for production as the UT-3.

Yak-1 (I-26)

Yakovlev soon jumped on the fighter bandwagon, submitting no fewer than four designs for the Soviet Air Force competition while other design bureaux entered only one. His proposals were the I-26 low and mid altitude tactical fighter, the I-27 (UTI-26) fighter-trainer, the I-28 high altitude air defence fighter, and the I-30 (I-26U) fighter. Unlike the other design bureaux, Yakovlev did not submit preliminary design documentation or mock-ups for the competition, but relied instead on his influential connections.

Compared with the other Yakovlev proposals, the I-26 (I - istrebitel, fighter, or literally 'destroyer') was more advanced. Development was initiated in May 1939, and eight months later the first aircraft was already complete. The manufacturing facilities used were quite modest, and the total workforce was only 45 engineers and 152 workers.

The I-26 was the forerunner of the whole family of Yak piston-engined fighters. It was single-seat monoplane of mixed construction, the forward fuselage being a steel truss

primary airframe structure with a duralumin skin. The rear fuselage being a fabric covered wooden structure. The wooden wing used the Clark 'YH' aerofoil, and the empennage, ailerons and flaps were made of duralumin.

The first prototype had to be powered by the Klimov M-106, and had to have a maximum speed at altitude of 620km/h (462kW). A landing speed of 74mph (120km/h) was required, and the aircraft had to be highly manoeuvrable and have a good climb rate and ceiling. The second prototype was to have a supercharged M-105 engine, and it was expected that this would enhance the fighter's altitude capability.

Designed by Vladimir Klimov, the M-105 was still in the prototype stage when the I-26 was rolled out. The engine had several special features; the M-105P had a hollow driveshaft to permit the internal installation of a ShVAK 20mm gun, negating the need for synchronisation, and two pairs of 7.62mm machine guns were mounted below and above the engine.

Built in a hurry, the I-26 had a gross take-off weight of 5,731lb (2,600kg), instead of the

5,070lb (2,300kg) predicted. First flights were made with the fuel tanks half full, and no ammunition was carried. Yakovlev promised Stalin that the aircraft would be rolled out by the beginning of 1940. The maiden flight of the ski-equipped aircraft was made on 13th January 1940, with Yakovlev chief test pilot Yulian Piontkovsky at the controls.

Alexander Yakovlev recalled the event as follows: 'The rotating propeller transforming into a silver disc and snow being blown back behind the aircraft indicated that the pilot had opened the throttle. The aircraft began its run. Finally it roared off and swept above our heads, making a steep climb'. The first flight was generally successful, but the pilot noticed a rise in oil temperature immediately after take-off and elected to make an early landing.

First phase of the test programme showed that the handling qualities and stick forces were acceptable. The maximum speed of 360mph (580km/h) at 16,400ft (5,000m) was close to the estimated figure, and the time to climb to that altitude was 5.2 minutes.

On the other hand, the new fighter exhibited a number of problems regarding both design and manufacture. The oil overheating noted in the first flight remained incurable, although the system was redesigned numerous times. The engine was changed five times, the propeller changed even more often, and the VISh-52 was replaced by a VISh-61P propeller. Some structural components proved to have insufficient strength; the landing gear jammed during retraction and the landing gear locks did not work properly. These flaws obviously contributed to the fatal accident on 27th April 1940, when the aircraft rolled over while flying at low altitude, entered a spin and hit the ground. Piontkovsky was killed, later being replaced by S Korzinschikov. The accident investigation board concluded that uncontrolled retraction of the landing gear had caused the accident.

At the time of the I-26's crash, the second prototype, which had an improved structure (including thicker skinning), had already been rolled out. In an attempt to improve engine cooling, the designers moved the oil radiator from its original aerodynamically efficient position between engine cylinders, positioning it underneath the engine.

During the development stage the Soviet government decreed that the most powerful water-cooled engine available, the M-107, was to be installed in the new aircraft. This requirement could not be met because even the M-107's predecessor had was not yet ready to power an aircraft. It was not until the end of the Second World War was the M-107 (by then designated VK-107A) sufficiently developed to be used as the powerplant of the Yak-9U fighter.

Only two of the four machine guns were retained in the I-26-2 second prototype, mainly because the centre of gravity had proved to be too far forward. The manufacturer's development test programme was fairly brief, and on 1st June 1940 the aircraft went to the Nauchno Issledovatelyskii Institut Voenno-vozdushniye Sily (NII VVS – scientific and research institute of the air forces of the USSR) for its state tests.

Shortly before this a government decree had been issued to organise large scale series-production of the aircraft at the plants in Moscow, Leningrad and Saratov. This unprecedented move was probably not due solely to the political abilities of Alexander Yakovlev, who had been made a Deputy of the People's Commissar of the Aircraft Industry, but also to a calculated risk taken by of Commissar of the Aircraft Industry Alexey Shakhurin, who was trying to establish production of apparently advanced fighter aircraft in the ongoing war.

A short flight test programme conducted under the supervision of leading engineer N Maksimov did not show any unexpected results. The aircraft's performance was high, with maximum speeds of 304mph (490km/h) at sea level and 363mph (585km/h) at 15,750ft (4,800m), a ceiling of 33,500ft (10,200m), and

a time to climb to 16,400ft (5,000m) of six minutes. As before, structural qualities were poor and test flights were performed at a gross take-off weight of 5,952lb (2,700kg), some 220lb (100kg) less than designed. There were strict limitations on aerobatics, and because of 'g' load restrictions at 3,300ft (1,000m) pilots Peotr Stefanovsky and A Nikolaev took 24 seconds to make a full turn.

A total of 123 design and manufacturing flaws were mentioned in the official flight test report, and for this reason the aircraft did not pass the state tests. It should be pointed out that the I-26's primary competitors, the Lavochkin I-301 and MiG I-200, received very similar assessments after corresponding test programmes. The fact that the I-26 had a maximum speed some 62mph (100km/h) faster than that of the I-16 was considered an advantage.

In their discussion of the results of the flight test programme, the industry and air force representatives noted the absence of the electric generator, altimeter and radio in the prototype. Alexander Filin, the head of the NII VVS, considered that even prototypes should be equipped with radio, whereas the chief designer stated that a flight test programme was intended only for evaluation of the flight envelope. Eventually it was decided to equip

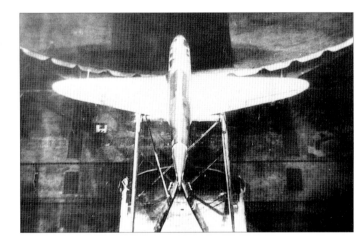

Yak-1 mock-up undergoing tests in the TsAGI wind tunnel.

The first I-26 prototype, on a non-retractable ski undercarriage.

production aircraft with such equipment. The machine's one-piece wooden wing gave rise to questions regarding maintainability and ease of transportation.

Production was initiated at the Aircraft Plant No.301 within Moscow, and by the summer of 1940 a run of 18 aircraft had been built for operational trials. The 11th Fighter Air Regiment, under Regiment Commander G Kogrushev, was the first unit to receive the new fighter.

The I-26 was favourably received by pilots. It was easy to handle, and there was no demand for familiarisation flights in the UTI-26 trainer when converting pilots from the I-16. Simulated aerial combats showed the new design's total superiority over the Polikarpov fighters. In spite of the lack of landing lights, the aircraft was successfully landed at night using only airfield illumination.

Five I-26s from the operational trial batch were flown in the air parade over Moscow on 7th November 1940. Test pilot A Yakimov, who evaluated the fighter under the orders of Commissar of Defence Klim Voroshilov, said: 'It seems that this is not a combat fighter but a primary trainer in terms of handling qualities'. On the other hand, operational trials revealed several new and serious flaws, such as jamming of the canopy in a dive and insufficiently strong undercarriage wheels.

Meanwhile, the third prototype, the I-26-3, was submitted for state tests. The extensively redesigned fighter had a maximum speed of 394mph (635km/h) in dive, the 'g' load limitations were removed, and a turn at 3,300ft (1,000m) took 20 to 21 seconds. The take-off gross weight was increased by some 220lb (100kg), and was expected to grow due to the installation of the equipment specified by the air force. Nevertheless, the aircraft retained its good handling qualities. During October and November 1940 the I-26-3 was flown by Pyotr Stefanovsky, A Kubyshkin, A Proshakov, Konstantin Gruzdev and A Nikolayev. By the end of December a report had been issued, stating that the I-26-3 had successfully passed its state flight tests.

Later, in the autumn of 1940, mass production was initiated. In addition to the relatively small GAZ-301 in Moscow, Plant No.292 in Saratov become involved in the production programme, the I-26 (already designated Yak-1) replacing the I-28 fighter designed by Vladimir Yatsenko at this factory. During December 1940 the production rate of the first Yak-1 batches was one aircraft per day. By April 1941 it had increased to two per day, and on the eve of war it had reached three per day, despite cancellation of production at Plant No.301 in Moscow.

The aircraft still had a number of defects, and all design alterations, such as strengthening the landing gear doors, inevitably led to an increase in the take-off weight. Yak-1 No.04-06, tested in February 1941, weighed 6,300lb (2,858kg). The performance of this aircraft can be considered standard for a 1941 Yak-1: maximum speed at sea level, 298mph (480 km/h); maximum speed at 16,250ft (4,950m), 358mph (577km/h); time to climb to 16,400ft (5,000m), 5.7 minutes; turning time at 3,300ft (1,000m), 20 to 21 seconds; landing speed, 85mph (137km/h); range at cruising speed, 434 miles (700km).

Starting in mid-May 1941, the 11th Fighter Air Regiment received 62 Yak-1s and eventually become a sort of training/conversion centre, where pilots of the 20th, 45th, 123rd, 158th and 91st fighter regiments converted to the new type before the outbreak of war. Most of the Yaks were concentrated near Moscow, but 105 were sent to five Western Military Districts before the war. However, only 36 pilots of the 20th Fighter Air Regiment based at Sambora, in the Kiev Special Military District, more or less mastered the Yak-1.

By early 1942 the Yak-1 had proved to be the best Soviet fighter with regard to overall performance, but it was still bettered in combat by the Messerschmitt Bf109F. When the Bf109F-2 was replaced by the 'F-4 with a more powerful, high altitude engine and improved armour and armament, the discrepancy was even more noticeable. In the words of Luftwaffe ace Gerhard Barkhorn, the Bf109F-4 represented the acme of the type's development. Its superiority over the Yak-1 in climb rate became more impressive, and manoeuvrability was of the same order. The 'F-4 also retained its superior speed, allowing Luftwaffe pilots to engage in combat at will or break off when the situation appeared unfavourable.

While the German fighters were being fitted with increasingly powerful engines, the Yak-1s did not gain so much as one horsepower in being converted from the M-105P to the M-105PA. It was therefore decided to augment the available engine.

The origin of the augmented M-105PA was unusual. In April 1942 a team of specialists from an engine plant and the NII VVS, headed by third rank engineer Boris Nikitin, was sent on a mission to the 236th Fighter Regiment commanded by Major Antonets, which was operating over the Western Front. In the course of this mission, on their own initiative, they converted seven Yak-1 M-105PAs to evaluate their operational performance with boost enhanced from 910 to 1,050mm Hg (1,050mm of mercury). This substantially improved performance, and the pilots were flying these aircraft willingly.

This afforded a simple means of improving the performance of all Yak-1s in service. Only minor changes to the M-105PA were required to increase the boost, and these could made under field conditions, without the need to take the aircraft off operations. The service debut of the augmented engines brought some unpleasant surprises. In hot weather, flight with the radiator intake fully closed for maximum speed could be maintained for only two minutes, after which time the water and oil temperatures exceeded the permitted limits. A boosted climb was also impossible because it was necessary to return to level flight to restore normal engine operating temperatures. Water and oil overheating was exacerbated by the radiator honeycomb cells becoming clogged with oil leaking through the breather and joints.

At the behest of the VVS Commandant, two of the seven modified Yak-1s were transferred to the NII for tests. The trials revealed that increasing the boost at nominal rpm resulted in an increase in maximum level speed of some 12.4 to 15.5mph (20 to 25km/h) at altitudes up to 11,500ft (3,500m), a one minute reduction in the time to climb to 16,400ft (5,000m), and a one second reduction in the time required to complete a 360° turn at 3,300ft (1,000m). Take-off performance also appeared to be improved. At the same time the augmented engine suffered from water and oil overheating. To keep the temperatures within permitted limits the nominal rpm had to be reduced from 2,700 to 2,400–2,500, which negated all the advantages of boost augmentation.

In the light of these findings it was decided to revise the cooling system and take measures to prevent oil leakage from the breather and engine seals. Certain modifications had to be introduced in the engine; the crankcase and gudgeon pins were re-inforced, and the carburettor jets were increased in diameter.

The boosted engine in series-production was designated M-105PF. Augmentation of the M-105PA resulted in increased power and poorer performance at altitude. The altitude at which the supercharger's first stage engaged decreased from 6,500 to 2,300ft (2,000 to 700m), while power increased from 1,100 to 1,260hp (820 to 940kW). Where supercharger's second stage was engaged, 8,900ft (2,700m), the M-105PF produced 1,180hp (880kW), compared with 1,050hp (783kW) at 13,200ft (4,000m) of the M105PA. At altitudes exceeding 13,200ft (4,000m) performances of the supercharged and and unsupercharged engines were practically the same.

In June 1942 M-105PF-powered Yak-1 No.1569 with an enlarged oil radiator underwent flight trials at the NII VVS. The trials revealed that the temperature regime was still critical. Weighing 6,430lb (2,917kg), typical for a Yak-1 without radio, the fighter attained maximum speeds of 316mph (510km/h) at sea level and 354mph (571km/h) at 12,000ft (3,650m), climbed to 16,400ft (5,000m) in 6.4

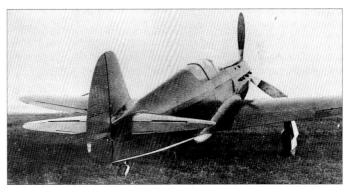

Top: **The second I-26 prototype, showing the distinctive format that remained throughout a very successful fighter family.**

Above, centre left and right: **Two views of an early production Yak-1, the first five of which were built at Plant No.292 in November 1940.**

Right: **An operational Yak-1 ready for action.**

minutes, completed a 360° turn at low altitude in 19 to 20 seconds and climbed to 3,200ft (980m) in an ascending turn.

To provide optimum performance, the engine's nominal speed at low altitudes was lowered to 2,550rpm, and the superiority of the Bf109F at these heights was reduced. A simulated combat between a Yak-1 M-105PF and a Bf109F at the NII VVS revealed that the Bf109F had only marginally superior manoeuvrability at 3,300ft (1,000m), though the German fighter could gain substantial advantage over the Yak-1 within four or five nose-to-tail turns. At 9,800ft (3,000m) the capabilities of both fighters were nearly equal, combat essentially being reduced to head-on attacks. As the Yak-1 was more manoeuvrable at altitudes over 16,400ft (5,000m), it was advantageous for the Russian fighter to draw the Bf109F to higher altitudes. It should be noted

that the supercharger of the Daimler-Benz DB601N engine did not provide a nominal boost in these tests. However, as it was flown under design operating conditions the DB601N ensured total superiority of the Messerschmitt over the Yak-1 M-105PF at altitudes exceeding 16,400ft (5,000m) as well. Moreover, by the summer of 1942, while the NII VVS was testing the earlier Bf109F-2, the Luftwaffe had converted to the 'F-4 with the more powerful DB601E engine, and this new variant completely outperformed the Yak-1 M-105PF.

A delay in the delivery of new Yak-1 fighters to the Soviet Air Force's active units in the Western Front Districts had unfortunate results. In June 1941 only regiment commanders and squadron leaders flew the aircraft; given another month, other pilots could have undergone sufficient training to fly it. Major B Suprun, of the 123rd Air Fighter Regiment, mastered the new fighter thoroughly. While repulsing the Luftwaffe air raids on the Fourth Army headquarters in Kobrin on 22nd June he flew four sorties, destroying three enemy aircraft, but failed to return from his last flight.

Yak-1 with upgraded M-105PF engine during NII tests in June 1942.

Naval pilots were among the first to master the Yak-1. On 4th June Lieutenant Y Shitov of the 9th Air Fighter Regiment shot down a Romanian reconnaissance aircraft, thereby becoming the first pilot of the Black Sea Fleet to gain a victory on the type. By the beginning of the war the 9th Air Fighter Regiment commanded by Major K Malikov had become the best-equipped unit, with nearly 90 combat aircraft, including three Yak-1s. Later, the regiment's total strength was reduced, but the number of Yaks grew steadily.

In the North West sector the new Yak-1s were concentrated in the 158th Air Fighter Regiment, at first was stationed near Pskov then becoming an organic part of the air defence units in Leningrad. Notable among its pilots was A Chirkov, who, in shooting down an enemy aircraft on 23rd June 1941, claimed the first victory in the skies over Leningrad. Chirkov initially flew the Polikarpov I-16, but he then mastered the Yak-1, and by the middle of August he had destroyed seven enemy aircraft. He was the first to engage in air combat as one of a pair.

The Yak-1's performance might have been better exploited but for a number of regrettable faults. When Leningrad was besieged by the Nazis the 158th Air Fighter Regiment passed their remaining Yak-1s to the 123rd Air Fighter Regiment, under Major B Romanov, before going to the rear. It transpired that there were twice as many faulty aircraft as those in good repair.

The M-105Ps caused a lot of trouble. Although they were more reliable than the AM-35A engines in the MiG fighters, they suffered breakdowns of magnetos and speed regulators, and emitted oil from the reduction shaft. One M-105P produced metal fragments on its second flight, and the pilot had to find open ground for an emergency landing when the engine seized.

On the eve of the German offensive against Moscow one in ten fighters on the front was a Yak. As the defects in the airframe and engine were eliminated and the teething troubles overcome, it became evident that the Yak-1 could carry on the struggle against the opposing fighters more successfully than other Soviet types. Luftwaffe experts assessed the fighter at that time in the following words:

'Apparently the Yak is the best Soviet fighter. Its speed and rate of climb exceed those of the MiG-3. The fighter was similar in performance to the Bf109F, but was inferior to it in speed. The Yak-1 was harder to attack from the rear than the MiG-3. It had a good rate of climb to [19,700ft] 6,000m, but its manoeuvrability deteriorated at the height. That is why pilots dived from high altitude when going into action'.

The 20th Air Fighter Regiment, mentioned above, considerably bolstered the defences on the Bryansk Front when the 2nd Armoured Group under the command of Hanz Guderian conducted a close enveloping manoeuvre around Moscow. That Regiment and the 42nd Air Fighter Regiment, equipped with MiG-3s, were based on the airfield near Karachevo. One of the pilots who flew the MiGs (and who later became an Air Marshal) wrote that, having examined the Yak-1 closely and sat in its cockpit, he envied his colleagues. At that time both regiments were attached to the 11th Soviet Air Division under the command of famous Soviet ace G Kravchenko. Command did everything in their power to enable the pilots to make good use of the capabilities of the Yak-1, and this soon bore fruit; Captain G Konev managed to shoot down two Junkers during one night in September.

Yaks bore the brunt of defending the skies over Moscow at the end of the summer and in the autumn. By 10th July 1941 133 Yak-1s were defending the capital, one in every six fighters being of that type. Only nine fighters were unserviceable, which testifies to the high level of combat readiness. The credit for the first victory of the Moscow Air Defence Corps also goes to a Yak. On 2nd July 1941 Lieutenant S Goshko of the 11th Air Fighter Regiment was pursuing an enemy reconnaissance aircraft. When his Yak's guns seized, Goshko rammed his adversary near Rzhev and landed his aircraft successfully.

Another pilot of the 11th Air Fighter Regiment, Captain K Zhitenkov, was noted for his great flying skill and courage. He was in action on 22nd July 1941, when the first air raid on the capital was dispersed, and the citation for his award stated: 'He flies on new types of aircraft at any time of day or night'. This was very important, because there were very few night fighter pilots. Zhitenkov shot down a Heinkel He111 during his first encounter with the enemy, and two days later he brought down a Junkers Ju88. On 29th July he shot down another He111. By 10th October 1941, when he was killed in an accident caused by bad weather conditions, his Yak-1 (No.2525) had gained six victories in 172 operational flights. These victories are even more impressive when it is taken into account that they were mostly won at night, and that the Yaks had no radio aids, navigation instruments or even landing lights.

After half a year of operational use it was possible to assess the first results. There were a great many defects in the Yak-1, and many complaints. The defects were not as dangerous as those on the MiG-3, and they did not impair flying as much as those on the LaGG-3, but they caused a lot of problems.

As before, the functioning of the undercarriage was unsatisfactory. When the landing gear retracted there were jerks and blows, and sometimes it stuck in an intermediate position and did not retract fully. In addition, it often folded during landing, and breakages of the tailwheel were brought about mainly by its insufficient angle of rotation.

The armament also proved troublesome. Many pilots considered it insufficiently powerful, and it often seized during firing. Heat in the cockpit, and emissions from the engine drain pipe which splattered the canopy and windshield with oil, made flying difficult.

The M-105PA, a modification of the M-105P, was installed in the Yak-1 by the summer of 1941. The M-105PA made extended inverted flight and negative 'g' dives possible. There were other changes, too, but it proved impossible to eliminate all of the defects. Oil emission, in particular, remained a problem.

The specialists of the Yakovlev OKB and the Saratov aircraft plant persisted in their efforts to improve the fighter's airframe. In November 1941 Yak-1 No.2029 underwent tests at the NII VVS with the following improvements installed:

- an 'unloading' cylinder was introduced to provide smooth retraction and extension of the landing gear;
- reliability of the armament was improved;
- a simplified non-retractable skid was installed;
- an easily removable propeller spinner was fitted;
- a trim tab was added to the rudder;
- a landing light was fitted;
- radio was installed;
- a special oil drain tank was fitted to prevent the emission of oil.

The aircraft's flying weight was increased to 6,468lb (2,934kg), and its performance was correspondingly reduced. Maximum speed at low altitude was 290mph (468km/h), and at 15,750ft (4,800m) it was 347mph (560km/h), so that the speed of the 'modernised' fighter was 7.4 to 10.5mph (12 to 17km/h) less than that of the normal Yak-1. It took 6.8 minutes to climbing to 16,400ft (5,000m), an increase of more than a minute.

As before, manoeuvrability remained adequate, a steep turn at a low altitude taking 19-20 seconds and 3,000ft (900m) being gained in a climbing combat turn. Use of the supercharger during take-off reduced the run by more than 5% and compensated for the increase in weight.

Aircraft No.2029 was the first of its kind to have a radio. The 1,000 Yak-1s produced up to that time had not even had elementary radio-receivers. Later, every tenth Yak-1 was fitted with radio aids, because the chief designer held the firm belief that such equipment only served to increase weight.

Previously, in October 1941, the Yak-1 had been equipped with rocket projectiles. Worthy of mention is the initiative of Major A Negoda, Commander of the 562nd Air Fighter Regiment, who flew four or five low-flying missions against the forward line of enemy troops without refuelling, landing only to replenish his supply of rockets. This was because the front line lay only six miles (10km) from the Regiment's airfield.

Only 195 Yaks had been equipped with rocket launchers at the factory by the end of 1941. The installation of six RS-82 rockets was welcomed by the pilots. Although the missiles increased the fighter's weight by 143lb (65kg) and reduced maximum speed by approximately 18.6mph (30km/h), they had a very demoralising effect when used against enemy aircraft, particularly in frontal attacks. On the rare occasions when a direct hit was scored the enemy aircraft simply broke up, but there was no need for a direct hit because the projectiles self-destructed, near bursts inflicting very effective damage. Even German bombers which survived an attack could often not remain airborne. However, the lack of a guidance system for the rockets and their imperfect design caused wide dispersion, and the probability of damaging a manoeuvring target was not high.

The preparation of winter modifications for the Yak-1 was a very important task at the end of autumn. A series-production aircraft was given a ski landing gear in place of wheels. Modifications for winter operations were:
- the wheel undercarriage was replaced by a retractable ski undercarriage;
- parts of the powerplant installation, including pipelines, radiators, oil tanks and drain tanks, were heated;
- the water-cooling system was refilled with anti-freeze;
- a quilted cover was used to prevent supercooling of the engine while the aircraft was stationary.

Water-based chalky distemper paint was applied over the summer camouflage to prevent aircraft being detected on snow-covered airfields. In its winter version weight of the Yak-1 increased by 154 to 176lb (70 to 80kg) and its speed was reduced by 18.6 to 24.8mph (30 to 40km/h) at all altitudes.

By 25th February 1942 830 'winter' Yak-1s had been produced. They could be used on airfields covered with deep snow without the need to clear a runway. No other fighter had such a wide-track ski undercarriage, which made landing on the rough surface easy. With a ski undercarriage the fighter became more stable and did not bounce. The take-off run was only 820ft (250m), and 902ft (275m) with flaps. The nose-over angle was considerably increased, resulting in a reduction of the danger of overturning.

Right: **Like the North American P-51 Mustang, the Yak-1 canopy evolved during its service career, from the 'turtle deck' illustrated to 'tear-drop'.**

Below right: **According to tradition, the call-number '1' was reserved for the regiment commander. This aircraft was flown by a deputy-commander.**

Below left: **Aircraft delivered to operational units had an inferior quality skin surface that impeded their performance.**

Intensive use of ski-equipped Yak-1s revealed that the ski runners had insufficient wear resistance and had a life of only 80 take-offs and landings. The pilots of the 236th Fighter Air Regiment observed that the only way to move an aircraft if its skis became stuck to the snow while it was parked was to swing it off with the help of ground personnel on the wings and tail.

Equipping the Saracombayn Plant No.292 with high production tooling and the adoption of a moving stand assembly system for the aircraft and its components played their part, and series-production of the Yak-1 had begun before the war. In June 1941 four fighters were produced daily, but by October the daily output had risen to eight. The time taken to produce individual units decreased considerably. For instance, fuselage assembly was reduced from 14 days to nine, and final assembly from seven days to three. The concentration of effort on series-production of the updated Yak-1 forced a decline in full scale production of the improved I-30. The Government's plan to develop full scale production of Yak-1 in Tbilisi and Kutaisi was not realised, production being concentrated in Saratov.

At first weight was not strictly controlled, and all structural changes made the aircraft heavier. But from early August 1941 that drawback was eliminated, designers and engineers being rewarded for each gramme of weight saved. In the middle of August, beginning with the 29th series, the normal weight of a Yak-1 without external loads and radio was 6,430lb (2,917kg).

A study of combat actions over a half-year period showed the Yak-1 to be the most successful Soviet fighter put into series-production before the war, although the number in service was not great. On 5th December 1941, the eve of the Soviet counter-offensive near Moscow, only 83 Yak-1s, about 8% of all available fighters, were serving in VVS combat units and of these, only 47 were operational. However, the aircraft had a great future.

In May 1942 the Yak-1 was re-equipped. By government decision the underwing rockets were removed to enhance speed, which appeared to be the critical element in air combat. At the same time production Yak-1s began to be fitted with two underwing stores shackles to enable them to carry a pair of 55 to 242lb (25 to 100kg) bombs, enabling the aircraft to serve as fighter-bombers. The Klimov M-105PA was not powerful enough to give the overweight aircraft the required performance. Loss of speed suffered was 18.6 mph (30km/h) and the controls became heavy. In this role the Yak-1 did not win the acclaim of service units.

Compared with the winter of 1941-42, the spring of 1942 saw a significant build-up of Luftwaffe forces, and especially fighter units, over Germany's Eastern Front. This forced the VVS to use the Yak-1 primarily in air combat, and only occasionally in the attack fighter role. Underwing stores shackles continued to be installed until series-production finished.

'Yak-1B'

The second development path taken by the Yakovlev Design Bureau was aimed at improving the Yak-1's pilot vision, armament and armour, and in June 1942 this activity resulted in significant modifications to one aircraft. To improve the view rearwards the fuselage top-decking behind the cockpit was cut down and a teardrop-shaped canopy was fitted. The curved windshield was replaced by a three-panel unit, thus reducing distortion. Pilot protection was enhanced by an armoured-glass screen and windscreen, plus an armoured headrest and armrests.

The two synchronised 7.62mm ShKAS machine guns were replaced by a single synchronised 12.7mm UBS machine gun, and the 20mm ShVAK cannon was re-instated. The PBP lens-type gunsight gave way to a primitive VV ring sight, in response to the repeated requests received from service units dissatisfied with poor quality of the optical sights. The control column was revised to make it similar to that of the Bf109, facilitating shooting during a manoeuvring dogfight.

On 1st July 1941 the fighter was moved to the NII VVS for testing. Pilots A Proshakov, Pyotr Stefanovsky, A Kochetkov, L Kuvshinov and V Khomyakov were very appreciative of the innovations. The report summarising the test results stated that the all-round vision through the armoured glass, and particularly vision aft through the transparent cockpit fairing, was the best to be found in a Soviet fighter. It was recommended that the modified fighter be placed in production as a standard type as soon as possible.

In September 1942 Plant No.292 succeeded in phasing these modifications on to its assembly lines, launching series-production of the modified Yak-1. This version, with the 12.7mm UBS machine gun and improved vision, was nicknamed 'Yak-1B', especially in the records of service units. Of a total of 3,474 Yak-1s built during 1942, 959 were the modified version powered by the M-105PF.

From December 1942 to January 1943 the modified Yak-1s underwent service tests with the 32nd Guards Fighter Regiment operating over the Kalinin Front and in the 176th Fighter Regiment on the Stalingrad Front. During that time 58 of the new fighters flew more then 700 missions, engaged in 38 combats and shot down 25 Luftwaffe aircraft. The Soviet losses amounted to six Yak-1s. The revised control column and improved rearwards vision were highly praised by Service pilots, who recommended that all fighter types should be so equipped. The other changes introduced by the Yakovlev Design Bureau were also approved.

The Bf109's main advantage lay in its vertical manoeuvrability, which was a result of its low power-to-weight ratio. The Soviet designers were forced to respond to this challenge in March 1942 by lightening the structure of the Yak-1. The work carried out was of a developmental nature, and resulted in the manufacture of a dozen interceptors.

A total of 25 changes were made to reduce the Yak-1's weight. The principal ones were: removal of the ShKAS machine guns and their ammunition tanks, removal of one of the two compressed air bottles, removal of a filter, replacement of the wooden empennage by an all-metal one similar to that of the Yak-7, and removal of fuel tank protection. These measures resulted in a weight saving of 357lb (162kg). One of the fighters was tested by Pavel Fedrovi, a chief pilot of the Yakovlev Design Bureau, who praised it highly. Ten lightened Yak-1s were issued to the 12th Guards Fighter Regiment of the 6th Fighter Corps, assigned to the Moscow air defence, for use as interceptors.

Attempts to evaluate the lightened Yak-1 in service were repeated in September 1942. Twenty of the aircraft were manufactured especially for distribution to units on the Stalingrad Front. Weighing 6,128lb (2,780kg), they were only marginally faster than production Yak-1s on the level, but substantially outperformed them in vertical manoeuvrability.

Lightened Yak-1s were supplied to the 512th Fighter Regiment, led by Hero of the Soviet Union Lieutenant Colonel N Gerasimov, and to the 520th Fighter Regiment, commanded by Major S Chirva. Two pilots of the 512th Fighter Regiment, I Motorny and V Makarov, shot down two Bf109G-2s while ferrying a pair of lightened Yak-1s from the Saratov plant. Air combat revealed that lightened Yak-1s flown by experienced pilots could counter Bf109F-4s and 'G-2s. According to statistics, the production Yak-1 succeeded in shooting down a German aircraft for every 26 missions, while the lightened Yak-1 gained a victory for every 18 missions, and also suffered fewer losses. It outclimbed the Bf109 marginally, and outperformed it completely in turning fights.

Admittedly, the armament of the lightened Yak-1 was inadequate for less-experienced pilots, and mass production of this version was not undertaken. The experience gained in lightening the Yak-1 was later put to good use by the Yakovlev Design Bureau during development of the Yak-3.

Above and right: **Two views of snow-camouflaged Yak-1 No.3855, used for the testing of retractable ski undercarriage. Note RS-82 rockets.**

In the late summer and autumn of 1942, during the fighting around Stalingrad, VVS activities were seriously hampered by the appearance of the new Bf109G-2. Owing to its more powerful, high altitude engine, the 'G-2 outperformed the Soviet fighters in level speed and especially in rate of climb.

Extraordinary measures were taken to improve the performance of Soviet aircraft, the Yak-1 being of primary concern. It was planned to install a more powerful M-106 engine with a single-speed supercharger. According to a government directive on the improvement of Yak-1 aerodynamics, issued in December 1942, maximum speeds of 326mph (525km/h) at sea level and 366mph (590km/h) at 12,300ft (3,750m) were required, 9.3 to 12.4mph (15 to 20km/h) higher than those of of the production Yak-1.

The aerodynamic improvements, coupled with the weight reduction achieved by the Yakovlev Design Bureau, resulted in numerous changes in the Yak-1's construction. Pressure bulkheads were installed in the fuselage, the tailwheel was made retractable, cowlings and fillets were retrofitted, exhaust pipes were faired and arranged to provide some measure of thrust augmentation, the air intake duct profiles were revised, and the finish of the skinning was improved.

Tests of the revised Yak-1 were conducted at the Letno-Issledovatel'skii Institut (LII - Ministry of Aviation Inudstry Flight Research Institute) by leading test engineer V Moichayev and test pilot V Kochenyuk, and the fighter proved to be 4.9 to 9.3mph (8 to 15km/h) faster than the production Yak-1. Work on Yak-1 improvements proceeded throughout 1943, and all of the modifications were phased on to assembly lines. The excellent results were evident in the tests of Yak-1 No.46139. At a loaded weight of 6,313lb (2,864kg) it attained speeds of 334mph (539 km/h) at sea level and 375mph (605km/h) at 13,500ft (4,100m), climbed to 16,400ft (5,000m) in 5.7 minutes, completed a 360° turn at low altitude within 17 to 18 seconds, and climbed to 3,500ft (1,050m) while performing an ascending turn. This was apparently the best performance that could be attained by a fighter of this type. Moreover, the low variations in performance of Yak-1s delivered in 1943 were due to well-controlled manufacturing standards at Plant No.292. When production was terminated in July 1944, to make way for the Yak-3, a total of 8,666 Yak-1s had been built.

Top left: **Modified Yak-1 undergoing field maintenance.**

Top right: **A '1943 Standard' Yak-1, one of the last of its type.**

Left: **Modified Yak-1 with a tear-drop canopy. Lisunov Li-2 in the background.**

Below: **Before the pilot has even had time to dismount, a Yak-1 is pushed into the trees and its 'hide'.**

Yak-1 M-106

In early 1941 serious consideration was given to the possibility of using the Vladimir Klimov M-106 engine, which was expected to provide 1,350hp 1,007kW at take-off and 6,500ft (2,000m), and 1,250hp (932kW) at 13,000ft (4,000m). Later the engine was uprated, being fitted with a one-speed supercharger developed by V Dollezhal which gave a boost of 1,175mm Hg. This increased the engine's output at altitudes above 13,000ft (4,000m) by 150 to 200hp (112 to 149kW) over that of its predecessor, the M-105PA/PF.

Another advantage came from its variation of output relative to altitude. The M-105PF, having a two-speed supercharger, suffered noticeable losses of power at 5,900 to 6,500ft (1,800 to 2,000m), whereas the Daimler-Benz engines had automatically-controlled superchargers that prevented power loss at operational altitudes. Luftwaffe pilots exploited this weakness in the Soviet engines by engaging the Yaks at their service ceiling. With the new supercharger the M-106's output varied smoothly with altitude, thus avoiding the speed drop at service ceiling.

The M-106 differed from its predecessor, the M-105PF, in having a lower pressure ratio, an increased flow rate in the main oil pump, and a stronger crankshaft, among other things. As the empty weight of M-106 engine was the same as that of the M-105PF, the aircraft's centre of gravity was unchanged.

The Yakovlev Design Bureau developed a new Yak-1 airframe to take the M-106. The wings had metal spars, and the empennage was of all-metal construction. Two fuel tanks of 87.9 gallons (400 litres) total capacity were installed in the wing outer sections, while the centre section housed two I-26-1 oil radiators. The engine cowling, armament and equipment of the new prototype were similar to those of a production Yak-1.

Tested in January 1943, the Yak-1 M-106 proved to have excellent performance. At a loaded weight of 6,078lb (2,757kg) it attained 342mph (551km/h) at sea level and 391mph (630km/h) at 11,200ft (3,400m), and climbed to 16,400ft (5,000m) in 4.5 minutes. The pilot, A Kokin, reported that the water and oil radiators allowed the engine to operate at nominal power only when the outside air temperature was +15°C or less, and he found it impossible to perform long duration flights.

The M-106 engine appeared to be underdeveloped, suffering from vibration, detonations, smoking and poor oil seals.

In parallel with these tests, engineers from the LII tested a production Yak-1 fitted with an M-106. The speed decreased by 12.4mph (20 km/h), and time to climb to 16,400ft (5,000m) was increased by 1.1 minutes.

In spite of its shortcomings the Yak-1 M-106 was put into production, and by 18th February 1943 the Saratov plant had built 47. However, these aircraft had not been tested and some were refitted with M-105PFs.

UTI-26

As related earlier, unlike the other design teams, Alexander Yakovlev's Opytno Konstruktorskoye Byuro (OKB – experimental design bureau) submitted three more combat aircraft, in addition to the I-26, for the air force contest. The first of these was the UTI-26 (UTI – uchebno-trenirovochny istrebitel – training fighter, also called the UTI-26-4, UTI-1 and UTI-27), on which the bureau began work at the beginning of 1940. On 4th March 1940 the government provided encouragement by issuing a resolution supporting the project.

Considering the Yakovlev OKB's great experience in designing trainers, it was thought that it would be more successful than other bureaux in developing the training fighter. Furthermore, it was believed that the new trainer would be generally similar to the I-26 prototype, minimising the chance of the project failing, as it would be a mistake to jeopardise the re-equipment of VVS units with the new-generation fighters.

And so it transpired. The first UTI-26 was indeed very similar to the I-26, the only difference being that the cockpits for the trainee pilot and the instructor were positioned in tandem beneath a single canopy, and the aircraft had full dual control. As there was no telephonic intercom, trainee and instructor communicated by means of a rubber speaking tube. Owing to the location of the second cockpit, the wing of the UTI-26 was a positioned a little further aft.

On 23rd July 1940 test pilot Pavel Fedrovi took the new trainer into the air for the first time. After a short manufacturer's test programme the aircraft went for its state flight tests, carried out by engineer A Stepanets and pilots Peotr Stefanovsky and A Kubyshkin from 28th August to 19th September.

On 30th August the undercarriage retracted during taxying, owing to poor design and construction. In general there were too many faults in the UTI-26's landing gear design: unsafe locks, wheels too weak for the take-off weight, a small anti-nose-over angle which

The UTI-26 arose from an urgent need for an advanced pilot trainer.

Rear view of a UTI-26 showing the neat second cockpit installation and the highly-polished finish typical of Yakovlev prototypes.

did not allow the use of brakes on landing, especially without an instructor in the rear cockpit. These shortcomings had all been present in the I-26, and were not new. Because of the defects it was impossible to use the training fighter in aviation schools with young pilots.

In addition, the pilots of the 11th Fighter Air Regiment who had made the delivery flight noticed very small elevator deflections in different flight modes, including landing, which would make its use as a trainer more difficult. However, the UTI-26 was intended as a transition type for the I-26, I-200 and I-301 production aircraft, so it was recommended for series-production. It was therefore decided to continue development on the modified second prototype.

The principal changes made to the UTI-26-2 were alteration of the ratio of the areas of the elevators and the tailplane and modifications to the undercarriage. The larger wheels conformed to the take-off weight and their different construction allowed an increase in the anti-nose-over angle, but a discrepancy arose between the wheels' plane of rotation and direction of movement which placed additional load on the axles.

Some rearrangement brought the centre of gravity forward, which improved dynamic stability. This was confirmed by test pilots who carried out intensive flying trials of the aircraft from the beginning of 1941, in practice all NII test pilots, headed by A Filin. The UTI-26 flight evaluation report included the following comments:

'The aeroplane has a good handling and sufficient dynamic stability, and performs all aerobatic manoeuvres pleasantly and easily. Cockpit visibility is satisfactory. Because of the canopy, flight without goggles is possible.

The aircraft enters a spin only after a considerable stall, and recovers very easily. It forgives basic mistakes in handling without fatal consequences. It has a wide safe speed range'.

Yak-7UTI

On 4th March 1941, following the release of the design report on the UTI-26, the Yak-7UTI was put into production at Plant No.301, where the Yak-1 had been manufactured.

In accordance with the nature of training operations, the tailskid was made non-retractable, engine revolutions were reduced, and instead of two ShKAS guns there was only one, on the port side. Weight of the production aircraft was about 6,172lb (2,800kg), and performance was close to that of production Yak-1s of the period.

On 18th May 1941 test pilot Pavel Fedrovi flew a production Yak-7UTI at the Central Moscow airfield. VVS regiments began to receive them just before the war, but they were generally operational in reserve air regiments only. They played a major role in accelerating the conversion of pilots to modern fighters.

On the basis of operational experience, at the beginning of August 1941 engineer Sharapov at Plant No.301 proposed that the Yak-7 be built with a fixed undercarriage to simplify production and increase output. That same month his idea was adopted for series-production aircraft. The main problem which beset the 87 production aircraft then in service concerned the landing gear pins, which failed by the dozen, and attempts to reinforce them proved futile.

A UTI-26 showing the many access panels on the type – inherited from the I-26.

Yak-7R

One of the first Yak-7UTI modifications centred on the development of a tactical reconnaissance variant. In accordance with Alexander Yakovlev's wishes, two aircraft were equipped with an AFA-1 aerial camera and an RSI-4 radio. To ensure the proper functioning of the latter the necessary bonding and screening was carried out, and in addition an armoured backrest was fitted and the glazing was changed. The aircraft's armament comprised a 20mm ShVAK cannon.

After the type was adopted by the Secret Service's NII, it was proposed that a small series of such aircraft be built.

Yak-7

In August 1941 the UTI-26/Yak-7V was modified into a combat fighter at Plant No.301, the project being headed by leading engineer K Sinelschikov. The following changes were introduced in the construction of production Yak-7UTI No.04-11:

- an armoured backrest was fitted in the rear cockpit;
- the camera gun was removed;
- the unprotected petrol tanks were replaced by protected ones;
- a fuel tank pressurisation system was devised, using an inert gas stored in a carbon dioxide bottle;

• the armament installed consisted of a 20mm ShVAK firing through the propeller hub (120 rounds), two 7.62mm ShKAS synchronised machine guns (1,500 rounds), and six rocket launchers (three underneath each wing) for RS-82s. Fire control of the rocket launchers was achieved using the bomb release mechanism in the cockpit. The rear cockpit canopy and skid remained the same, and for this reason the Yak-7 single-seater looked like the Yak-7UTI two-seat fighter.

The designers reported the results of their work to Alexander Yakovlev. Although he was sceptical at first he approved it, and after he had reported to the government about the creation of a fighter based on the trainer the work was encouraged and supported.

Two reports issued in August required that the Yak-7UTI be fitted with armament like that of the Yak-1 from 15th September. Curiously, there were some mistakes in the texts of these reports.

According to the reports, Moscow Plant No.301 and, after evacuation, Novosibirsk Plant No.153, were to produce the Yak-1. In reality Yak-1s were never built there, although this had been planned. Up to the end of 1941 186 Yak-7s had been built in Moscow (51 of them fighters) and 21 in Novosibirsk (11 of them fighters).

From the outset references to the Yak-7 were complimentary, and when the aircraft was formally accepted on 2nd October 1941, the OKB technical commission reported the Yak-7's advantages when compared with the Yak-1. Its undercarriage wheels were of sufficient strength for the machine's flying weight, its detachable engine mounting made repair easier and allowed the installation of alternative engines, and the increased ground angle allowed the pilot to brake harder during landing without the danger of hitting the propeller of overturning.

The retained second cockpit could be used to carry technical personnel and cargo during unit redeployments, to rescue pilots from emergency landing sites, for additional tanks, photographic equipment or bombs, and for other purposes. Nearly all of these uses were later realised.

The Yak-7's performance was quite similar to that of the Yak-1. At 6,525lb (2,960kg), 352lb (160kg) more than the Yak-7UTI, without external stores and with the canopy closed, the Yak-7 had a maximum speed of 292mph (471km/h) at ground level and 347mph (560 km/h) at 16,400ft (5,000m), and could climb to that height in only 6.8 minutes. In manoeuvrability it was inferior to the Yak-1: 24 seconds were required for a 3,300ft (1,000m) banked turn, and it climbed 2,500ft (750m) during the combat turn. However, there was

a good point to its handling. A Lazarev, the test pilot at Plant No.153, describing its spinning properties, observed that the Yak-7's spin recovery was: 'Very easy, without any tricks. The aircraft immediately stopped turning and began to dive as soon as you centralised the pedals and the control column'.

In September 1941 the Yak-7 underwent successful armament trials. Thanks to the fighter's good dynamic stability, dispersion during firing on ground targets was less than that of LaGG-3 and the Yak-1, and rather less than that of the MiG-3.

The first Yak-7 combat operation was connected with the offensive near Moscow. One squadron (the 172nd Fighter Air Regiment) with Yak-7s (another two had LaGG-3s and Yak-1s) followed Ilyushin Il-2 attack aircraft (from the 65th ShAP) and attacked enemy forces during the Soviet offensive in the Volokolamsk area of the Teryaev Sloboda-Ruza region. At the time there were only eight Yak-7s in Soviet aviation, and only three were combat capable. The necessity of evacuating factories from Moscow (including Plant No.301) held up deliveries to the squadrons, but modernisation of the aircraft continued.

Before the redeployment to Novosibirsk the 'winter standard' version of the Yak-7 had been prepared. Because the fighting did not allow the work of strengthening the Yak-7's armament to be completed, it was planned to mount two ShVAK synchronised cannon on the engine.

Yak-7M

A very interesting modification of the Yak-7V was undertaken in August 1941, though it was not the work of the Moscow or Novosibirsk plants that were producing the Yak-7. The modification originated with a team of engineers engaged in setting up a Yak-1 production line at the Saratov Plant, No.292. It is difficult to understand how this development came about, but many innovations developed on the I-30 were introduced into the trainer's construction. As a result the Yak-7M (modifikatsirovannii – modified) appeared.

All equipment was removed from the rear cockpit. The single ShKAS machine gun was replaced by three 20mm ShVAK cannon; one engine-mounted and two wing-mounted, the latter firing outside the the radius of the propeller disc. The salvo firepower of the Yak-7M was greater than that of all other Soviet and German production fighters.

The most significant changes concerned the wings. The span was reduced from 32ft 9¾in to 31ft 11in (10 to 9.74m), and the wingtips were rounded at greater radius owing to the extended slats. Installation of the

cannon and ammunition boxes in the wing reduced the capacity of the outer wing tanks. The wing construction was strengthened and the area of the landing flaps was increased. To regain the lost fuel capacity, an additional 17.5 gallon (80 litre) tank was positioned behind the cockpit back armour.

In October 1941 the Yak-7M was moved to the NII VVS for testing, and immediately attracted the attention of leading engineer A Stepanets and a test pilot V Khomyakov. They pointed out that, owing to the slats, the handling proved to be markedly simplified despite the increase in gross weight to 6,966lb (3,160kg). The risk of entering a spin owing to pilot error was completely eliminated, and stability, particularly directional, was improved. These features ensured improved flight safety. The speed at which aerobatics could be performed could be further reduced by some 18.6 to 24.8mph (30 to 40km/h).

The cannon tests showed that they performed reliably throughout the entire flight envelope. It was obvious that the Yak-7M's armament could be effectively used against both air and ground targets.

Consideration was given to the series-production of the Yak-7M, but this appeared to be impossible in winter of 1941-42. The introduction of the Yak-7M would have required major reorganisation of the production lines, and this could not be contemplated by the aircraft industry at that time.

Yak-7A

The Yak-7 underwent considerable changes in 1942. While retaining all the main features of its trainer predecessor early in the year, late in the year it became one of the best fighters of the time. In the winter of 1941-42 the Novosibirsk Plant No.153 produced six or seven Yak-7s monthly (the main production aircraft of the plant was the LaGG-3), but by August 1942 that was its daily output.

In early January 1942 production Yak-7 No.14-13 was moved to the NII VVS for the joint development and state acceptance trials, in which it was flown with both wheel and ski landing gear. The tests revealed the degradation of flight performance compared with that of the UTI-26. Maximum speed was 295mph (476km/h) at sea level and 341mph (550km/h) at 16,400ft (5,000m), and this altitude could be reached in only 6.8 minutes.

The ski undercarriage and chalky winter paint applied over the camouflage reduced the aircraft's speed by some 18.6 to 24.8mph (30 to 40km/h). Its climb rate, range and take-off were also adversely affected, but the landing run decreased by 492ft (150m) due to the greater friction. Some 300 landings validated the reliability of the undercarriage fitted with the wooden skis produced by Plant No.153. The tail ski was fixed.

After modification in which aerodynamic improvement was of primary concern, with a wheeled undercarriage it reached a maximum sea level speed of 307mph (495km/h), and at 16,400ft (5,000m) a speed of 354mph (571km/h) was attained, the time to climb to 16,400ft (5,000m) being 6.4 minutes. Under the designation Yak-7A production started at Novosibirsk on the first day of 1942. Most of modifications justifying the new designation were introduced later, mainly in spring of 1942. Among the main changes were:

- installation of radio, mast, and aerial;
- replacement of the fixed tailwheel by a semi-retractable one;
- fitting the undercarriage wells with additional cover doors;
- replacement of the aft-sliding rear canopy with a sideways-hinging plywood hood providing a smooth transition from the canopy to the fuselage decking;
- engine supercharging was used to reduce the take-off run;
- retrofitting of an oxygen system;
- rearrangement of the instrument panel.

Thus modified, the Yak-7A became one of the fastest Soviet fighters, although it was marginally inferior to the Yak-1 in manoeuvrability (with the same armament).

Early in the summer of 1942 several dozen Yak-7As were distributed to the service units operating over the Volkhov and Western Fronts. In his report to Alexander Yakovlev, the Commander of the 283rd Fighter Regiment, Major A Morozov, pointed out certain shortcomings of the Yak-7A, including inadequate armament, poor speed and the weakness of the engine.

Yak-7B

The Yakovlev OKB tried to eliminate the faults found in the Yak-7A and as a result the Yak-7B M-105PA was created. This had more powerful armament and improved aerodynamics.

The two 7.62mm machine guns were replaced by two 12.7mm UBS machine guns, the 20mm hub-mounted ShVAK cannon being retained. In the overload condition six RS-82 rocket projectiles or two bombs of up to 220lb (100kg) each could be carried beneath the wings.

Aerodynamic improvements were based on the recommendations of the Tsentral'nyi Aerogidrodynamichesky Institut (TsAGI – Central Aerodynamic and Hydrodynamic Institute). Redesigned air intakes increased service ceiling and exploited dynamic pressure more effectively. The external surface finish was improved, and revised water and oil pipelines were installed as well.

Due to the installation of the radio equipment and new armament resulting in distortion of the upper cowling, the normal loaded weight was increased by about 220lb (100kg). Nevertheless the Yak-7B's performance was slightly higher than that of the Yak-7 and 'A.

With the pair of UBS machine guns replacing the ShKAS weapons the Yak-7B met the service requirements for a weight of fire of 5.9lb/sec (2.72kg/sec), 3.5 times greater than that of the Bf109F (according to the results of test carried out in the USSR), 1.35 times greater than that of the latest LaGG-3 variant, and over 1.5 times greater than the weight of fire of the Yak-1 and Yak-7A.

By comparing the Yak-7B with other indigenous fighters as well as German and Lend-Lease aircraft, the LII concluded that it was one of the best regarding stability and handling qualities.

Following state acceptance trials, the State Defence Committee issued a directive that Yak-7A production was to be converted to Yak-7B. As early as April 1942 the first production Yak-7B was rolled off the assembly line at Novosibirsk Plant No.153, and the fighter at once began to reach the front line units. From late May the rocket projectiles were removed to improve performance, though the underwing bomb racks were retained.

The first operational problem encountered by service units at the South Western Front was an unacceptable decrease in the Yak-7B's

Photograph on the opposite page:

Production of Yak-7s under way at Plant No.153 in Novosibirsk. The plant earned a reputation for building more than targets required, hence the notation on the propeller blades of the aircraft in the foreground: 'Extra to the Plan – Bound for the Front'.

Photographs on this page:

Top left: **The Yak-7B fighter effectively was a Yak-7UTI with an empty rear cockpit.**

Top right: **Plant No.153 built Yak-7B of the first production series under test by the NII VVS.**

Centre: **A Yak-7B with redesigned undercarriage doors undergoing static testing.**

Above left: **Yak-7B No.22-03 from the 22nd production series under test and evaluation at the NII.**

Above right: **Modified pre-production Yak-7B No.41-01 of the 41st series with tear-drop canopy and cut-down rear fuselage.**

Top: **Another view of modified pre-production Yak-7B No.41-01 of the 41st series with tear-drop canopy and cut-down rear fuselage.**

Above: **Yak-7Bs lined up at the pilot school named in honour of Josef Stalin.**

Photograph on opposite page:

Pilots were afraid of the canopy jamming on the Yak-7 and flew with it open, thus lowering performance. A canopy jettison system was introduced, illustrated under test in a wind tunnel.

nose-over angle owing to the forward shift of the centre of gravity as a result of the greater weight of armament. The use of brakes during landing was dangerous. Anti-nose-over provisions resulted in the installation of an additional 17.5 gallon (80 litre) fuel tank in the rear cockpit of production Yak-7Bs from late May 1942. Pilots were extremely displeased by this innovation, which, compounded by lack of tank protection, increased the risk of fire in the cockpit. Moreover, the increase in the Yak-7B's loaded weight was manifested in worsened performance (especially with regard to vertical manoeuvrability). Consequently in service units these tanks were removed without official approval.

The pilots of the 434th Fighter Regiment, operating in the zone of action of the 8th Air Army, were among the first to receive the Yak-7B M-105PA. This regiment reported to the Chief of the VVS Inspectorate, Colonel Vasily Stalin, the leader's son. The regiment, led by Hero of the Soviet Union Major Ivan Kleshchyov, was formed with highly experienced pilots, including four women: K Nechaeva, K Blinova, A Lebeda and O Shahova.

From its first flights using Yak-7Bs on 13th June until 3rd August 1942 this regiment flew 827 missions. A total of 55 Luftwaffe aircraft were shot down, exceeding the victories claimed by any other Soviet fighter division during the same period. The regiment's losses amounted to only three aircraft.

Engine augmentation was of primary concern during Yak-7B modification during the summer of 1942. The Yakovlev Design Bureau participated in an experiment to enhance boost from 910 to 950, 1,000 and up to 1,050 mm Hg. The influence of boost enhancement on speed and other performance parameters was also studied. The results were extremely encouraging, and formed the basis for a government directive obliging Vladimir Klimov, chief designer of the M-105 engine, to convert it from normal to augmented operation in the shortest possible time. The gudgeon pins were re-inforced and carburettor adjustment was changed to give reliability in the boosted regime. Designated M-105PF, the boosted engine had no other exceptional features compared with its predecessor.

Besides the engine uprating, provision was made to improve the Yak-7B's aerodynamics and decrease its loaded weight, mainly by lightening the airframe components while retaining their strength and the aircraft's operational qualities. Among the main changes introduced beginning with the 22nd batch were a lightened fuselage frame and undercarriage, along with the removal of the wiring to the rocket projectile launchers. As a result the Yak-7B M-105PF with the same armament and equipment proved to be 66 to 77lb (30 to 35kg) lighter than its progenitor.

In the course of the NII VVS tests, Yak-7B No.2241, powered by the M-105PF, reached maximum speeds of 319mph (514km/h) at sea level and 354mph (570km/h) at 12,000ft (3,650m). It climbed to 16,400ft (5,000m) in 5.8 minutes, and completed a 360° turn in 19 to 20 seconds. Height during an ascending turn increased from 3,300ft (1,000m) to 6,400 to 6,600ft (1,950 to 2,000m). Such a performance made it possible to fight the Bf109 successfully at low and middle altitudes.

On 20th August 1942 a whole division equipped with Yak-7B M-105PFs (the 288th Fighter Division led by Lt Colonel Konovalov) was committed over Stalingrad. From 7th to 12th September the 4th Fighter Regiment, acknowledged as the best in this Division, succeeded in shooting down 29 Luftwaffe aircraft, mainly Bf109Fs, in 30 combat missions, for the loss of nine Yak-7Bs. Achievements of other regiments of this division were more modest, and losses were higher.

Konovalov considered the Yak-7B to be outclassed by the German fighters with regard to performance. In a letter to Joseph Stalin he noted that the performance figures according the NII VVS test results, particularly maximum level speed, were unattainable under service conditions, and demanded that urgent measures be taken to rectify this.

Investigation by a commission sent to the front immediately revealed that the fighter's capabilities had not been properly exploited. It transpired that most pilots flew with their cockpit canopy open, owing to their anxiety about the hood locking in an emergency, and operated the engines at the reduced nominal rpm, thus reducing the fighter's performance by some 24.8 to 31mph (40 to 50km/h).

Another set of problems, not associated with the pilots, were traced to poor surface finish and ill-fitting hatches, cowlings and fairings as a result of field maintenance.

To show the pilots of the 288th Fighter Regiment the Yak-7B's capabilities given good maintenance and operational conditions, test pilot A Zaitsev flew a repeatedly repaired aircraft with a total operational flying time of 60 hours. Zaitsev achieved at sea level speed of

307mph (495km/h), compared with the 290 mph (467km/h) clocked before the aircraft was refinished.

The modifications to production Yak-7Bs were permanently adopted. In the winter of 1942-43, due to improved finishing, the maximum level speed of Yak-7Bs of the 41st batch increased by some 13.6 to 15.5mph (22 to 25km/h) compared with aircraft from the 22nd batch, and vertical manoeuvre was improved as well.

Yak-7R

Apart from the mass produced Yak-7 versions, several modifications of this aircraft were built in small batches or for development purposes. In August 1941, according to Alexander Yakovlev, two Yak-7R reconnaissance prototypes were tooled at Plant No.301 in Moscow. The prototypes, developed on the basis of the Yak-7UTI, were equipped with an AFA-IM camera and an RSI4 radio. This version was not put into production because of a front line demand for the single-seat Yak-7.

The Yak-7B version adapted for the reconnaissance role had the same structure as the Yak-7Rs produced in 1941, and was intended for reconnaissance at altitudes ranging from 1,000 to 10,000ft (300 to 3,000m). About 300 Yak-7 reconnaissance aircraft were manufactured at Plant No.82. Provision was made for the installation of the AFA-IM camera in production Yak-7Bs under field conditions.

Yak-7-37

Modification of the Yak-7B M-105PA to replace the 20mm ShVAK cannon by the Boris Shpitalny 37mm cannon (an installation developed on the LaGG-3), received the designation Yak-7-37. Offering a weight of fire of 9lb/sec (4.15kg/sec), the Yak-7-37 considerably outperformed all of the fighters engaged in combat at that time. Because of the new armament, certain changes were introduced in the fighter's structure. To accommodate the gun breech and keep the centre of gravity within an admissible range, the pilot's cockpit was moved 15.7in (400mm) aft and the rear cockpit was eliminated. The tailwheel was enlarged, and the wing was fitted with slats to prevent entry into a spin at low speeds and high angles of attack.

After brief tests in April-May 1942, a directive was issued authorising manufacture of a small batch of Yak-7-37s, and 22 without slats were produced at Novosibirsk in August 1942. For service trials these were transferred to the 42nd Fighter Regiment, operating over the North West Front. In 12 air battles in which the Yak-7-37s took part, ten German aircraft were shot down at the cost of four Soviet fighters lost and three damaged. The MPSh-37 cannon proved to be a troublefree and formidable weapon, a shell hit in a fuel tank causing an explosion and a hit in the wing resulting in a hole of 10.7ft² (1m²). One shell was practically sufficient to destroy an aircraft.

The fragmentation-incendiary and armour-piercing incendiary tracer shells, with an initial speed up to 3,000ft/sec (900m/sec), were not only used against air and ground targets, but also against ships of small displacement.

Yak-7 M-82

One of first attempts to achieve a radical improvement in the Yak-7's performance by adapting its airframe to take the air-cooled Shvetsov M-82 radial engine had been undertaken as early August 1941. The estimated performance of the Yak-7 M-82 prototype included maximum speeds of 320mph (515 km/h) at sea level and 382mph (615km/h) at 21,000ft (6,400m), and the ability to climb to 16,400ft (5,000m) in 5.6 minutes.

In January 1942, when Yakovlev OKB chief pilot Pavel Fedrovi began flying the new fighter, it became obvious that the attempt had failed. The anticipated considerable gain in speed was not achieved, at sea level the maximum speed being only 311mph (501km/h). The poor performance was mainly due to the inadequacy of a propeller diameter of 9ft 1in (2.8m), but the undercarriage was too short to allow the required 10ft 6in (3.2m) diameter propeller to be used. In May 1942 development of the Yak-7 M-82 was abandoned.

Yak-7PD

In creating the Yak-7PD high altitude fighter, the Yakovlev Design Bureau continued the line originating with the I-28 (Yak-5) of 1940.

Unlike the I-28 prototype, the Yak-7PD had a production airframe (from the 22nd batch) modified to take the prototype M-105PD fitted with the Ye-100 supercharger designed by V Dollezhal. At the same time the aircraft was fitted with an improved air intake, front and rear armoured glass and revised aft fuselage decking and cockpit canopy, other changes also being incorporated.

To keep the all-up weight to a minimum the armament was reduced to a single 20mm ShVAK cannon, increasing service ceiling to 37,000ft (11,300m) at the cost of the armament. This was the highest ceiling attained among Soviet aircraft in production at the time (the MiG-3 had been withdrawn from production by then). The inadequacy of the armament becomes obvious if the low probability of a second attack at altitudes close to the service ceiling is taken into account.

The manual control of the Yak-7PD's supercharger hydraulic governor proved a great distraction to pilots. Moreover, they could not simply keep up the necessary boost in accordance with a barometric pressure, and this hampered performance. Development of an automatically controlled hydraulic governor in October-November 1942, while updating of the M-105PD engine continued, proved unsuccessful.

Yak-7V

In late 1941 Plant No.301 and then Plant No.153 were converted to production of the single-seat fighters, and delivery of the fighter trainers was discontinued, the Yak-7UTI having been the only such variant to have been placed into production. By the middle of 1942 these Yak trainers were reaching the ends of their lives, and the VVS Combat Training Administration repeatedly appealed to the industry to develop a transitional aircraft to facilitate conversion from the Polikarpov U-2 to fighters.

The modifications to Yak-7V (vyvoznoy – introductory, or in western terms, advanced or conversion trainer) standard, carried out in late 1941 and based on operational experience with the Yak-7UTI, resulted in such an aircraft. Unlike its predecessor the Yak-7V was fitted with a fixed undercarriage that increased its operational life and excluded the probability of undercarriage collapse due to failures or errors by cadets. The trainer differed from the Yak-7 fighter in having its undercarriage legs mounted vertically to ease manufacture. There was no armament at all, and consequently the cowling had no cutouts or knock-out panels.

The Yak-7V was reliable and quite easy to master, yet could perform practically all the

aerobatic manoeuvres. Up to late 1943 510 had been delivered, thus meeting the VVS demands completely.

Yak-7PVRD and Yak-7L

As with other types, the Yak-7 was employed in test and experimental work. Based upon a UTI-26 airframe, the Yak-7PVRD (Pryamotochnii Vozdushno-Reaktivnii Dvigatel) carried a pulse jet under each wing to boost performance. Those who witnessed the test flights said that the engines sounded very similar to continuous cannon firing!

Another use of the Yak-7 for aerodynamic research was the Yak-7L (Laminarny) for investigation into laminar flow wings.

Yak-7D and Yak-7DI

The Yak-7D (Dalny – long range) was a forerunner of the Yak-9. Late in spring 1942, Alexander Yakovlev charged engineer Nikolay Skrzhinsky with the responsibility of developing a long range reconnaissance variant of the fighter to meet a military requirement. While designing the aircraft in May 1942, a series-produced Yak-7V fuselage incorporating elements of a Yak-7B fighter was used. The main structural innovation was an experimental wing that differed essentially from any designed before. Its framework consisted of two one-piece spanwise duralumin spars connected by six duralumin ribs and two wooden wingtip ribs. This framework was covered by a bonded Bakelite plywood and veneer skin.

With the same area of 184.6ft² (17.15m²) the wing span was reduced from 32ft 9½in (10m) to 31ft 11in (9.74m). The wingtips were less rounded owing to the possible installation of the slats. Eight fuel tanks with a total capacity of 183 gallons (833 litres) were packed into the wing, and one more tank of 20 gallons (92 litres) capacity was installed in the fuselage. The Yak-7D had no equal in range, flying 1,419 miles (2,285km) in 6.5 hours.

Photographs on the opposite page:

Top left: **The large gun barrel protruding from the spinner signifies a Yak-7-37, fitted with a lethal 37mm cannon.**

Top right: **The Yak-7 M-82 did not achieve the performance results hoped for it in state tests.**

Centre: **Work under way to achieve the M-82 powered Yak-7.**

Bottom: **High altitude Yak-7B with sealed cockpit.**

Above and left: **Two views of a Yak-7V conversion trainer on fixed ski undercarriage. Note that the undercarriage bay was partially faired over.**

Below: **Yak-7PVRD, fitted with two underwing pulse jets.**

Above: **Front view of the Yak-7L test-bed.**

Left: **The rear bay of the Yak-7PVRD housed photographic equipment to monitor the pulse jet's performance.**

Plan and front view, Yak-7A

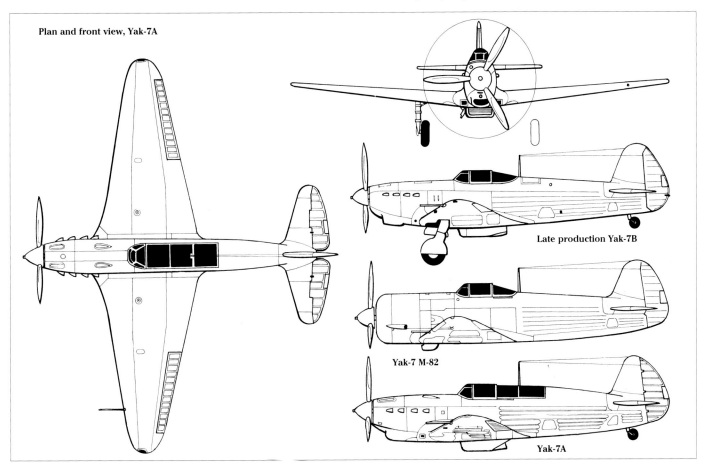

Late production Yak-7B

Yak-7 M-82

Yak-7A

In the middle of June 1942 Alexander Yakovlev gave an order to convert the Yak-7D into a long range fighter, designated Yak-7DI. Actually this was a production Yak-7B fuselage with an M-105PF engine and the Yak-7D experimental wing, in which only four protected tanks of 673 litres (500kg) were placed. An important innovation was the connection of all four fuel tanks with a supply tank by means of check valves, unlike the systems of the Yak-1 and Yak-7.

The rear fuselage fairing of the Yak-7DI was lowered and a teardrop canopy fitted, and the starboard UBS machine gun was removed to lighten the aircraft. Later, no modification of the Yak-9 with the M-105PF engine had such a machine gun.

The Yak-7DI could be used in two main forms; normal, and lightened by 440lb (200 kg) by limiting the fuel and oil carried. The flying weight in the first case was 6,690lb (3,035kg), and the Yak-7DI's performance was similar to that of the Yak-7B in series-production during the summer and autumn period of 1942, though its range was much greater. As a long range fighter this version could conduct long combat air patrols, bomber escorts, and similar tasks.

The lightened version weighed 6,250lb (2,835kg), and was light and pleasant to fly, being very manoeuvrable. Simulated aerial combat with a Messerschmitt Bf109F showed that at low altitude the Yak-7DI climbed 820ft (250m) higher than the German fighter during combat turns and, as a result, came close to the Messerschmitt's tail in three to four turns.

After brief production tests, the Yak-7DI successfully completed state testing in August 1942. Leading engineer A Stepanets wrote in the report that: 'the possibility of using the Yak-7DI in many versions, and its perfect performance, put it in first place among the other Soviet series-produced fighters'.

It was recommended that the Yak-7DI be placed into series-production just as soon as possible, and this was done without delay. During full scale production the aircraft was designated Yak-9.

Top: **Single-seat Yak-7D.**

Second from top: **Two-seater version of the Yak-7D.**

Third from top and bottom left: **Two views of the Yak-7DI, precursor of the exceptional Yak-9.**

Yak-9

Yakovlev's third basic fighter design after the Yak-1 and Yak-7, the Yak-3 was also used extensively during the Great Patriotic War. Structurally, it was a further development of the Yak-7, being much like the latter in shape but a better aircraft. On one hand this was quite natural, because the design of the new fighter benefited from two years' experience of production and combat operation of the Yak-7. On the other hand, the use of duralumin was now widespread, and no longer the problem it had been for the Soviet aircraft industry at the start of the war, and this enabled structural weight to be reduced. This saving could be used either to increase the fighter's fuel capacity or to give it more powerful armament or special equipment.

The Yak-9 was the most commonly used fighter of the Soviet Air Force. By the summer of 1944 the total number of Yak-9s, Yak-9Ts and Yak-9Ds in service was greater than the sum total of all other fighters in the Air Force inventory, and they replaced to a great extent the Yak-1, Yak-7B and LaGG-3, in addition to the Mikoyan MiG-3 and Polikarpov fighters.

The Yak-9 was produced at three large aircraft plants: No.82 in Moscow, which manufactured only the Yak-9 M-107A; No.166 in Omsk; and No.153 in Novosibirsk. The last plant had a daily output of 17 aircraft in mid-1944. The main characteristic of the Yak-9 was its easy adaptability to suit different applications and combat roles, including those of tactical fighter with conventional and heavy armament, long range escort fighter, fighter-bomber, photo-reconnaissance fighter, high altitude fighter interceptor, special purpose two-seat unarmed passenger aircraft and two-seat fighter trainer.

The Yak-9 underwent 22 basic modifications, and 15 of these went into series-production. It could be equipped with five new and modified powerplants, six number and volume combinations of fuel tanks, seven armament variations and two of special equipment. During six years of production, from October 1942 to December 1948, 16,769 series-produced Yak-9 fighters were delivered, 14,579 before the end of the war.

At first, Plant No.153 produced the lightened Yak-7DI fighter, without the two additional wing tanks. Although the flying weight increased by 77 to 88lb (35 to 40kg) compared with the prototype, owing to the usual penalties of mass production, the aircraft's performance did not suffer at all. Tests of the first Yak-9 production fighters showed that they retained their perfect manoeuvrability, which enabled them to outperform all of their contemporaries.

In late December 1942 Yak-9s took part in the Soviet counter-offensive at the battle of Stalingrad, the aircraft having entered service with the 1st Air Army on the Western Front a little earlier. Plant No.153 in Novosibirsk began to produce the Yak-9 from October 1942, and Plant No.166 in Omsk from January 1943, but in spite of all its advantages, production of this Yak-9 version was short-lived. Late in 1942 the Yakovlev OKB developed two more versions of the fighter which promised to be very successful. They replaced the current model, of which 500 had been built up to that time.

Yak-9T

The Yak-9T (Tyazhelowooruzhenny, heavily armed) was the first modification. It differed from prototype and series-production Yak-9s in having a 37mm OKB-16 gun (also designated 11P-37), later redesignated NS-37, in place of the 20mm ShVAK.

The design of this gun was begun in 1941 by a group of engineers led by A Nudelman and A Suranov, who continued the work of Y Taubin and M Baburin in designing large calibre aviation cannon. By the time the weapon attracted Alexander Yakovlev's attention, it had undergone successful flight tests on an LaGG-3. The gun was placed between the Yak-9's engine cylinders, as on the LaGG-3, firing through the hollow gearbox shaft and propeller hub, and was attached at two points to the engine and airframe. Its barrel projected 6⅓in (160mm) from the propeller spinner, increasing the length of the fighter from 27ft 10½in to 28ft 5in (8.5 to 8.66m).

The installation of this large and heavy 37mm gun, weighing 330lb (150kg), required considerable changes in the Yak-9's structure. The primary fuselage structure was strengthened, and in order to position the gun breech correctly and keep the centre of gravity in the same place the cockpit was shifted 15½in (400mm) rearward, improving the rearward view and making the fighter more manoeuvrable. Installation of the gun demanded improved standards of assembly, especially with regard to the fitting of pipelines, because the gun's great recoil when fired (approximately 12,000lb – 5,500kg) caused cracks and the destruction of whole pipeline units.

The Yak-9T was produced by the Yakovlev in January 1943, and underwent armament testing at the aviation armament firing ground in February 1943, under leading engineer L Los, and flying tests at the NII VVS in March, with leading engineer A Stepanets in charge.

At a weight of 6,668lb (3,025kg) the Yak-9T had a speed of 331mph (533km/h) at sea level and 370mph (597km/h) at 12,900ft (3,930m). Time-to-climb to 16,400ft (5,000m) was 5.5 minutes. Manoeuvrability proved sufficient, the time of turn being 18 to 19 seconds and climb during a combat turn being 3,600ft (1,100m). In March 1943 the Yak-9T was put into production. By the end of March three aircraft had been built, and in April the total was 75. Soon, 100 per month were being built.

Operational combat trials were conducted on the Central Front from 5th June to the 6th August 1943, during the Battle of the Kursk 'bulge', using 34 Yak-9Ts of the 16th Air Army. Half of the 110 enemy aircraft shot down fell to Yak-9Ts, the remainder being brought down by Yak-1s, Yak-7Bs and Yak-9s, Combat losses of the Yak-9T totalled 12, a third of the losses suffered by Yak fighters. While it was necessary to expend an average of 147 ShVAK rounds to bring down an enemy aircraft, only 31 rounds were required using the NS gun.

The appearance of the Yak-9T on the front had a great psychological influence on German troops. The Focke-Wulf Fw190A, with its great survivability and powerful armament, was used successfully in head-on attacks on Soviet fighters, but after the appearance of the Yak-9T head-on attacks were avoided by the Luftwaffe. The 37mm gun gave the Yak-9T considerably increased firing range, and as a result the likelihood of being shot down while attacking a bomber or reconnaissance aircraft head-on was greatly reduced.

The firing range for bombers was 1,600 to 2,000ft (500 to 600m), and for enemy fighters less than 1,300ft (400m). To disturb a bomber formation it was possible to fire from 3,300 to 4,000ft (1,000 to 1,200m), using fragmentation shells with time fuzes. Unfortunately, imperfect sights and limited ammunition supplies greatly hampered efficient exploitation of the Yak-9T's powerful armament.

The Yak-9T pilot had to fire short, aimed salvos of one, two or three shells, because 'long' salvos, amounting to only 30-32 shells of 37mm calibre, wasted ammunition and lost the sighting line by lowering the aircraft's nose, making it necessary to aim again.

Stability in flight while firing the gun depended on flying speed and the length of salvo. The higher the speed and the shorter the salvo, the better was stability. Lt Colonel F Shinkarenko, together with other commanders of the 240th Fighter Air Division, noted that the Yak-9T was considerably more stable while firing than the LaGG-3, which he had flown previously.

Yak-9Ts were highly appreciated by flying personnel and were widely used. By 1st July 1943 only a few dozen of the 153 Yak-9 tactical fighters deployed had the 37mm gun, but the Yak-9T soon became one of the principal Soviet fighters, 2,748 of the type being produced up to the end of war. Rapid mastering of production and operation of this combat aircraft played an important role in the attainment of air superiority by the Soviet Air Force.

Top: **View from above (note cockpit windscreen at left) of the engine compartment of the Yak-9T.**

Centre: **Yak-9T No.0121 was used for trial installation of the 45mm gun used on the Yak-9K.**

Bottom: **The gun barrel on the Yak-9T protruded considerably from the spinner.**

Yak-9D

The Yak-9D (Dalny – long range) was another mass produced modification of the Yak-9. In this variant the Yak-7DI's fuel system was introduced into series-production, four fuel tanks of 142 gallons (650 litres) capacity replacing the 96 gallon (440 litres) capacity tankage of the previous Yak-9 variants. In addition, the capacity of oil system was increased to 105lb (48kg). The need for such a fighter had arisen in 1943, when Soviet troops began to make deep penetrations of the German defences. The rapid advances and the lack of prepared forward airfields meant that the ground troops were in danger of being left without air support.

The Yak-9D had been developed by Yakovlev in January 1943 and was under state tests at the NII VVS until the end of February that year, under leading test pilot V Golofastov and leading flight test programme engineer I Rabkin. The tests showed that although the Yak-9D's maximum speed was equal to that of the Yak-9, the increase in flying weight to 6,871lb (3,117kg) made it less manoeuvrable.

A turn was completed in 19 to 20 seconds, time to climb to 16,400ft (5,000m) was 6.1 minutes, and the combat turn climb was 3,100ft (950m).

The aircraft was quickly put into series-production. A decision to produce the first 100 long range fighters was made before the official state tests had been completed, and all of the aircraft were assembled in spring 1943. Operational combat trials were held in the 18th Guard Fighter Air Regiment, commanded by Hero of the Soviet Union Lieutenant Colonel A Golubov, on the Western Front in August and September 1943.

The regiment had three Yak-9Ds in its inventory, plus 12 Yak-9Ts and seven Yak-9s, all of which were uniformly distributed among three squadrons and performed the same tasks. It carried out joint combat tasks with the Normandie squadron, which was based in the neighbourhood and had nine Yak-9Ds and eleven Yak-9s in August 1943. The French pilots plugged the outer wing fuel tanks and used only the wing root tanks.

During their operational trials with the 18th, three Yak-9Ds made 58 flights (average mission time 1.25 hours) and participated in seven air combats. Two Junkers Ju87s, two Focke-Wulf Fw190s and one Heinkel He111 were brought down. One Yak-9D was shot down and one damaged.

The combat experience showed that the joint combat operation of the Yak-9D and other Yak-9 versions was pointless, because all Yak-9 versions except the Yak-9D had less fuel capacity and consequently less endurance. In service with the 303rd Fighter Air Division, including the 18th Guard Fighter Air Regiment, the Yak-9D on average used only 59 gallons (270 litres), or 40% of its total fuel capacity, per flight. The remaining fuel only increased flying weight and made the aircraft more vulnerable.

While making a reconnaissance flight in a Yak-9D after the operational trials, Golubov, commander of the 18th Guard Fighter Air Regiment, came under anti-aircraft fire. The shells hit the cantilever fuel tank and the aircraft caught fire, and the pilot baled out of his burning machine at a low altitude almost at the moment it exploded. The heavily wounded commander was hospitalised.

As a result of the operational trials it was concluded that the Yak-9D was suitable for special combat tasks which the Yak-1, Yak-7B and La-5, with their limited fuel supplies, were unable to perform.

In the summer of 1943 the Yak-9D was put into series-production, and by June 1944 two plants had manufactured 3,058 of the type. Some series had a large calibre NS gun instead of the usual armament, effectively being revisions of the Yak-9T. These aircraft were given the designation Yak-9TD.

The Yak-9D was widely used for bomber escort missions deep into the rear of enemy territory, for air support of offensive tank operations, for combat air patrols, and in situations when the weather changed very quickly and it was difficult to return to airfields. It would undoubtedly have been more useful had it been provided with navigational equipment, in particular a gyro horizon and a radio compass (without which the possibility of flight in bad weather was limited), and there was also a great difference between its 562 miles (905km) range at cruising speed and the two-way radio communication distance of only 37 miles (60km).

In dogfights with German Fw190A-4 and Bf109G-6 fighters the Yak-9D had an advantage in horizontal manoeuvrability up to an altitude of 11,500ft (3,500m), but was inferior in speed even at low altitudes. This was why, during the official state tests of Yak-9D No.08-85 in January and February 1944, the speed was increased by 12,4mph (20km/h) due to fulfilment of the TsAGI recommendations; the fuselage and cowlings were sealed, the finish of the wing surface was improved, etc. The speed increased to 332mph (535km/h) at ground level and 367mph (591km/h) at 12,000ft (3,650m), while all other performance data remained the same.

The Yak-9D was not only used by the Red Army VVS. Late in 1944 some were turned over to the Bulgarian Air Force. The most successful Bulgarian pilot was Z Zakhariev, honoured with the title Hero of the Soviet Union.

Yak-9 M-106

While series-production continued, the Yakovlev Design Bureau designed further prototypes based on the Yak-9, one of the first being the Yak-9 M-106. The installation of the unsupercharged M-106 engine was similar to

One of the first production Yak-9 (No.0118) undergoing flight test at NII VVS.

Yak-9 among a variety of other types at the Byuro Novoy Tekhniki – Bureau of Modern Technology – part of TsAGI.

that in the Yak-1. Tests of the aircraft at the NII VVS showed an increase of maximum speed to 374mph (602km/h) at 10,600ft (3,250m), while the climb rate and take-off performance were improved.

The Yak-9 M-106 proved superior in simulated aerial combat with a Bf109G-2/R-6 seized during the Battle of Stalingrad. Test pilots noted that it was easier to handle compared with the overloaded Messerschmitt, which explained why the Yak-9 M-106 could gain the advantage in a dogfight. The cockpit visibility of the Soviet fighter was also better, but it was inferior in firepower and in performance at high altitudes. Insufficient development of the M-106 was the main problem in placing it into production in Novosibirsk, as it had been in Saratov with the Yak-1 M-106.

Yak-9P and Yak-9TK

Most effort was concentrated on improving the Yak-9's armament. The synchronised 12.7mm UBS machine gun with 200 rounds of ammunition replaced the ShVAK (SP-20) gun with 175 rounds. The modification was not difficult and the performance of the aircraft, designated Yak-9P (Pushechny, literally 'gunship', another way of referring to a high calibre armed fighter), was unaffected, although the salvo weight increased in proportion when compared with the Yak-9. The firing of the synchronised gun and machine gun though the propeller arc proved safe in all flight regimes and manoeuvres, but it did not enter series-production as it was decided to install a more powerful, larger calibre gun.

This thinking led to the next variant, the Yak-9TK (Tyazhelowooruzhenny, heavily armed; Krupnokaliberny, large calibre), to be used in the development of engine-mounted heavy cannon. In response to VVS requirements the aircraft was designed for the first time to mount any of the following guns: the 20mm ShVAK, the 23mm VYa, and the 37mm and 45mm NS. To install any of these weapons it was necessary only to change the attachment point and gun ammunition supply unit, and this could be done even under field conditions.

Pilot V Khomyakov and armament engineer A Aronov, who conducted flight tests of the Yak-9TK in October 1943, noted that the flying weight, centre of gravity position, handling qualities and performance varied in accordance with the gun installed. When firing the ShVAK and VYa cannon the recoil was imperceptible even at a minimum manoeuvring speeds, whereas the recoil of the NS-37 greatly affected handling. At an indicated airspeed of 186 to 217mph (300 to 350km/h) the aircraft swung violently, and it was only possible to aim the first salvo. With the NS-45, only a single shot could be fired at near top speed.

Yak-9K

Universal gun mountings found their application on the Yak-9 a later, when the Yak-9U went into series-production. The NS-45 attracted the designers' attention because of its unusual firepower, and work on its installation was continued on the Yak-9K. The fighter was modified to allow for the peculiarities of the NS-45. It had a thin-walled barrel and a small radial clearance between the barrel and the hollow engine gearbox shaft, owing to the small opening of the shaft (only 2.1in – 55mm). The recoil force of the 45mm gun was 40% greater than that of the 37mm cannon, so to reduce the recoil the barrel was fitted for the first time with a powerful muzzle brake that absorbed 85% of the recoil energy. The muzzle brake projected well forward of the spinner, making the overall length of the Yak-9K 29ft 1in (8.87m), as against 28ft 5in (8.66m) for the Yak-9T and 27ft 10½in (8.50m) for the standard Yak-9. The NS-45 was fed by a belt feed, as on NS-37. The ammunition comprised 29 shells, the pilot having a shell store counter in the cockpit.

Photographs on the opposite page:

Top left: **Yak-9D (No.0104) with four wing tanks instead of the Yak-9's normal two.**

Top right: **Field maintenance under way on a Yak-9D.**

Left: **Yak-9D in front line service.**

With its massive one-second salvo of 12.2 lb/sec (5.53kg/sec), the Yak-9K outperformed all other Soviet fighters and a great many foreign ones, only 'flying gun batteries' such as the Fw190A-6/R1 or Bf109G-6/R-6 having more powerful armament. But their two to four guns were installed under the wings, considerably reducing their performance, while the Yak-9K was similar to the main versions of the Yak-9 (it weighed 6,675lb – 3,028kg). The Yak-9K was developed by the Yakovlev OKB late in 1943, and underwent official state tests from the beginning of 1944 at the NII VVS.

From April to June 1944, after the results of the tests had been taken into consideration, a pre-production batch of 53 Yak-9Ks was produced at the Novosibirsk plant. Almost all were delivered to the 3rd Fighter Air Corps commanded by Lieutenant General Evgeny Savitsky. The first combat operation by these powerful fighters occurred in the middle of August 1944, when German bombers were seldom flying on the Eastern front, their function having been taken over by Fw190 and Bf109 fighter-bombers. The Yak-9K was used mainly to intercept these aircraft. In addition, the Yak-9Ks were often used as attack fighters against ground troops. With a single shot they could set on fire a vehicle, a wooden building or a locomotive, for example.

A participant in the operational tests, Major A Nikishin of the 812th Fighter Air Regiment, formulated the following Yak-9K combat tactics for use against German aircraft:

'The Yak-9K must be used together with Yak-3 light fighters, which provide cover. Dogfighting the heavy Yak-9K with light enemy fighters is undesirable because, owing to insufficient engine power, it has poor manoeuvrability in the vertical plane. It is necessary to attack enemy bombers suddenly from cloud or out of the sun, and to try to break up a combat formation. It is worth making the first attack from above at a distance of [1,300 to 2,000ft] 400 to 600m. A hit by one or two shells in any part of the bomber is sufficient to ensure its destruction'.

The structure of the Yak-9K was very strong. One aircraft was hit by a 20mm Oerlikon gun, suffering damage to a 10.7ft² (1m²) area of skin. Despite this, it was flown more than 62 miles (100km) and made a successful landing at its base.

However, drawbacks were also noted. The great recoil of the NS-45 affected the aircraft's structure, causing leakages of water and oil through pipe seals, and cracks in the pipes,

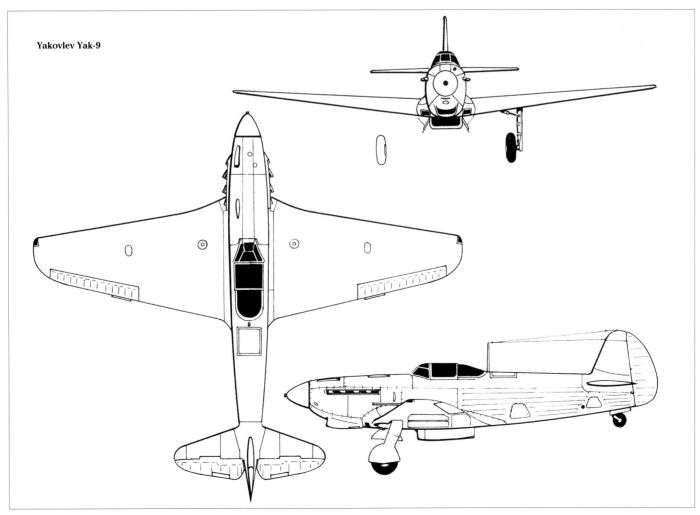

Yakovlev Yak-9

coolers etc. Insufficient reliability of NS-45 was the main reason that the Yak-9K was not put into mass production.

Yak-9B

A modification of the Yak-9D series-production aircraft, the Yak-9B tactical bomber was put into small scale production. (B for 'bombardirovschik – bomber; it was initially given the factory designation Yak-9L – lyukovy, literally 'doors'.) The modification consisted of replacing the rear cockpit with a bay housing four bomb bays, placed in pairs one behind the other, in each of which were suspended four FAB-100 220lb (100kg) bombs. Alternatively, four clusters of PTAB 2kg anti-tank bombs could be carried. The gun armament was the same as for the Yak-9D. The of bomb bay, considerably increased the aircraft's

combat capabilities. Without bombs Yak-9Bs could be used as tactical fighters; with bombs they became high speed fighter-bombers for use against small, well protected targets.

The normal bomb load was limited to 440lb (200kg) to comply with the centre of gravity position and the limits of longitudinal static stability. The flying weight with that load was 7,398lb (3,356kg), and the aircraft could be flown by pilots of average skill. Yak-9Bs carrying the 661 to 881lb (300 to 400kg) bomb load were considered overladen, and thus loaded was used only for special operations and flown only by highly skilled pilots.

Yakovlev completed conversion of the tactical fighter into a fighter-bomber rather quickly, and in March 1944 the Yak-9B was ready for flight testing. State flight tests were conducted in four stages, and continued throughout the summer. During that time stability and controllability were assessed, and spin tests were conducted.

A series-production batch of 109 Yak-9Bs was then built, and in December 1944 the aircraft were delivered to the 130th Fighter Air Division, commanded by F Shinkarenko. By 20th February the Yak-9Bs had flown some 2,500 bombing missions, destroying 29 tanks, 11 armoured vehicles, more than 1,000 vehicles and numerous depots and trains. Despite this, the Yak-9B's operational trials proved unsatisfactory. The main reasons were the lack of a special bomb sight and bad handling qualities when loaded with bombs.

Principal defects included a tendency for the bombs to hang up in a shallow dive, and difficulty in loading the bomb bay. In adopting the report of the operational tests, A Novikov, Commander-in-Chief of the Red Army VVS, wrote: 'The Yak-9B had very severe limitations in combat operation; it is not expedient to deliver it to combat units. Pilots did not want to fly the aircraft. The chief designer must redesign the aeroplane'.

Photographs on the opposite page:

Top: **Another of the heavy weapon Yak-9 versions; the Yak-9-37 with a 37mm gun mounted between the engine cylinder blocks.**

Left: **Yak-9P prototype, with three 20mm guns, during flight tests, 1943.**

Right: **Wreckage of a German aircraft with a hole blown in it courtesy of a Yak-9K.**

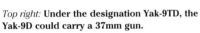

Top right: **Under the designation Yak-9TD, the Yak-9D could carry a 37mm gun.**

Above left: **Yak-9K with 45mm cannon, which underwent service testing with the 3rd Fighter Wing in August and September 1944.**

Left: **The 45mm NS-45 cannon.**

Above: **Another gun permutation, the Yak-9-23 prototype.**

Below: **The Yak-9TK was capable of being armed with any cannon from 20mm to 45mm calibre.**

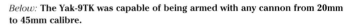

Yak-9DD

Born of the same idea that created the Yak-7D – the Yak-9DD followed the same modifications. (Production designation was Yak-9Yu; Dalny – long range, the 'DD' perhaps indicating extra long range!) In 1944 a fighter with a range over 1,242 miles (2,000km) was needed, and the main innovation of the Yak-9DD was its wing structure. After first strengthening the wing ribs, the designers installed eight metal fuel tanks in the wing, and the resulting 185 gallon (845 litre) fuel capacity allowed the fighter to fly 823 miles (1,325km) at high speed and 1,419 miles (2,285km) at optimum cruising speed.

Only one 20mm ShVAK gun was retained from the type's original armament, but great attention was devoted to special equipment. A gyro horizon, an RPK-10 radio compass and an American-built SCR-174N radio were installed; enlarged oxygen bottles were also incorporated. The new radio provided two-way communication at 3,300ft (1,000m) over a range of 93 miles (150km), and reception at 23,000ft (7,000m) over 186 miles (300km).

In spite of its increased take-off weight of 7,466lb (3,387kg), complex handling and inferior manoeuvrability, the Yak-9DD could be operated even from remote airfields. Its great range and endurance permitted its use as an escort fighter and for special missions behind the forward battle area.

From May 1944, following state tests, full scale production of the Yak-9DD was initiated, 399 aircraft being manufactured. These differed from the prototype mainly in their navigational equipment.

The first batch of 40 Yak-9DDs underwent operational trials in the 368th Fighter Air Regi-

ment, commanded by Major M Zhylin, during the period when German troops were being routed in Eastern Prussia. The aircraft were used to provide cover for Petlyakov Pe-2 and Tupolev Tu-2 bombers. It proved very difficult to escort the Tu-2 because its speed was almost equal to that of the Yak-9DD. The fighter's great flying weight, great mass and lack of power were the main reasons for the deterioration in its performance and manoeuvrability. Its pilots nicknamed it the 'flying cistern'.

Many complications arose during its operational use, including rapid tyre wear and fatigue failure of the tailwheel forks. Irregular flow of fuel from the tanks led to airlocks, causing engine cut-outs in flight.

Nevertheless, the Yak-9DD amply demonstrated its ability as a long range fighter in August 1944, when 12 aircraft led by Major I Ovcharenko made a 807 miles (1,300km)

Yak-9L fighter-bomber prototype, as tested in 1944.

Maly Teatr, a famed Russian theatre, sponsored a squadron of Yak-9B fighter-bombers, the legend reads, 'From the Maly Theatre to the Front Line'.

Top left: **Production Yak-9B with Guard insignia under going operational tests with the 130th Fighter Division.**

Top right: **One of the major drawbacks with the Yak-9B was the difficulty in loading the bombs into its tiny bomb bay. They had to be hoisted by cable through the dorsal hatch.**

Above: **A Yak-9B damaged by the bombs it was carrying.**

Right: **Bomb release by a Yak-9B. A lack of a bomb sight hampered the type's capability.**

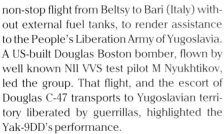

non-stop flight from Beltsy to Bari (Italy) without external fuel tanks, to render assistance to the People's Liberation Army of Yugoslavia. A US-built Douglas Boston bomber, flown by well known NII VVS test pilot M Nyukhtikov, led the group. That flight, and the escort of Douglas C-47 transports to Yugoslavian territory liberated by guerrillas, highlighted the Yak-9DD's performance.

During the whole period of the type's presence in Bari there were no failures. During each combat mission (of which they flew a total of 155) they twice crossed the Adriatic Sea, flying from 248 to 372 miles (400 to 600km) over water and landing on small airfields amidst mountains, in fair winds or strong crosswinds.

Yak-9M

The Yak-9M, with the Klimov VK-105PF (designated M-105PF before spring 1944), was a modification of the Yak-9D. It differed from latter only in having the cockpit moved 15¾in (400mm) rearwards, similar to the Yak-9T. This modification was favourable in manufacturing terms, allowing use of the fuselage structure of either the Yak-9T or Yak-9D, depending on production requirements. Moreover, the Yak-9M was considerably changed and developed to improve operational capabilities and maintenance. All structural and manufacturing defects mentioned in the NKAP and VVS defect lists and protocols were removed.

Here a digression must be made. Late in spring 1943 a manufacturing defect was introduced in Yak aircraft built at Novosibirsk, and as a result a considerable proportion of the Soviet fighter force was rendered unfit for action. Alexander Yakovlev recalled:

'In June 1943 I and Deputy People's Commissar [of the Aircraft Industry] Peotr Dementiev, being in charge of series-production, were summoned to the headquarters of the Supreme Commander in Chief [Joseph Stalin]. Marshals Vasilevsky and Voronov were also in the office with Stalin. We at once noticed pieces of cracked wing fabric on the table, and understood what was the matter. The forthcoming conversation promised to be unpleasant.'

'It was pointed out that, at one of the eastern factories where Yak-9s were manufactured, the wing skins had begun to crack and come off. The delamination of wing skins during flight had become a common occurrence, and was caused by the poor quality of the cellulose nitrate paint delivered by one of the chemical enterprises on the Ural, where the product was checked in a hurry and substitutes were used in the production process.'

'The paint was unstable, and when subjected to the influence of atmospheric conditions it cracked and the fabric skinning of the wing began to come away from the plywood.'

'We already knew about this defect, and had been trying hard to eliminate it.'

'Stalin, pointing out to the pieces of cracked skin on the table, asked: "Do you know anything about that?", and read a report from the Air Army, stationed near Kursk, sent together with samples of the skin.'

'We answered that we knew of some cases of delamination of the skin. He interrupted us: "What cases? The whole fighter force is unfit for action. There are dozens of such cases. The pilots are afraid of flying. Why is it so?"'

'Joseph Stalin took up a piece of fabric, the paint surface of which was completely cracked and was falling off, and showed it to us. "Oh, but do you know that only the most perfidious enemy could do such a thing? Producing aircraft at the plant that proved unfit for service at the Front. The enemy could not damage us so cruelly; he could invent nothing worse. This is work for Hitler!"'

The two deputies of the People's Commissar of the Aircraft Industry understood perfectly what could become of them with such an accusation of sabotage, and promised to take special measures immediately. Demen-

tiev began to act especially energetically and effectively to remove all the defects. Thanks to special measures taken by the People's Commissariat, the wing skins of many hundreds of aircraft were strengthened in the space of two or three weeks. But, unfortunately, the defect was still in existence later on, though not on such a large scale.

This problem was solved on the Yak-9M when the wing was re-inforced. The thickness of the skin was increased, a Bakelite plywood was used and the area of skin stuck to the fuselage was increased, and as a result the strength of the wing and fuselage met the technical requirements.

Fuel tankage and armament of the Yak-9M were similar to those of the Yak-9D, while the arrangement of the pilot's cockpit resembled that of the Yak-9T. Moving the cockpit rearwards by 15½in (400mm) as compared to the Yak-9D did not reduce the pilot's view, but considerably improved the aeroplane's anti-nose-over angle. In addition a jettisonable pilot's cockpit canopy, an automatic water temperature controller, a radio control button and an engine intake dust filter were fitted.

The handling qualities and performance of the Yak-9M were basically the same as those of the Yak-9D and Yak-9T. The modification was undertaken at Plant No.153, where the Yak-9D and the Yak-9T were manufactured. All Yak-9s commencing from the 25th batch were designated Yak-9Ms. The Yak-9M of the pilot batch underwent official state tests at NII VVS in December 1944, under leading test pilot V Ivanov and engineer G Sedov.

With a weight of 6,823lb (3,095kg) the fighter attained a maximum sea level speed of 321mph (518km/h) and 356mph (573km/h) at 12,300ft (3,750m), and its climb rate and manoeuvrability were similar to those of the

Externally, only the larger radio aerial shows this to be a long range Yak-9DD.

Yak-9. Such a performance was unsatisfactory in late 1944. It is sufficient to say that the Yak-9M was 31mph (50km/h) slower than the Yak-3, and it was also inferior to the updated Focke-Wulf and Messerschmitt fighters.

The Yak-9M was in series-production from May 1944 until June 1945, when production of the Yak-9U with the VK-107A was commenced, a total of 4,239 aircraft being built. From October 1944 VK-105PF2 boosted (for the second time) engines began to be delivered to Plant No.153, and these were installed at the Yak-9M. Before that, all VK-105PF2 engines had been installed in the Yak-3.

Yak-9PD

The Yakovlev OKB continued the design work on the Yak-9PD high altitude fighter that had begun with the I-28 and continued with the Yak-7PDs. The work began in November 1942, but owing to the delay in the delivery of the M-105PD engine the aircraft were not ready until April 1943. Their structure was the same that of series-production Yak-9s, but they had only one 20mm ShVAK gun.

All five Yak-9PDs went for operational trials with the 12th Guard Fighter Air Regiment of the Moscow Air Defence Force, commanded by Major K Marenkov. By 25th June the high altitude fighters had completed 69 flights, 39 of which were flown at altitudes greater than 32,800ft (10,000m). These tests showed that the engine was underdeveloped. In particular, continuous climb at optimum rate was impossible; at 23,000ft (7,000m) the water and oil temperatures exceeded their limits, and in order to continue the flight it was necessary to break off from the climb and fly level to allow the engine to cool. Naturally, this greatly reduced the climb rate.

According to the resulting report, operational trials of the Yak-9PD failed because of the engine defects, insufficient service ceiling (38,200ft – 11,650m) and poor armament.

In the summer of 1943 the main threat to Moscow Air Defence was the Junkers Ju86R-1 high altitude reconnaissance aircraft, with its turbosupercharged engines and pressurised cockpit. It often appeared high in the sky over Moscow. On 2nd June 1943 an attempted interception of a Ju86 was made by a Yak-9PD flown by Lt Colonel L Sholohov, Air Corps inspector of handling qualities. The Soviet pilot took off from the Central Airfield in Moscow and quickly caught up with his quarry, which was 3,300 to 4,900ft (1,000 to 1,500m) higher.

Sholohov saw the aircraft's yellow markings and the vague shapes of the Luftwaffe crosses, and was ready to open fire, but then his engine's oil pressure fell sharply and the windshield became covered with ice. Having lost sight of the Junkers, the Soviet pilot broke off his pursuit and was forced to land.

Other attempts to intercept Ju86R-1s were also unsuccessful. On 23rd August 1943 the Commander-in-Chief of Western Front Air Defence, G Gromadin, reported to the VVS Command that the question of a high altitude fighter was still unsolved.

But the Yakovlev Design Bureau continued its work in concert with the LII. One was fitted with an experimental M-105PD engine with the gear ratio of the centrifugal blower increased from 8.48 to 9.72. The service ceilings of the water, oil and fuel systems were also increased.

The Yak-9PD prototype was given a new wing of increased area and 3ft 3⅜in (1m) greater span. Together with a reduction of the weight to 6,272lb (2,845kg), this increased the aircraft's service ceiling to 41,000ft (12,500m), but many of the defects of the previous model remained. The next step was the installation of the prototype M-106PV engine, with service ceiling increased from 27,900 to 31,200ft (8,500m to 9,500m). On 16th October 1943 this machine reached an altitude of 43,000ft (13,100m).

In 1944 Yakovlev undertook one further and what proved to be the most successful attempt to develop a high altitude fighter interceptor. As before, the main aim in the effort to increase the service ceiling of the aircraft was improvement of engine capabilities and the powerplant installation in general at high altitudes, plus a lightening of the airframe.

The fighter was powered an M-106PV. To reduce air temperature with supercharger the engine had a water-methanol system (50% methanol plus 50% water). The cooling system permitted a continuous climb up to the service ceiling of 44,300ft (13,500m) without intermediate levelling off. An additional pump in the fuel system provided a normal fuel supply at high altitude. The weight of the aircraft's structure was reduced to 5,511lb (2,500kg), the lowest of all Yak-9 variants.

The success of this work allowed the construction of a batch of 30 Yak-9 M-106PVs, the combat performance of which was not put to the test because there was not a single flight by a German aircraft over Moscow in the summer of 1944.

The greatest shortcoming of the Yak-9 high altitude aircraft was its lack of a pressurised cockpit. A prototype developed by Alexey Scherbakov was not ready until May 1944, and subsequent unsuccessful tests proved it to be a failure.

Yak-9R

The Yak-9R short range reconnaissance aircraft was developed from the two fuel tank Yak-9, while the long range variant was based on the airframe of the Yak-9D. The latter was lightened by the removal of a machine gun and its ammunition, and was equipped with AFA-IM or AFA-3S/50 cameras, installed behind the cockpit.

This retrofitting was often carried out under field conditions, but in the summer of 1943 35 Yak-9Rs were produced at Plant No.166 in Omsk for operational testing by the 48th

The cockpit position on the Yak-9M was moved rearwards. Comparison of the cockpit to the under fuselage radiator could define the model.

Production Yak-9Ms in front line operation.

Guards Air Regiment, commanded by Lt Colonel Sadov.

Although the tests were successful, they showed that in spite of its high speed and manoeuvrability the Yak-9R could not replace the Petlyakov Pe-2 heavy twin, especially in the face of strong counter-attacks by German aircraft.

Yak-9V

The work of designing a two-seat 'introductory' fighter based on the Yak-9 continued. The Yak-9V differed from its forebear in having a retractable undercarriage and armament, comprising a 20mm ShVAK engine-mounted gun. These aircraft were produced in series only after the Second World War. Yak-9Vs also formed the basis of the Yak-9 Kur'yer (Courier) liaison aircraft.

Yak-9U

Yakovlev understood that, for all its good qualities, the Yak-9 could not meet the requirements needed of a fighter in the last days of the war, so it was decided to improve the structure as far as possible without crucially changing the technology of Yak-9 production. The development of such ideas in November 1943 resulted in a production standard for the following year. This, the most updated version of the Yak-9, was designated Yak-9U (Uluchshenny – improved).

Essentially, its aerodynamics were improved, but an attempt was also made to reduce flying weight, increase reliability in operational use, and improve the pilot's working environment. Most of the innovations were taken from the Yak-1M, highly praised by the specialists.

The following differences are especially worthy of mention:

Wing: The centre section was changed owing to the installation of an oil-cooler of the Yak-1M type.

Fuselage: The fabric skin replaced one of plywood and airtightness was improved. Control of the aircraft on the ground was enhanced.

Armour: The armoured backrest was cut off at the top, front and rear armoured glass was installed, and armoured head rest and arm rests were provided to increase pilot protection in combat.

Powerplant: By increasing the boost from 1,050 to 1,100mm Hg, the power of the engine was also increased. A further increase in speed was obtained by using a redesigned propeller.

New and more powerful water and oil coolers were installed in line with TsAGI recommendations, and the structure of the inlet pipe was changed. The self-sealing fuel tanks were made of varying thickness to reduce vulnerability and to reduce weight.

The Yak-9PD with both oil and water coolers. It wears the white fin tip of the 12th Guard Air Regiment, part of Moscow's air defence system.

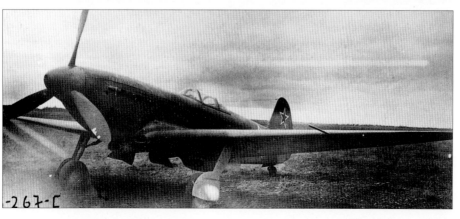

One of the Yak-9PD high altitude fighter prototypes with refitted VK-106PV engine and increased span wings.

In Yakovlev's opinion the optimum armament would consist of a single 23mm gun and two 12.7mm UBS large calibre machine guns. But because only the VYa-23 gun was in production in November 1943, this was installed between the cylinders. The better NS-23, which was lighter and had a higher rate of fire, was later incorporated in the Yak-9S, but unfortunately that gun was not used in combat by Yak aircraft. The VYa-23 was a powerful and safe weapon, giving a good account of itself on the Ilyushin Il-2. The high initial speed of the VYa-23 shell, combined with its ability to inflict heavy damage, permitted successful combat not only against airborne targets, but also against ground targets. A shell hit in a fuel tank caused an explosion, and one in the wing would produce a large rupture. Such VYa shells could punch a hole in 1in (25mm) armour. Even so, VVS Command thought that the VYa-23 gun was too heavy and had too low a rate of fire to be introduced it into the fighter armament inventory, and only an experimental batch was built.

Great attention was devoted to the comfort of the pilot. The radio was controlled by buttons on the throttle quadrant, and the arrangement of the equipment was rational and close to the standard.

Externally, Yak-9Us differed from Yak-1Ms only in having a shorter undercarriage and unslotted flaps.

When he flew the Yak-9U in January 1944, pilot V Khomyakov noted that it did not differ from production aircraft in handling, remaining stable in flight, easy to control and not tiring to fly.

The aerodynamic refinements and increase in engine power markedly improved performance. Maximum speed at sea level rose to 346mph (558km/h), and at 12,600ft (3,850m) it increased to 385mph (620km/h). Reduction of the aircraft's weight to 6,393lb (2,900kg) improved vertical manoeuvre; time to climb to 16,400ft (5,000m) was 4.8 minutes – less than a Messerschmitt. In a combat turn the Yak-9U climbed 3,900ft (1,190m), while the best Bf109 variant, the 'G-10, climbed only 3,940ft (1,200m).

In the state test report it was recommended that all of the aerodynamic and weight improvements mentioned above be introduced on production aircraft.

If the Yak-9U VK-105PF2 was part of an evolutionary line of development, the intensive growth of the power of the water-cooled-engine was 'revolutionary'. An engine created by the Vladimir Klimov Design Bureau and designated M-107A had undergone 50 hour tests as long ago as late 1942. In a test report of December 1942 it was noted that the M-107A could be used in combat operations, though it could not be the principal engine for mass production at that time.

Yak-9 Kur'yer (Courier) liaison aircraft, a version of the Yak-9V.

The first series-produced engines were installed in the Yak-9, and production tests of the Yak-9 M-107 were conducted by Pavel Fedrovi. On 25th February 1943 test pilot Peotr Stefanovsky was conducting the last test of the aircraft before it went for its official state tests when an accident occurred. Stefanovsky remembered:

'Having climbed to an altitude of [3,300ft] 1,000m, I began to make a level pass over the airfield to determine the maximum speed. The aircraft sped along faster and faster. Glancing at the cowling, I noticed smoke. A moment later flames leapt up. The engine was on fire'.

While trying to land the burning aircraft the pilot became unconscious, and as a result the aircraft was damaged beyond repair. Despite this mishap, Pavel Fedrovi wrote to Alexey Shakhurin, People's Commissar of the Aviation Industry, saying that the Yak-9 M-107A could be compared only with Nikolay Polikarpov's I-185 prototype. The latter achieved about the same speeds, but its handling was trickier and manoeuvrability worse because of its greater weight. Fedrovi asked the Commissar to issue an order that M-107As be installed in 10 to 15 production Yak-9s as a priority, for operational tests. However, the accident and difficulties with the completion of the as yet unperfected powerplant delayed the work by more than a year.

Not until December 1943 was a new prototype ready as a 'back-up' of the Yak-9U with a VK-105PF2 used in the initial tests. The engine mounting was changed, the radiators were given greater cooling surface, and fuel and oil

capacity was increased. Compared with the first model, a standard 20mm ShVAK engine mounted cannon was installed. Because of the heavier engine, flying weight increased to 6,944lb (3,150kg).

In its official tests in January-February 1944, in the charge of pilot A Proshakov and leading engineer A Stepanets, the aircraft reached a speed of 372mph (600km/h) near the ground and 434mph (700km/h) at an altitude of 18,000ft (5,500m). Following these tests, the NII VVS concluded: 'With regard to its performance at altitudes ranging from ground level to [19,700ft] 6,000m, the Yak-9U with VK-107A is best among the known Soviet and foreign fighters'.

The Yak-9U VK-107A's handling qualities were good and within the capabilities of pilots of average skill, to the same extent as the Yak with the VK-105PF. Series production began in April 1944 at three aviation plants. At that time Plant No.166 in Omsk was undoubtedly the most advanced, and it was there that the first production Yak-9U was built. It proved to be aerodynamically inferior to the prototype. However, at a weight of 7,041lb (3,194kg) and with the engine full out (3,200 rpm), the aircraft reached a speed of 349mph (562km/h) at ground level and 406mph (654 km/h) at 16,900ft (5,150m), and the time to climb to 16,400ft (5,000m) was 5.2 minutes, so the performance was sufficiently high.

But defects in the new engine adversely affected the production aircraft more than the prototype. The faults of the VK-107A the leakage of oil from the breather and the front seals of the reduction gear's hollow shaft, an unacceptable drop in oil pressure in the climb, and vibration with a silencer and under other conditions. However, the main defect was undoubtedly the overheating of oil and water,

The Yak-9U VK-107A prototype.

The Yak-9U with VK-105PF2 entered flight test in 1943.

which also occurred at the combat power setting (3,200 rpm). At maximum level flying speed the temperature became unacceptably high, even with the radiator intakes fully open.

Climb at the optimum rate had to be interspersed with short horizontal flights to allow the oil and water to cool. Pilots in combat units found it very difficult to operate the aircraft, and often failed to get the best performance from their machines.

The 42nd Guard Fighter Air Regiment, commanded by Y Alexandrovich, was among the first units to receive the Yak-9U VK-107A. To gain a visual comparison of the manoeuvring qualities of the Yak-9U and Bf109G, the command organised an unusual competition. Test pilot L Kuvshinov arrived at the front line aerodrome and piloted a captured Messerschmitt in mock combats and vertical fights against the Yak. Kuvshinov's 'enemies' from the 42nd regiment, I Gorbunov and G Pavlov (both Heroes of the Soviet Union) outmanoeuvred him despite his skill. During combat the Yak-9U climbed 4,100 to 4,200ft (1,250

to 1,300m) and always seemed higher than Bf109G. This demonstration gave the pilots of the regiment confidence.

Wide use of the new fighters began at the end of the summer of 1944, and the enemy became acutely aware of the new aircraft and their good combat qualities. At the same time great difficulties were encountered in front line operational servicing. Overcoming these difficulties with minimal cost to the fighter's performance was the main task facing technical personnel.

It was therefore recommended that use of the engine combat power setting be avoided until the powerplant was perfected and maximum speed flights at 3,000rpm had been successfully accomplished. Although this meant a slight decrease in speed and rate of climb, it made flying safer.

In October 1944 the VVS Command decided that it was now possible to organise operational tests of the Yak-9U. All 32 test aircraft were taken from the assembly line of Plant No.82 in Moscow, which had just begun production of the modern fighter. Necessary

finishing of the fuselage and the engine was carried out before the tests started.

The important task of carrying out the tests was entrusted to the pilots of the 163rd Fighter Air Regiment of the 3rd Air Army (regiment commander Lieutenant Colonel V Ukhanov). The main opponents in air combats were Fw190As, 'Fs and 'Gs trying to prevent the annihilation of Baltic troop concentrations.

During the tests, which continued almost to the end of 1944, 398 flights were made by the Yak-9Us and 299 air combats took place. According to the regiment's documentation the combat loss ratio was 28 to 2 in the Yak's favour. Moreover, in one of the two losses the pilot of the damaged aircraft managed to get back across the front line before baling out.

In combat with the different Fw190 variants the Yak-9U showed complete superiority, particularly in vertical fights. Especially noteworthy was the achievement of Lieutenant Petrov, who shot down five German aeroplanes. Lt Kapustin fought alone against two Focke-Wulfs and shot them both down.

Not only the performance, but also the servicing of the Yak-9U was highly praised by the command, pilots and technicians of the 163rd Fighter Air Regiment. It was noted that young pilots and technicians of average skill could soon master the aircraft. The fighter was easy to service, preparation for combat not exceeding 30 minutes.

The enemy also formed a high opinion of the Yak-9U. After landing in Soviet territory by mistake, a German pilot said at his interrogation: 'Luftwaffe Command issued an order not to fight with the Yak-type aircraft with no aerial masts'. At the end of the war German air ace Walter Wolfrun, who flew the Bf109G and was an experienced pilot with many victories, wrote:

'The best fighters I met in combat were the American P-51 Mustang and Russian Yak-9U. Both of these types obviously exceeded all Bf109 variants in performance, including the 'K'. The Mustang was unmatched in altitude performance, while the Yak-9U was champion in rate of climb and manoeuvrability.

Tests carried out at the NII VVS at the end of 1944 and the beginning of 1945, using an Omsk series-production Yak-9U, showed that most of the defects mentioned earlier had been overcome. Speeds of 357mph (575 km/h) at ground level and 417mph (672km/h) at 16,400ft (5,000m) were reached, close to official requirements.

A total of 3,921 Yak-9Us was built, about 2,500 of them before the end of the war, and the type was widely used on all fronts.

Yak-9UT

The Yak-9U and the other Yak variants were used to test a range of armament alternatives; 23mm, 37mm and even 45mm guns. To install the last of these it was necessary to remove the synchronised machine guns, B-20 synchronised guns being installed instead.

Production Yak-9U (No.0316) at NII VVS.

The device in front of the windshield of this operational Yak-9U is a camera-gun.

The possibility of installing different engine-mounted guns without the need for airframe modification was the design's most valuable feature, allowing a rapid change of armament, according to VVS requirements, during series-production. The aircraft was designated Yak-9UT. Clearly, each armament installation a different effect upon weight, centre of gravity position and flying performance, but the speed was the same as the Yak-9U. Handling was almost the same except for elevator load, which was heavy, this being the aircraft's most serious shortcoming.

Main advantage of the Yak-9UT was its heavy salvo weight, 13.2lb/sec (6kg/sec), using the NS-37 and two B-20s. This was a formidable figure at the end of the Second World War, even for the Germans, who were trying to increase the salvo weight of their aircraft as much as possible for combat with the redoubtable Boeing B-17 Flying Fortress.

Testing of the Yak-9UT began in March 1945 and was completed, very successfully, after the war's end, but many of the 282 built took part in air combats over Berlin during the last days of the war.

Yak-9UV

The Yakovlev OKB completed its work on a piston-engined fighter trainer, developing the Yak-9UV (Uluchshenny Vyvoznoy, improved introductory trainer), with a VK-107A. Armament consisted of a single engine-mounted B-20 gun and special equipment allowed it to operate at altitudes up to 13,100 to 14,750ft (4,000-4,500m) in daylight in clear visibility conditions.

Although new coolers were installed, the engine still frequently overheated in nominal

performance regimes (3,000rpm) owing to the frequent take-offs and landings. For this reason engine power was limited up to 2,800rpm and speed reduced by 21.7 to 56mph (35 to 90km/h), depending on altitude.

Shortly after the war the Yak-9UV was delivered for its official state tests, but its time was past. The VVS now needed new jet aircraft, and consequently new jet fighter trainers were also required.

Yak-9P

The ultimate development of the Yak-9 series was the Yak-9P (Pushyechnyi, cannon) fighter, which differed from the Yak-9U mainly in having an all-metal wing. The war's end brought a change of requirements. A mixed structure was rational when the front line constantly demanded more aircraft and there was a shortage of duralumin, and it facilitated mass production. Its disadvantages were its comparatively short service life, subject to the influence of weather and climatic conditions, its rapid loss of strength and, as a result, deterioration of the machine's aerodynamics.

The new requirements for peacetime fighters were long life and high production quality of airframe, engine, armament and equipment. The change to all-metal construction had taken place gradually during the war, as the USSR's production of duralumin increased. The first step in that direction was the development of the Yak-7DI, a prototype of the Yak-9 fighter, in the summer of 1942. This aircraft had duralumin spars instead of heavy wooden T-section units. Finally, the all-metal Yak-9P was designed in 1946.

Modification of the Yak-9P was carried out during 1946-47. The all-metal version of this variant had increased fuel capacity (as in the Yak-9D), and equipment included a radio compass, a radar identification system, an ultra-violet lamp to illuminate the instrument panel, and a camera gun.

The Yak-9P was in series-production until December 1948. In total 801 were built, including 29 with metal wings and 772 all-metal aircraft. It was the last Yakovlev piston-engined fighter.

I-28 (Yak-5)

While previous aircraft developed by the Yakovlev OKB were intended for operation at low and middle altitudes, the I-28 (also called Aeroplane No.28, I-26V or high altitude I-28V) offered maximum performance at higher altitudes to operate as an interceptor in service air defence units.

Unlike other Russian designers, Alexander Yakovlev had a taken an interest in the prototype Klimov M-105PD engine, equipped with the Ye-100 two-stage supercharger designed by V Dollezhal. This supercharger was provided with an hydraulic governor to ensure smooth variation of the supercharger impeller in accordance with altitude. In contrast to the automatically controlled supercharger of the German DB601E engine, the Dollezhal supercharger was manually controlled, increasing pilot workload and preventing effective exploitation of engine output.

The I-28 was built within three months and made its maiden flight, with Pavel Fedrovi at the controls, on 1st December 1940. It differed from the I-26 in having landing gear taken from the UTI-26 (Yak-7UTI) and somewhat extended slats. The wingspan was reduced from 32ft 9¾in to 31ft 11in (10 to 9.74m), and the rounded wingtips were of greater radius.

The estimated performance of the I-28 was: maximum speed, 320mph (515km/h) at sea level and 403mph (650km/h) at 29,500ft

(9,000m) with supercharging; time-to-climb to 16,400ft (5,000m), 5.2 minutes; service ceiling, 39,400ft (12,000m). Because of the manually controlled supercharger, engine output had to be varied smoothly while changing from one supercharger speed to another. In contrast, the M105P engine had a two-stage, two-speed, mechanically-controlled supercharger which caused a drop in the performance of I-26 and I-301 fighters within the altitude range where supercharger speed had to be reset.

However, the M-105PD engine appeared to be underdeveloped. It emitted smoke, vibrated and leaked oil, and the pilot had to make an emergency landing on the first flight. Although the engine was uprated and underwent trials in February-March 1941, the Yak-5 programme had been already cancelled. In 1942 the design bureau continued the development of a high altitude fighter based on the the production Yak-7.

I-30 (Yak-3 of 1941)

The I-30 prototype fighter was the last of the pre-war family of Yakovlev Design Bureau prototypes including the I-26, I-28 and UTI-26. In the creation of the I-30, all of the experience gained while developing its predecessors was exploited, thus enhancing the the I-30's qualities.

The propeller was fitted with an easily removed spinner, the exhaust pipes provided some measure of thrust augmentation and the control column was refined, being similar to that of the Messerschmitt Bf109. The I-30's wing structure featured metal spars and removable outer panels to accommodate two unsynchronised 20mm ShVAK cannon. The engine mounting was made detachable.

Certain features of the earlier prototypes, such as further-forward centre of gravity position, landing gear similar to that of the UTI-26 and slats like those installed on the I-28, were inherited by the I-30. According to the pilot's reports the radio equipment met the tactical fighter operational requirements. Reliable two-way communication with the ground was ensured up to 124 miles (200km).

The I-30, powered by an M-105PD, made its first flight on 12th April 1941, with Pavel Fedrovi at the controls. The intended M-105PD engine fitted with the Dollezhal Ye-100 supercharger was unfinished, and was be replaced by the M-105P, and with this engine installed the fighter underwent state trials. At a loaded weight of 6,900lb (3,130kg) it achieved maximum speeds of 295mph (476km/h) at sea

Photographs on this page:

Top: **The barrel of a 37mm cannon protruding from the spinner of a Yak-9UT.**

Centre: **Just discernible in this view of a Yak-9UT is the muzzle damper on the nose cannon.**

Bottom: **Yak-9UT undergoing tests at the NII VVS in winter 1945.**

Top: **First production Yak-9UV trainer, built at Plant No.82 with the unusual production No.0000.**

Centre: **Manufacture of Yak-9Us continued after the end of the war. Illustrated is a 1946 standard example under test at the NII VVS.**

Bottom: **A Yak-9P undergoing spinning tests post-war. Note the spin recovery parachute housed on the special rig underneath the rudder and the bay for photographic equipment behind the cockpit.**

level and 354mph (571km/h) at 16,000ft (4,900m), climbed to 16,400ft (5,000m) in seven minutes and reached a service ceiling of 29,500ft (9,000m). The increased weight raised the landing speed to 88mph (142 km/h), but due to the effective use of brakes the landing run remained the same.

The slats decreased the minimum flying speed and almost eliminated the risk of entering a spin owing to incorrect handling. The increase in total fuel capacity from 672 to 844lb (305 to 383kg), plus the installation of an auxiliary tank, improved the fuel system and gave the aircraft a range of 605mph (975km) at long range cruising speed. On 8th April 1941 a government directive was issued to withdraw the Yak-4 twin-engined attack aircraft from production at the Moscow plant in favour of the I-30, which was designated Yak-3. On 12th April 1941 it was decided to place the Yak-3 in production at the Saratov plant.

Yakovlev did not hesitate to replace the Yak-1 with its successor, the Yak-3. Responding to Yak-1 critics at a pre-war conference, he repeatedly assured them that the Yak-3 (I-30) would have none of the Yak-1's drawbacks.

However, the Yak-3 (I-30) had not entered series-production. At first, the setting up of Yak-3 production was postponed until 1942, but then the decision to put the aircraft into series-production was abandoned. The reasons given included the shortage of aluminium owing to the industry's redeployment to the east, and the fall in fighter mass production associated with the introduction of new aircraft at the beginning of the war.

Yakovlev continued to revise the structure of the I-30 prototype. In May 1941 tooling of the second prototype had begun. The cockpit developed for it was made the standard for all VVS fighters. Aiming at large scale production, Yakovlev reverted to the wooden, integral wing without slats. Fitted with an M105PD engine, the second prototype, crashed in the course of its flight tests at the LII and was not rebuilt.

Yak-3

The Yak-3 was the last and most attractive member of the Yakovlev fighter family of the Second World War. Development of this fighter, which benefited from experience gained during the first two years of war, produced an essentially new aircraft. It represented the culmination of a considerable amount of work carried by the Yakovlev OKB, production plants and research organisations seeking to improve the aerodynamic characteristics, structure and combat performance of fighter aircraft, and embodied all changes incorporated in the earlier Yak-1, Yak-7 and

Yak-9. When it reached the tactical regiments in the summer of 1944 the Yak-3 fitted with the VK-105PF was the lightest and most manoeuvrable of all fighters on both sides.

By comparison with its brother, the Yak-9 with VK-107A, the Yak-3 was marginally inferior in performance but had a better power-plant providing more reliable operation and greater capability. The Yak-3 VK-108 prototype reached 462mph (745km/h), the highest speed ever attained by a Soviet piston-engined aircraft and close to the pre-jet era limit.

The Yak-3's immediate predecessor was the Yak-1M prototype, nicknamed 'Moskit'. Its wing was of similar construction to that of the Yak-9, comprising a set of metal stringers, metal and wooden ribs, and plywood skinning. Compared with its predecessors, the wing area of the Yak-3 was reduced by 24.7ft^2 (2.3m^2) to 159.8ft^2 (14.85m^2), and its span was also reduced, to 30ft 2in (9.2m). The outer wing panel attachments allowed a damaged unit to be replaced under field conditions.

The fighter's control system, fuselage and undercarriage were taken from the production Yak-1. Unlike that machine, however, the Yak-3 had three fuel tanks with a total capacity of 595lb (270kg); two in the outer wing panels and a feeder tank in the wing centre section. The engine cooling system had a more powerful ventral coolant radiator with deeper accommodation in the fuselage. Two circular oil radiators arranged in parallel were installed in the wing centre section, beneath the cockpit floor, allowing the engine to have a smooth lower cowling and improving the aircraft's lines.

Armament, instrumentation and armour were nearly the same as those of the Yak-1 with improved pilot view, armour and armament. The Yak-1M's loaded weight was 5,853lb (2,655kg), roughly 551lb (250kg) less than a production Yak-1. This weight saving was achieved mainly by the reduction in wing area and substituting wooden longerons for duralumin ones (330lb – 150kg).

The prototype was completed in the middle of February 1943. Its refinement continued for the whole of the spring under the direction of chief engineer M Grigorev, who had played an active role in the development

Top: **The I-28 was the first aircraft to be powered by the turbosupercharged M-105PD.**

Second from top: **View of the I-28 showing the M-105PD engine, water cooler and synchronised machine gun. Note the pitot head carried under the port wing.**

Third from top: **The first I-30 showing off the generous flap area.**

Bottom: **The second I-30 took advantage of developments to date.**

and construction of the Yak-1M. The initial test flight was performed by Pavel Fedrovi, the chief pilot of the Yakovlev Design Bureau. Flight trials at the NII VVS continued for the whole of June 1943, with A Proshakov as senior pilot and A Stepanets as chief engineer. The aircraft displayed excellent performance.

The design bureau believed that the potential of the aircraft was not exhausted. On Yakovlev's insistence additional tests were performed to evaluate the changes resulting from augmenting the boost of the M-105PF engine from 1,050 to 1,100mm Hg. Initially Vladimir Klimov, the chief designer of the engine, increased the boost in the first stage of the turbosupercharger. The additional tests revealed that the boost augmentation increased maximum speed by 3.7 to 4.3mph (6 to 7km/h) at low altitudes, reduced the time to reach 16,400ft (5,000m) by 0.1 minute, increased the altitude increment in a 360° turn by 164ft (50m), improved take-off performance and had no noticeable effect on water and oil temperatures.

Later the supercharger's second stage was also augmented. The engine with its supercharging increased to 1,100mm Hg was designated M-105PF-2.

Because of its excellent flying and combat capabilities the Yak-1M was among the best fighters at the end of Second World War. According to NII VVS test results it excelled the production Yak-9 in maximum speed by at least 15.5 to 21.7mph (25 to 35km/h) over the whole altitude range, the German Fw190A-4 at altitudes up to 27,250ft (8,300m) and the Bf109G-2 at altitudes up to 18,700ft (5,700m). The Yak-1M displayed extraordinary superiority at low altitude, while at higher altitudes the German aircraft had the edge. At 23,000ft (7,000m), for instance, the Bf109G-2 was nearly 31mph (50km/h) faster than the Soviet fighter. In climb rate up to 16,400ft (5,000m) the Yak-1M was unrivalled among the world's fighters, including various Bf109 sub-types.

The reduction in wing area did not adversely affect the aircraft's take-off, diving and spinning qualities. Due to good handling qualities the Yak-1M, like the Yak-1 and Yak-9, could be flown by pilots of average or lower abilities.

The trial report noted: 'as far as control effectiveness and tractability are concerned (with regard to the effort exerted on control levers), the Yak-1M, like the Spitfire [which had been tested in the NII VVS in June 1943], is a model for any fighter either domestic or foreign'. Insignificant deficiencies typical of Yak fighters, such as oil overheating at the optimum climb rate, poor venting, oil leakages, and limited radio transmission range, did not mar the overall impression.

In parallel with the state trials of the first Yak-1M, work on the second prototype was completed under the direction of Grigorev.

Construction of this aircraft was better in every respect. For example: fuel tank compartments were separated from the cockpit by hermetically sealed partitions; fabric skinning was replaced by plywood and the canopy was jettisonable. A VISh-105SV-01 propeller with a lightweight hub and profiled blade root section was used.

Changes were introduced in the armament as well. The ShVAK cannon gave way to the ShA-20M experimental cannon designed by Boris Shpitalny, and a pair of 12.7mm Berezin UBS machine guns were installed using the same arrangement as in the Yak-7B.

The navigation equipment was improved. Among the appreciated innovations was a remote radio control using a button on the throttle lever. The aerial mast was rejected on the second prototype in favour of a single beam antenna.

The take-off weight was kept the same at 5,864lb (2,660kg). After brief development tests the Yak-1M was moved to the NII VVS at the beginning of October 1943 for its state trials. These were successfully completed in ten days by pilot A Proshakov and engineer G Sedov. In addition to its enhanced performance (the second prototype reached 354 mph – 570km/h at sea level and 404mph – 651km/h at 14,100ft – 4,300m, and completed a 360° turn at low altitude in only 16 to 17 seconds), an improvement in engine temperatures had been achieved by a more effective radiator bath installation, modification of the intake duct profiles, and increasing the angle of air-duct flap deflection.

The Yak-1M became the first Yakovlev fighter capable of performing long duration level flight at maximum speed, as well as climbing at the maximum climb rate with an engine operating at nominal revolutions of 2,700rpm. Thorough wiring and screening increased the radio reception range to 56 miles (90km), a noteworthy achievement for Soviet fighters of the time.

Test pilot V Khomyakov, who made the initial flight tests of the aircraft, wrote:

'The cockpit is comfortable. The forward vision is improved. The disposition of the instrumentation and control levers is suitable and almost completely meets the standard cockpit requirement. Handling is tractable: the aircraft is stable in flight and easy to handle. It has excellent climb rate and manoeuvrability in both the vertical and horizontal planes. By comparison with its predecessor the Yak-1M's performance has been markedly improved'.

This report and others triggered a Government directive to launch production of the Yak-1M in its second prototype form under the designation Yak-3 in October 1943.

Preparations for Yak-3 production started immediately, but the production tempo could not be allowed to falter during conversion to the new aircraft. So Plant No.292 mastered the manufacture of the fighter in the winter of 1944 while maintaining its average monthly output of 250 Yak-1s. First production Yak-3 was rolled out on 1st March 1944.

Production aircraft differed from the second prototype in numerous but minor ways. Initial production Yak-3s had exactly the same armament as the Yak-1, as production of the ShA-20M cannon had not yet begun. Because of low manufacturing standards, production Yak-3s had poorer flight performance than the second prototype. The loss of speed was about 9.3 to 12.4mph (15 to 20 km/h), and time to attain an altitude of 16,400ft (5,000m) increased by 0.5 minute. Increased loads on the control surfaces had an adverse effect on horizontal manoeuvrability.

The new warplanes began to reach fighter aviation regiments during the summer of 1944, when the Soviet Command was preparing to launch large scale offensives. Yak-3 service tests were conducted by the 91st Fighter Regiment of the 2nd Air Army, commanded by Lt Colonel Kovalev, in June-July 1944. The regiment was tasked with gaining supremacy in sky. In the course of the L'vov operation almost half of its pilots flew their first combat mission, and all of the regiment's pilots had begun a higher standard of training. During the service tests 431 missions were flown, including interception, on-call missions, missions for building up forces, and freelance operations. Twenty Luftwaffe fighters and three Junkers Ju87 bombers were shot down in air combats, while Soviet losses numbered two Yak-3s shot down, plus three that were damaged by German anti-aircraft defences but managed to reach Soviet-held territory.

Operations showed that the innovative Soviet fighter could catch its German counterparts in horizontal flight as well as in climbing and diving manoeuvres. The Yak-3 gained a substantial advantage over the Fw190A within two nose-to-tail turns, and over the Bf109G within three turns.

A large dogfight occurred on 16th June 1944. Both sides built up their forces, with the result that 18 Yak-3s opposed 24 German fighters, and 15 Luftwaffe aircraft were shot down for the cost of one Soviet fighter destroyed and one damaged. Next day, Luftwaffe activity over that section of the front had virtually ceased.

Service tests indicated that the Yak-3 appeared to be most suitable for air defence missions. Its use for close support of ground troops, bomber escort and so on was less worthwhile owing to its limited supply of fuel, average mission duration being limited to about 40 minutes.

The tests also revealed certain short-comings of the initial production Yak-3.

Right: **Yak-1 with improvements following joint TsAGI recommendations. It was very similar to the Yak-1M.**

Centre: **The second Yak-1M which served as the prototype Yak-3 with the oil cooler mounted in the wing root leading edges.**

Bottom: **The second Yak-1M (Yak-3) undertook 24 test flights in the space of one week during 1943 and was highly acclaimed.**

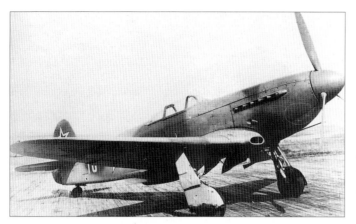

Top left: **Production Yak-3 with VK-105PF from the Saratov Plant No.292.**

Top right: **Yak-3 No.0111 was tested by the NII VVS.**

Centre: **Also tested at NII VVS was Yak-3 No.9626.**

Bottom left: **The team of NII VVS test pilots and engineers in front of the Yak-3. Aleksey Stepanets is in the centre of the group.**

Bottom right: **The lightweight, high speed and manoeuvrable Yak-3 became a favourite of Soviet pilots.**

Photographs on the opposite page:

Top: **Yak-3s could easily operate from unprepared surfaces.**

Below: **Pilots of the French Normandie-Niemen unit brought their Yak-3s home to France.**

Instances were pointed out when a main undercarriage leg folded during take-off or land-ing and taxying, owing to failure of the undercarriage ram and oleo strut attachment. However, in general the Yak-3 was easy to operate, and maintenance crews and pilots found it easy to adapt to the new aircraft.

Assessing the fighter, Lieutenant General Walter Schwabedissen wrote in the book *The Russian Air Force in the Eyes of German Commanders*: 'Whereas the German Bf109G and Fw190 models were equal to any of the afore-mentioned Soviet fighter models in all respects, this cannot be said of the Soviet Yak-3, which made its first appearance at the front in the late Summer of 1944. This aeroplane was faster, more manoeuvrable and had better climbing capabilities than the Bf109G and Fw190, to which it was inferior only in arma-ment'.

Luftwaffe fighters in combat with the Yak-3 tried to exploit surprise. This happened on 17th September 1944, when Fw190s attacked a formation of three Yak-3s of the 66th Fighter Air Regiment over the Riga district of the front by coming out of the sun, shooting down two of the Soviet aircraft. On 23rd September the regiment gained its revenge when a Yak-3 formation led by Major I Vitkovsky shot down seven Fw190s in a single dogfight.

During the autumn a set of modifications was introduced in Yak-3 construction. Starting from the 13th batch, the second 12.7mm UBS machine gun was reinstated, since such armament appeared to be more suited to the needs of service units. Starting from the 16th batch the capacity of the fuel tanks was increased by about 4.4 gallons (20 litres).

Initially there was lack of close control of the loaded weight of production Yak-3s, which reached 5,974lb (2,710kg). From August 1944 to April 1945 the weight ranged between 5,795 and 5,934lb (2,629 and 2,692kg), these limits being regarded as satisfactory.

To discover the reasons behind the deterioration in performance, an investigative study was undertaken by the Yakovlev Design Bureau in co-operation with the LII, TsAGI and the production plants. As result the performance level was restored in October 1944. This work was conducted in parallel with an escalation of production. While the Yak-3's share of the total output of the Saratov aircraft plant in May 1944 was 29%, in June it comprised 52%, in July it was 84% and in August it had already reached 100%. Thus the production line's conversion to the new fighter had proceeded without any reduction in overall output.

Plant No.31 in Tbilisi mastered the Yak-3 even more successfully. The fighters manufactured there were of higher quality and had more powerful armament than those made in Saratov. But most important was the weak-

ening of the wing caused by unsatisfactory bonding of the wing skin with the structure. For this reason more than 800 Yak-3s built at Plant No.292 at the end of 1944 were withdrawn from operations at the order of A Novikov, Commander-in-Chief of the Red Army Air Force, and sent for repair.

Fighters from one of Plant No.31's first batches were flown operationally and with success by the 303rd Fighter Division, commanded by Major-General Georgy Zakharov. The Division incorporated the French Normandy volunteer regiment. The Normandie-Niémen converted rapidly to the Yak-3, and shot down 29 Luftwaffe aircraft without any losses to themselves on 16th October 1944. M Alber, R De LaPuap, J Andrew and M Lefevre, pilots and commanders of the Normandy Regiment, were made Heroes of the Soviet Union. After the war's end the regiment departed for France with 40 Yak-3s that had been presented to it. These served in the regiment and then in French training schools until 1956, without an accident. One example has survived and is displayed in the Musée de

l'Air near Paris. In Russia, a single Yak-3 is preserved in the Yakovlev Design Bureau Museum. This aircraft was presented to Major Boris Yeremin by Ferapont Golovaty, a collective farmer.

In total, 4,848 Yak-3s were produced, of which 3,840 were built at the Saratov main plant and 737 were delivered after the war.

Yak-3P

The Yak-3P variant was largely delivered after the war, its distinctive feature being its modified armament comprising three of the new B-20 cannon, one hub-mounted and two synchronised. These provided a total weight of fire of 7.2lb (3.25kg), compared with the 5.9lb (2.72kg) of the standard Yak-3, but did not increase the aircraft's 'dry' weight.

The Yak-3P was stable during cannon firing throughout the speed range and in all evolutions, and the effect of recoil on aiming was insignificant. Trials of the modified Yak-3P

Soviet and French pilots stand in front of a Yak-3 carrying a Guards logo on the nose. Second from the left is Major General G Zakharov, Commander of the 303rd Fighter Air Division, which incorporated the Soviet-French Normandie-Niemen squadron, later made up to an air regiment.

were undertaken at the NII VVS during March and April 1945, and it was then placed in production. A total of 596 Yak-3Ps was built at both plants.

Yak-3T

Even more powerful armament was installed in the Yak-3T, built at the Yakovlev Design Bureau in January 1945. The synchronised cannon were mounted in a similar fashion to those of the Yak-3P, but the 20mm engine-mounted cannon was replaced by the lightweight 37mm N-37 engine-mounted cannon designed by A Nudelman. The Yak-3T differed externally from the production Yak-3 in having a muzzle brake protruding from the propeller spinner. This absorbed up to 75% of the N-37's recoil energy.

This powerful cannon installation resulted in some redesign of the basic structure, the cockpit being moved 15¾in (400mm) aft, similar to that of the Yak-9T, fuel tank capacity being reduced by 3.7 gallons (17 litres) and the fuel tank protection being removed. In spite of the effort devoted to reducing the aircraft's weight it rose to 6,075lb (2,756kg), resulting in some deterioration in performance.

Trials showed that the fighter was still easy to handle and the armament was effective against air targets as well as trains, trucks and armoured personnel carriers. In firing three or four rounds the recoil did not affect sighting, and this allowed aiming fire for long bursts that could not be achieved on the Yak-9.

However, significant shortcomings were also revealed. The powerplant, along with the new cannon, posed certain problems. Faulty engine operation was evident in smoke emission, ignition spark failure, and drops in oil and fuel pressure, which made it difficult to fly normally. These problems ruled out production of the Yak-3T.

Yak-3PD

On the basis of the Yak-3 airframe, Yakovlev created its best high altitude interceptor. On 8th September 1944 the high altitude version of the VK-105PF, equipped with the Dollezhal supercharger and designated VK-105PD, was installed in a production airframe, and the aircraft underwent trials at the NII VVS just before the end of the war. According to the LII report, the aircraft had its wing area increased by 5.4ft² (0.5m²), the engine drove a prototype high altitude propeller, and the intake duct was moved in front of the water radiator tunnel. To reduce the temperature in the supercharger the engine was provided with a system of water/spirit solution injection between the supercharger stages.

Take-off weight was reduced to 5,767lb (2,616kg) by limiting the armament to a single engine-mounted NS-23 cannon. Test pilot Sergei Anokhin reached 37,750ft (11,500m), but it was estimated that a service ceiling of 42,500ft (13,000m) was attainable. A speed of 430mph (692km/h) was reached at 35,600ft (10,850m).

The VK-105PF engine was then installed, but before new trials commenced at the LII some refinements were introduced at the initiative of test pilot I Shumeyko, who was responsible for flight testing. This resulted in the installation of a system for bleeding air from the supercharger into the atmosphere, providing steady engine running at high altitudes, permitting flights at over 43,600ft (13,300m) with normal engine operation.

On 26th June 1945 Shumeyko achieved 441 mph (710km/h) at an altitude of 36,000ft (11,000m), and on 6th July he attained a ceiling of 42,600ft (13,000m). It was pointed out that flights above 42,600ft (13,000m), using an oxygen mask, were required for special high altitude training.

Yak-3RD

A fighter prototype embodying a mixed powerplant was developed by conversion of a Yak-3. In addition to its VK-105PF2 piston engine, the aircraft was fitted with an RD-1 rocket motor developed by Valentin Glushko, for use as a booster.

The RD-1, which gave 661lb (300kg) thrust for three minutes, was installed in the extreme tail, beneath the rudder. It was mounted on a special support and housed in a cowling that was easily removed and did not protrude beyond the external lines of the fuselage. The modified aeroplane was designated Yak-3RD (Reaktivnii Dvigatel – rocket motor).

In the course of the development tests, test pilot Viktor Rastorguev performed 21 flights, in eight of which the RD-1 was used. In one flight, on 11th May 1945, the aircraft reached 485mph (782km/h) at 25,600ft (7,800m). The RD-1's automatic control system was prone to fail, causing a spontaneous engine cut-out during the flight. An accident resulted in destruction of the motor nozzle.

The Yak-3RD was being prepared to appear in the flying parade on Air Fleet Day, but two days before the event it crashed and pilot Victor Rastorguev was killed. Although the cause of the accident was not determined, it was evident that the RD-1 had not exploded and had not been destroyed. It is presumed that there was a failure in the flight control system.

With the advent of turbojets in the postwar period, the work of fitting piston engined aircraft with liquid rocket boosters lost its urgency and was abandoned.

Yak-3 VK-107A

An important part of the Yakovlev Design Bureau's work on the Yak-3 concerned the mating of the airframe with more powerful engines. The installation of the VK-107A did not require significant changes to the airframe, although the cockpit had to be moved aft by 15¾in (400mm). The more powerful engine made it necessary to increase fuel tankage to 1,141lb (518kg), armament being reduced to a pair of synchronised B-20 cannon mounted over the engine.

Two prototypes were built at the beginning of 1944. The first undertook the development tests until the end of November 1944, being flown by Pavel Fedrovi. The second was used for the State Acceptance Trials.

Although its loaded weight had increased to 6,578lb (2,984kg), the Yak-3 VK-107A was acknowledged as a fighter of low weight and small dimensions, and having some excellent qualities; wing loading was 41lb/ft² (201 kg/m²) and power loading was 44lb/hp (20kg/hp). These characteristics, coupled with its aerodynamically clean lines, gave the aircraft an outstanding performance. Its maximum speed at sea level was 379mph (611 km/h), increasing to 447mph (720km/h) at 18,800ft (5,750m), and it could reach 16,400ft (5,000m) in 3.9 minutes and gain 5,00ft (1,500m) while performing a climbing turn. All of these figures are recorded in the test records.

Test pilots Yu Antipov and A Proshakov noted that, owing to destruction of their main

bearings, VK-107A engines had failed to meet their anticipated Service life expectancy.

On the basis of the state trials it was concluded that the Yak-3 VK-107A was the best among indigenous and foreign fighters with regard to flight and combat performance at altitudes ranging from sea level to a service ceiling of 38,700ft (11,800m). However, although the Red Army Air Force needed such an aircraft, it was further noted that a large number of serious defects, especially in the powerplant, needed to be resolved before it was put into production.

Yak-3 VK-108

The VK-107A engine providing a maximum output of 1,500hp (1,119kW) was replaced by the VK-108 with a maximum output of 1,550hp (1,156kW) in the critical heat regime. Test pilot Viktor Rastorguev pointed out the outstanding flying qualities of the aircraft.

On 21st December 1944 the Yak-3 powered by the VK-108 was accelerated to 462mph (745km/h) at 20,600ft (6,290m). This was only 6.2mph (10km/h) lower than the absolute world record set in 1939 by the Messerschmitt Me 209V-1. The Yak-3 reached a height of 16,400ft (5,000m) in only 3.5 minutes, and made almost a three-point take-off. But engine troubles again precluded regular flight tests, and vibration and smoke emission led to the abandonment of the trials and the work was discontinued.

Yak-3U

In the Yak-3U the Yakovlev OKB attempted to combine the good aerodynamics of its fighter with the merits of Arkady Shvetsov's engine. In January 1945, when the aircraft was being tooled, the Shvetsov ASh-82FN was acknowledged as a reliable and developed engine, while the Klimov VK-107A (not to mention the VK-108) was capricious and frequently failed. The bureau succeeded in creating an exceptionally lightweight fighter to be mated with the ASh-82FN.

While the Yak-3U's gross take-off weight was only 6,155lb (2,792kg), compared with 7,164lb (3,250kg) for the Lavochkin La-7, its maximum speed of 438mph (705km/h) at 20,000ft (6,100m) was higher than that of the La-7 and its climb rate was excellent. However, the wing had been moved forward to improve stability, and the consequent decrease in nose-over angles had an adverse effect on the aircraft's landing and taxying qualities.

Although the Yak-3U was completed, there was no need for it and the project was cancelled in October 1945.

The Musée de l'Air at Le Bourget proudly displays a Yak-3 painted in Normandie-Niemen colours.
Ken Ellis

Top: **Yak-3 from the Tbilisi plant, No.31.**

Centre: **The Yak-3 with the VK-107A was a superb combination.**

Bottom: **Judging by the shell hole just behind the cockpit, the pilot of this Yak-3 was extremely fortunate to walk away from a forced-landing.**

Photographs on the opposite page:

Top: **French Yak-3 in post-war markings.**
Philip Jarrett collection

Centre left: **Peasant farmer Ferapont Golovaty and Soviet ace Guard Major Eremin at the hand over of Golovaty's second gift to the VVS, a Yak-3.**

Centre right: **Yak-3P with three 20mm B-20 guns.**

Bottom: **Golovaty's gift Yak-3 survives to this day and is preserved in Moscow.**

Top left: **Yak-3 fitted with exhaust shrouds to increase the aircraft's maximum speed.**

Centre left: **The cannon protruding from the spinner defines a Yak-3T.**

Bottom: **The VK-107A-powered Yak-3 in which Yuri Antipov reached the speed of 447mph (720km/h).**

Photographs on the opposite page:

Top left: **Many of the later Yak-3s built at Tbilisi were natural metal with a red stripe.**

Top right: **The VK-108 engined Yak-3 prototype.**

Bottom: **Yak-3 flown by René Chatte of the Normandie-Niemen squadron.**
Philip Jarrett collection

Yak-3UA

In June 1993 a Yak-3 could be found in the static at the Paris Airshow as part of the Yakovlev exhibition. The Yakovlev OKB had come to an arrangement with a company in California, USA, to build a run of 20 'new production' Yak-3s with the designation Yak-3UA for the growing number of 'warbird' owners.

Construction is undertaken at Orenburg and many of those working on the project worked on late production Yak piston-engined fighters and trainers, having come out of retirement. The aircraft are powered by Allison V-1710 V-12 which powered the Curtiss P-40, among other types. The first 'production' Yak-3UA was delivered to the Museum of Flying at Santa Monica in 1991.

For technical data, see Tables F and G, pages 177 and 178.

Yakovlev Yak-3.

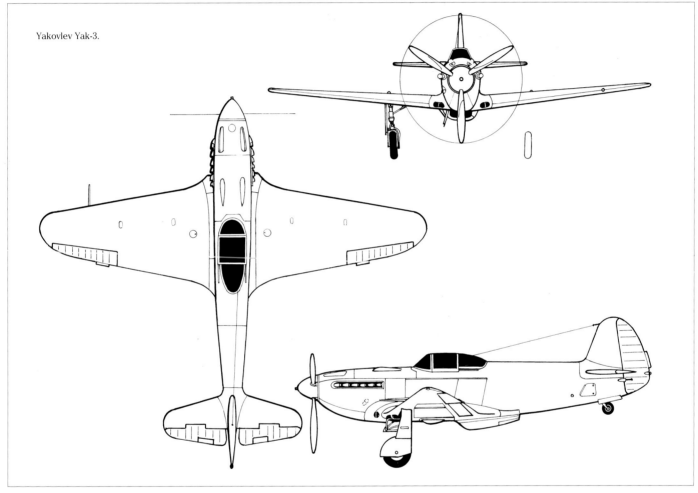

171

Yatsenko

I-28

Vladimir Yatsenko's OKB was among the first to design a new fighter in the late 1930s. In the summer of 1939 the bureau handed over a monoplane powered by an air-cooled engine for flight testing. It was similar in shape to the Polikarpov I-16, which had already been operational for some years, but its structure and performance were considerably different.

Designated I-28 (I - istrebitel, fighter, or literally 'destroyer'), it was heavily armed. The first prototype had four synchronised machine guns; two 7.62mm ShKAS and two 12.7mm ShVAK (on the basis of the latter the 20mm ShVAK gun was produced under the same designation). In overload the I-28 could carry four RS-82 rockets or bombs up to a total weight 220lb (100kg) beneath the wings.

The I-28 was of mixed structure. The fuselage was a wooden monocoque, moulded from veneer. Its two-spar, single-piece wing of 'inverted gull' type was also made of wood, while the control surfaces had a duralumin framework and fabric skin. The undercarriage was pneumatically retracted into the wing. The cockpit had a sliding canopy.

Two prototypes were built, the first being completed on 30th April 1939. It was powered by the 950hp (708kW) Tumanskii M-87A radial engine, though it was intended to have the more powerful M-90 which was still in the design stage. The results of the first flight tests were so promising that, without waiting until the end of the tests, one of the biggest aircraft plants started to prepare its shops and facilities for series-production of the I-28.

The tests of the first prototype were conducted from 1st June to 4th July 1939. Its maximum speed was 256mph (412km/h) at sea level and 338mph (545km/h) at 19,700ft (6,000m), it climbed to 16,400ft (5,000m) in 6.3 minutes and service ceiling was 34,000ft (10,400m). Flying weight during the tests was 5,864lb (2,660kg). On the final test flight the engine cowling was torn off by the extreme aerodynamic load imposed during a dive from 26,250ft (8,000m) at 450mph (725km/h) speed, and a piece of it damaged the tail. Fortunately test pilot Peotr Stefanovsky had the canopy open, and his life was saved when he was thrown from the cockpit.

The second prototype, powered by a 1,000hp (746kW) M-88, underwent tests from 20th April to 15th May 1940 in the hands of test pilot A Kubyshkin. At a take-off weight of 6,018lb (2,730kg) the maximum speed at 23,000ft (7,000m) increased to 351mph (566 km/h), the time to climb to 16,400ft (5,000m) was reduced to 6.1 minutes and the service ceiling increased by 1,312ft (400m). However, it required considerable modification.

Following the accident to the first prototype, series-production was halted. Only five aircraft were delivered of 30 ordered, and these only progressed as far as their taxying tests. All work on the aircraft was stopped in June 1940, and with the appearance of the more advanced I-301 (LaGG-3), I-26 (Yak-1) and I-200 (MiG-1) the I-28 became obsolete. Nevertheless, the experience gained in producing this design proved useful to the plant, for series-production of the Yak-1 proceeded more rapidly as a result.

For technical data, see Table E, page 177.

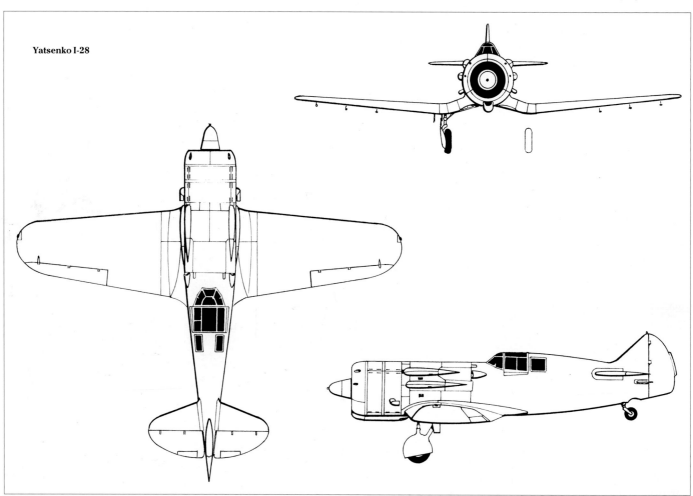

Yatsenko I-28

Four views of the second prototype Yatsenko I-28, powered by an M-88.

Table A

Lavochkin, Gorbunov and Gudkov Fighters

	I-301	LaGG-3 production	LaGG-3 production	LaGG-3 production	LaGG-3-37	LaGG-3	LaGG-3M-82 (La-5 prot)	La-5 production	La-5F production	La-5	La-5 'doubler'	La-5FN production	La-5UTI	La-5M-71	La-5TK	La-5 *	La-5 ** standard
Year of Production	1940	1941	1941	1942	1942	1942	1942	1942	1943	1943	1943	1943	1943	1943	1943	1943	1944
Powerplant	M-105P	M-105P	M-105P	M-105PA	M-105PF	M-105PF	M-82	M-82	M-82F	M-82	M-82FN	ASh-82FN	M-82	M-71	ASh-82FNV	M-82FN	ASh-82FN
Power at altitude – (hp)	1,050	1,050	1,050	1,050	1,180	1,180	1,330	1,330	1,330	1,330	1,470	1,470	1,330	1,670	1,470	1,470	1,470
– (kW)	783	783	783	783	880	880	992	992	992	992	1,096	1,096	992	1,245	1,096	1,096	1,096
Length – (m)	8.81	8.81	8.82	8.82	8.9	8.82	8.71	8.7	8.67	8.67	8.67	8.67	8.71	–	8.67	–	8.6
– (ft-in)	28-11	28-11	28-11	28-11	29-2¼	28-11	28-6¾	28-6½	28-5¼	28-5¼	28-5¼	28-5¼	28-6¾	–	28-5¼	–	28-2½
Wingspan – (m)	9.8	9.8	9.8	9.8	9.8	9.8	9.8	9.6	9.6	9.6	9.8	9.8	9.6	–	9.8	9.8	9.8
– (ft-in)	32-1¾	32-1¾	32-1¾	32-1¾	32-1¾	32-1¾	32-1¾	31-6	31-6	31-6	32-1¾	32-1¾	31-6	–	32-1¾	32-1¾	32-1¾
Wing area – (m²)	17.51	17.51	17.51	17.51	17.51	17.51	17.51	17.37	17.27	17.27	17.27	17.59	17.37	–	17.56	17.59	17.59
– (ft²)	188.4	188.4	188.4	188.4	188.4	188.4	188.4	186.9	185.8	185.8	185.8	189.3	186.9	–	189.0	189.3	189.3
Empty weight – (kg)	2,478	2,573	2,610	2,531	2,832	–	2,790	2,681	2,590	2,600	2,582	2,678	2,576	2,840	–	–	2,605
– (lb)	5,462	5,672	5,753	5,579	6,243	–	6,150	5,910	5,709	5,731	5,692	5,903	5,679	6,261	–	–	5,742
Gross weight – (kg)	2,968	3,346	3,280	3,100	3,363	2,865	3,380	3,360	3,220	3,200	3,168	3,322	3,210	3,526	–	3,445	3,265
– (lb)	6,543	7,376	7,231	6,834	7,414	6,316	7,451	7,407	7,098	7,054	6,984	7,323	7,076	7,773	–	7,594	7,197
Speed at sea level – (km/h)	515.0	498.0	457.0	446.0	501.0	497.0	515.0	509.0	551.0	518.0	595.0	573.0	552.0	612.0	–	630.0	597.0
– (mph)	320.0	309.4	283.9	277.1	311.3	308.8	320.0	316.2	342.3	321.8	369.7	356.0	343.0	380.2	–	391.4	370.9
Speed at altitude – (km/h)	605.0	575.0	535.0	518.0	560.0	564.0	600.0	580.0	590.0	600.0	648.0	620.0	600.0	685.0	–	684.0	680.0
– (m)	4,950	5,000	5,000	6,750	4,000	4,000	6,450	6,250	6,150	6,500	6,300	6,150	2,300	5,500	–	6,150	6,000
– (mph)	375.9	357.2	332.4	332.4	347.9	350.4	372.8	360.4	366.6	372.8	402.6	385.2	372.8	425.6	–	425.0	422.5
– (ft)	16,250	16,500	16,500	16,750	13,500	13,000	21,000	20,500	20,000	21,250	20,750	20,000	7,500	18,000	–	20,000	19,750
Climb to 5,000m – (min)	5.05	8.0	8.5	7.1	7.3	6.0	6.0	6.0	6.0	5.5	6.1	4.7	4.7	5.7	–	5.2	4.45
– (16,400ft – min)	5.85	6.8	8.5	7.1	7.3	6.0	6.0	6.0	6.0	5.5	6.1	4.7	4.7	5.7	–	5.2	4.45
Service ceiling – (m)	9,600	9,100	9,300	9,300	9,000	10,200	–	9,500	9,550	9,650	11,200	10,700	–	–	–	–	10,750
– (ft)	31,500	29,750	30,500	30,500	29,500	33,500	–	31,000	31,250	31,750	36,750	35,000	–	–	–	–	35,250
Turn time – (seconds)	20	–	20	26	22	19	25	22.6	20	19	18.5	19	19	–	–	–	–
Operational range – (km)	556	870	705	466	–	–	–	655	450	900	480	580	–	–	–	–	–
– (miles)	345	540	438	289	–	–	–	407	279	559	298	360	–	–	–	–	–
Take-off run – (m)	355	500	545	515	465	–	310	400	350	–	285	290	350	–	–	–	–
– (ft)	1,164	1,640	1,788	1,689	1,525	–	1,017	1,312	1,148	–	935	951	1,148	–	–	–	–
Landing roll – (m)	400	460	460	560	610	–	470	500	475	–	485	510	475	–	–	–	–
– (ft)	1,312	1,509	1,509	1,837	2,001	–	1,541	1,640	1,558	–	1,591	1,673	1,558	–	–	–	–
Armament – (mm)	1 x 23 / 2 x 12.7	3 x 12.7 / 2 x 7.62	1 x 20 / 1 x 12.7 / 2 x 7.62	1 x 20 / 1 x 12.7	1 x 37 / 1 x 12.7	1 x 20 / 1 x 12.7	2 x 20	2 x 20	2 x 20	1 x 20 / 1 x 12.7	2 x 20	2 x 20	1 x 20	2 x 20	2 x 20	2 x 20 / 12.7	3 x 20 / 1 x 12.7
Page in main text	23	25	25	25	35	25	39	41	43	41	41	49	51	51	41	41	41

* aircraft No.39210206   ** Standard for 1944   See the Glossary and Notes, pages 12 and 13, for details of measurement units etc.

Table A – continued

	La-7 production	La-7 production	La-7TK	La7ASh-71	La-7UTI	105 No.1	105 No.2
Year of Production	1944	1945	1944	1944	1945	1943	1943
Powerplant	ASh-82FN	ASh-82FN	ASh-82FN	ASh-71	ASh-82FN	M-105PF	M-105PF2
Power at altitude – (hp)	1,470	1,470	1,470	2,000	1,470	1,180	1,240
– (kW)	1,096	1,096	1,096	1,492	1,096	880	925
Length – (m)	–	8.6	8.6	–	–	8.82	8.82
– (ft-in)	28-2½	28-2½	28-2½	–	–	28-11	8.82
Wingspan – (m)	9.8	9.8	9.8	9.8	9.8	9.8	9.8
– (ft-in)	32-1¾	32-1¾	32-1¾	32-1¾	32-1¾	32-1¾	32-1¾
Wing area – (m²)	17.59	17.59	17.59	17.59	17.59	17.51	17.51
– (ft²)	189.3	189.3	189.3	189.3	189.3	188.4	188.4
Empty weight – (kg)	–	–	2,711	2,849	2,724	2,234	2,285
– (lb)	–	–	5,976	6,280	6,005	4,925	5,037
Gross weight – (kg)	3,250	3,315	3,280	3,505	3,372	2,875	2,875
– (lb)	7,164	7,308	7,231	7,727	7,433	6,212	6,338
Speed at sea level – (km/h)	612.0	613.0	600.0	–	–	541.0	554.0
– (mph)	380.2	380.9	372.8	–	–	336.1	344.2
Speed at altitude – (km/h)	658.0	661.0	676.0	–	–	612.0	618.0
– (m)	5,900	6,000	8,000	–	–	3,400	3,400
– (mph)	408.8	410.7	420.0	–	–	380.2	384.0
– (ft)	19,250	19,750	26,250	–	–	11,250	11,250
Climb to 5,000m – (min)	5.1	5.3	4.5	–	–	5.1	4.8
– (16,400ft – min)	5.1	5.3	4.5	–	–	5.1	4.8
Service ceiling – (m)	11,300	10,450	11,800	–	–	10,250	10,750
– (ft)	37,000	34,250	38,750	–	–	33,750	35,250
Turn time – (seconds)	20.5	–	–	–	–	–	–
Operational range – (km)	665	–	–	–	–	–	535
– (miles)	413	–	–	–	–	–	332
Take-off run – (m)	340	350	–	–	–	188	–
– (ft)	1,115	1,148	–	–	–	616	–
Landing roll – (m)	540	–	–	–	–	–	–
– (ft)	1,771	–	–	–	–	–	–
Armament – (mm)	2 x 20	3 x 20	2 x 20	2 x 20	1 x 20	1 x 20 / 12.7	1 x 23 / 1 x 12.7
Page in main text	53	53	53	53	58	36	36

See Glossary and Notes, pages 12 and 13, for details of measurement units etc.

Lavochkin LaGG-3, built by Plant No.21, undergoing testing, August-September 1941.

A view of a late version of the MiG I-220(A) series.

Table B

Mikoyan-Gurevich Fighters

	I-200	MiG-1	MiG-3	MiG-3	MiG-3M-82 (MiG-9)	I-211(E)	MiG-3U (I-230)	I-231(2D)	I-220(A) No.1	I-220(A) No.1	I-220(A) No.2	I-221(2A)	I-222(3A)	I-224(4A)	I-225(5A)
Year of Production	1940	1941	1941	1942	1941	1942	1943	1943	1942	1942	1942	1943	1944	1944	1944
Powerplant	AM-35A	AM-35A	AM-35A	AM-38	M-82	M-82F	AM-35A	AM-39A	AM-38F	AM-39	AM-39	AM-39A*	AM-39B-1†	AM-39B †	AM-42B †
Power at altitude – (hp)	1,200	1,200	1,200	1,500	1,330	1,330	1,200	1,500	1,500	1,500	1,500	1,500	1,500	1,500	1,750
– (kW)	895	895	895	1,119	992	992	895	1,119	1,119	1,119	1,119	1,119	1,119	1,119	1,305
Length – (m)	8.155	8.155	8.25	8.25	8.078	7.954	8.62	8.62	9.603	9.603	9.603	9.55	9.603	9.51	9.603
– (ft-in)	26-9	26-9	27-0¾	27-0¾	26-6	26-1	28-3⅓	28-3⅓	31-6	31-6	31-6	31-4	31-6	31-2½	31-6
Wingspan – (m)	10.2	10.2	10.2	10.2	10.2	10.2	10.2 (11.0)	10.2	11.0	11.0	11.0	13.0	13.0	13.0	11.0
– (ft-in)	33-5½	33-5½	33-5½	33-5½	33-5½	33-5½	33-5½ (36-1)	33-5½	36-1	36-1	36-1	42-7½	42-7½	42-7½	36-1
Wing area – (m^2)	17.44	17.44	17.44	17.44	17.44	17.44	17.44(18.0)	17.44	20.38	20.38	20.38	22.44	22.44	22.44	20.38
– (ft^2)	187.7	1877	187.7	187.7	187.7	187.7	187.7 (193.7)	187.7	219.3	219.3	219.3	241.5	241.5	241.5	219.3
Empty weight – (kg)	2,475	2,602	2,699	2,780	2,720	2,528	2,612	2,583	2,936	3,013	3,101	3,179	3,167	3,105	3,010
– (lb)	5,456	5,736	5,950	6,128	5,996	5,573	5,758	5,694	6,472	6,642	6,836	7,008	6,981	6,845	6,635
Gross weight – (kg)	2,968	3,099	3,350	3,325	3,328	3,100	3,285	3,287	3,574	3,835	3,647	3,888	3,790	3,780	3,900
– (lb)	6,543	6,832	7,385	7,175	7,336	6,834	7,242	7,246	7,879	8,454	8,040	8,571	8,355	8,333	8,597
Speed at sea level – (km/h)	508.0	486.0	505.0	519.0	475.0	–	560.0	–	572.0	550.0	571.0	–	–	574.0	590.0
– (mph)	315.6	301.9	313.8	322.5	295.1	–	347.9	–	355.4	341.7	354.8	–	–	356.6	366.6
Speed at altitude – (km/h)	648.0	628.0	640.0	592.0	565.0	670.0	660.0	707.0	630.0	668.0	697.0	698.0	682.0	693.0	729.0
– (m)	6,900	7,200	7,800	3,400	6,150	7,000	5,000	7,100	7,000	7,000	7,000	7,000	6,700	13,100	8,520
– (mph)	402.6	390.2	397.6	367.8	351.0	416.3	410.1	439.3	391.4	415.0	433.1	433.7	423.7	430.6	452.9
– (ft)	22,750	23,750	25,500	11,000	20,000	23,000	16,500	23,250	23,000	23,000	23,000	23,000	22,000	43,000	28,000
Climb to 5,000m (min)	5.3	5.9	5.3	7.9	6.7	4.0	6.2	4.5	–	4.5	4.5	4.6	6.0	4.8	4.5
– to 16,400ft (min)	5.3	5.9	5.3	7.9	6.7	4.0	6.2	4.5	–	4.5	4.5	4.6	6.0	4.8	4.5
Service ceiling – (m)	12,000	12,000	12,000	9,500	–	11,300	11,500 §	11,400	9,500	–	11,000	14,500	14,500	14,100	12,600
– (ft)	39,500	39,500	39,500	31,000	–	37,000	37,750	37,500	31,000	–	36,000	47,500	47,500	46,250	41,330
Operational range – (km)	730	580	820	–	1,070	1,440	1,350	–	960	630	630	–	1,000	1,000	1,300
– (miles)	453	360	509	–	664	894	838	–	596	391	391	–	621	621	807
Take-off run – (m)	–	238	268	380	410	–	–	–	–	–	–	–	–	230	257
– (ft)	–	780	879	1,246	1,345	–	–	–	–	–	–	–	–	754	843
Landing roll – (m)	–	400	400	400	535	–	–	–	–	–	–	–	–	440	450
– (ft)	–	1,312	1,312	1,312	–	–	–	–	–	–	–	–	–	1,443	1,476
Armament – (mm)	1 x 12.7	1 x 12.7	1 x 12.7	1 x 12.7	3 x 12.7	2 x 20	2 x 20	2 x 20	4 x 20	4 x 20	4 x 20	2 x 20	2 x 20	2 x 20	4 x 20
	2 x 7.62	2 x 7.62	2 x 7.62	2 x 7.62	–	–	–	–	–	–	–	–	–	–	–
Page in main text	66	66	6767	74	74	75	76	76	76	76	76	80	80	81	81

* with TK-2B supercharger; † with TK-300B supercharger; § I-230 speed at 691m (12,500ft). See the Glossary and Notes, pages 12 and 13, for details of measurement units etc.

Table C

Polikarpov Biplane Fighters

	I-5 production	I-5 standard	I-15 'doubler'	I-15 production	I-15 production	I-15*bis* prototype	I-15*bis* production	I-15*bis* production	I-152 standard	DIT-2	I-153 prototype	I-153 production	I-153 production	I-153 production	I-153TK	I-190
Year of Production	1932	1933	1933	1934	1934	1937	1937	1938	1938	1939	1938	1939	1939	1940	1940	1939
Powerplant	M-22	M-22	Cyclone	Cyclone	M-22	M-25V	M-25V	M-25V	M-25V	M-25V	M-25V	M-25V	M-62	M-63	M-62	M-88
Power at altitude – (hp)	480	480	625	625	480	750	750	750	750	750	750	750	820	1,100	820	1,100
– (kW)	358	358	466	466	358	559	559	559	559	559	559	559	611	820	611	820
Length – (m)	6.81	6.81	6.10	6.10	6.10	6.27	6.27	6.27	6.27	6.27	6.175	6.175	6.175	6.175	6.175	6.48
– (ft-in)	22-4	22-4n	20-1	20-1	20-1	20-6¾	20-6¾	20-6¾	20-6¾	20-6¾	20-3	20-3	20-3	20-3	20-3	21-3
Upper wingspan – (m)	9.65	9.65	9.75	9.75	9.75	10.2	10.2	10.2	10.2	10.2	10.0	10.0	10.0	10.0	10.0	10.2
– (ft-in)	31-7¾	31-7¾	31-11¾	31-11¾	31-11¾	33-5½	33-5½	33-5½	33-5½	33-5½	32-9½	32-9½	32-9½	32-9½	32-9½	33-5½
Wing area – (m^2)	21.0	21.0	23.55	23.55	23.55	22.5	22.5	22.5	22.5	22.71	22.14	22.14	22.14	22.14	22.14	–
– (ft^2)	226	226	253	253	253	242	242	242	242	244	238	238	238	238	238	–
Empty weight – (kg)	943	1,032	949	960	1,106	–	1,243	1,373	1,251	–	1,307	1,338	1,219	1,547	–	1,761
– (lb)	2,078	2,275	2,092	2,116	2,438	–	2,740	3,026	2,757	–	2,881	2,949	2,687	3,410	–	3,882
Gross weight – (kg)	1,355	1,415	1,358	1,369	1,415	1,700	1,640	1,700	1,648	1,759	1,650	1,680	1,762	1,902	1,860	2,212
– (lb)	2,987	3,119	2,993	3,018	3,119	3,747	3,615	3,747	3,633	3,877	3,637	3,703	3,884	4,193	4,100	4,876
Speed at sea level – (km/h)	–	285.5	324.0	315.0	286.0	321.0	325.0	318.0	314.0	315.0	360.0	368.0	365.0	365.0	363.0	420.0
– (mph)	–	177.4	201.3	195.7	177.7	199.4	202.0	197.6	195.1	195.7	223.7	228.6	226.8	226.8	225.5	261.0
Speed at altitude – (km/h)	252.0	259.0	352.0	367.0	350.0	360.0	367.0	367.0	372.0	362.0	425.0	424.0	443.0	427.0	422.0	450.0
– (m)	2,000	3,000	2,000	3,000	3,000	5,000	2,900	–	2,900	3,200	–	–	4,600	5,100	5,000	7,050
– (mph)	156.6	160.9	218.7	228.0	141.6	223.6	228.0	–	231.1	224.9	–	–	275.3	265.3	262.2	279.6
– (ft)	6,500	10,000	6,500	10,000	10,000	16,500	9,500	–	9,500	10,500	–	–	15,000	16,750	16,500	23,000
Climb to 5,000m (minutes)	10.9	12.0	6.2	6.1	11.0	6.7	7.0	–	7.3	8.05	6.1	–	–	–	–	5.0
– 16,400ft (minutes)	10.9	12.0	6.2	6.1	11.0	6.7	7.0	–	7.3	8.05	6.1	–	–	–	–	5.0
Service ceiling – (m)	7,500	7,520	8,000	9,800	7,520	–	9,100	9,600	9,100	8,500	8,600	8,700	9,800	10,600	–	10,600
– (ft)	24,500	24,700	26,250	32,100	24,700	–	29,800	31,500	29,800	27,800	28,200	28,500	32,100	34,750	–	34,750
Turn time – (seconds)	10.0	10.1	8.0	–	8.5	11.0	10.5	–	11.5	12.5	–	–	–	–	–	–
Operational range – (km)	660	–	535	480	–	–	–	–	–	–	–	–	–	–	–	–
– (miles)	410	–	332	298	–	–	–	–	–	–	–	–	–	–	–	–
Take-off run – (m)	100	–	–	–	70	–	–	–	–	200	130	200	200	373	–	–
– (ft)	328	–	–	–	229	–	–	–	–	656	426	656	656	1,223	–	–
Landing roll – (m)	200	–	–	–	70	–	–	–	–	420	250	250	265	145	–	–
– (ft)	656	–	–	–	229	–	–	–	–	1,377	820	820	869	475	–	–
Armament – (mm)	2x7.62	2x7.62	2x7.62	2or4x7.62	2or4x7.62	4x7.62	4x7.62	4x7.62	4x7.62	2x7.62	4x7.62	4x7.62	4x7.62	4x7.62	4x7.62	4x7.62
Page in main text	86	86	87	87	87	90	90	90	90	90	91	91	91	91	91	91

See the Glossary and Notes, pages 12 and 13, for details of measurement units etc.

First prototype Yatsenko I-28.

Side elevation of the Nikitin IS-1.

TsKB-3, the prototype for the Polikarpov I-15.

Polikarpov I-16 Type 24 with six unguided rockets.

Table D

Polikarpov Monoplane Fighters

	I-16 (TsKB-12)	I-16 Type 4	I-16 Type 5	I-16 Type 10	I-16 Type 12	I-16 Type 17	I-16 Type 18	I-16 Type 24	I-16 Type 29	I-180 No.2	I-180 No.3	I-180 production	I-185	I-185	I-185 standard	ITP (M-1)	ITP (M-2)
Year of Production	1934	1935	1936	1939	1937	1939	1939	1939	1940	1939	1940	1939	1941	1941	1942	1942	1943
Powerplant	Cyclone	M-22	M-25A	M-25V	M-25A	M-25V	M-62	M-63	M-63	M-87B	M-88R	M-88R	M-71	M-82A	M-71	VK-107	AM-39A
Power at altitude – (hp)	625	480	715	750	715	750	820	1,100	1,100	950	1,100	1,100	1,625	1,330	1,625	1,650	1,700
– (kW)	466	358	533	559	533	559	611	820	820	708	820	820	1,212	992	1,212	1,230	1,268
Length – (m)	5.86	5.86	5.86	5.86	5.86	5.86	6.13	6.13	6.13	6.79	6.88	6.88	7.68	8.10	8.05	8.9	9.2
– (ft-in)	19-2½	19-2½	19-2½	19-2½	19-2½	19-2½	20-1⅓	20-1⅓	20-1⅓	22-3¼	22-7	22-7	25-2¼	26-6¾	26-5	29-2¼	30-2
Wingspan – (m)	9.004	9.004	9.004	9.004	9.004	9.004	9.004	9.004	9.004	10.05	10.09	10.09	9.79	9.8	9.8	10.0	10.0
– (ft-in)	29-6	29-6	29-6	29-6	29-6	29-6	29-6	29-6	29-6	32-11½	33-1	33-1	32-1⅓	32-1¾	32-1¾	32-9½	32-9½
Wing area – (m^2)	14.54	14.54	14.54	14.54	14.54	14.54	14.54	14.54	14.54	16.11	16.11	16.11	15.53	15.53	15.53	16.50	16.50
– (ft^2)	156.5	156.5	156.5	156.5	156.5	156.5	156.5	156.5	156.5	173.4	173.4	173.4	167.1	167.1	167.1	177.6	177.6
Empty weight – (kg)	1,040	–	1,145	1,336	1,263	1,425	1,410	1,437	1,545	1,847	2,020	2,046	2,846	2,717	3,130	2,960	2,910
– (lb)	2,292	–	2,524	2,945	2,784	3,141	3,108	3,167	3,406	4,071	4,453	4,510	6,274	5,989	6,900	6,525	6,415
Gross weight – (kg)	1,420	1,355	1,530	1,726	1,696	1,810	1,846	1,878	1,966	2,240	2,429	2,456	3,500	3,328	3,735	3,570	3,570
– (lb)	3,130	2,987	3,373	3,805	3,738	3,990	4,069	4,140	4,334	4,938	5,354	5,414	7,716	7,138	8,234	7,870	7,870
Speed at sea level – (km/h)	362.0	362.0	429.0	398.0	393.0	385.0	411.0	440.0	408.0	408.0	455.0	470.0	556.0	549.0	600.0	568.0	540.0
– (mph)	224.9	224.9	266.5	247.3	244.2	239.3	255.4	273.4	253.5	253.5	282.7	292.0	345.4	341.1	372.8	352.9	335.5
Speed at altitude – (km/h)	437.0	346.0	475.0	448.0	431.0	425.0	464.0	489.0	461.0	540.0	575.0	585.0	630.0	615.0	680.0	655.0	650.0
– (m)	2,900	3,000	3,000	3,160	2,400	2,700	4,400	4,780	4,350	5,850	7,000	7,150	6,170	6,470	6,100	6,300	2,500
– (mph)	271.5	215.0	295.1	278.3	267.8	264.1	288.3	303.8	286.4	335.5	357.3	363.5	391.4	382.1	422.5	407.0	403.9
– (ft)	9,500	10,000	10,000	10,400	8,000	9,000	14,500	15,750	14,250	19,000	23,000	23,500	20,250	21,250	20,000	20,750	8,200
Climb to 5,000m (min)	6.8	9.2	7.35	8.2	–	–	–	–	–	6.25	5.6	5.0	5.2	6.0	4.7	5.9	6.0
– 16,400ft (minutes)	6.8	9.2	7.35	8.2	–	–	–	–	–	6.25	5.6	5.0	5.2	6.0	4.7	5.9	6.0
Service ceiling – (m)	8,800	8,440	8,300	8,260	8,340	8,240	9,470	10,800	9,800	10,250	11,050	–	–	–	–	10,400	11,500
– (ft)	29,000	27,750	27,250	27,000	27,400	27,000	31,000	35,500	32,000	33,500	36,250	–	–	–	–	34,000	37,750
Turn time – (seconds)	–	–	–	16.5	–	–	16	18	16	21	19.5	–	–	22	22.5	–	–
Operational range – (km)	–	–	–	–	–	–	–	–	–	800	900	–	835	1,015	–	1,280	980
– (miles)	–	–	–	–	–	–	–	–	–	497	559	–	518	630	–	795	608
Take-off run – (m)	–	150	–	–	–	–	–	400	–	–	240	–	300	404	–	350	375
– (ft)	–	492	–	–	–	–	–	1,312	–	–	–	–	984	1,325	–	1,148	1,230
Landing roll – (m)	–	130	–	–	–	–	200	180	420	–	200	–	370	348	–	375	390
– (ft)	–	426	–	–	–	–	656	590	1,377	–	656	–	1,213	1,141	–	1,230	1,279
Armament – (mm)	2 x 7.62	2 x 7.62	2 x 7.62	4 x 7.62	2 x 20	2 x 20	4 x 20	4 x 7.62	1 x 12.7	4 x 7.62	2 x 12.7	2 x 12.7	3 x 20	3 x 20 *	3 x 20	1 x 37	3 x 20
	–	–	–	–	2 x 7.62	2 x 7.62	–	–	2 x 7.62	–	2 x 7.62	2 x 7.62	–	–	–	2 x 20	–
Page in main text	99	100	101	102	102	102	102	102	103	109	109	109	112	112	112	115	115

* or 2 x 12.7 and 2 x 7.62

See the Glossary and Notes, pages 12 and 13, for details of measurement units etc.

Table E

Other Fighter Types

	I-207 No.1	I-207 No.2	I-207 No.3	I-207 No.4	I-28 No.1	I-28 No.2	I-21 (IP-21)	SK-2	IS-1	IS-2	'110'	'BI'	Su-1 ('330')	Su-3 ('360')	Il-2I	Il-1	Su-7R	Gu-37 (Gu-1)
Year of Production	1939	1939	1939	1941	1939	1939	1940	1940	1940	1941	1942	1942	1940	1941	1943	1944	1945	1943
Powerplant	M-62	M-63	M-63	M-63P	M-87A	M-88	M-105P	M-105	M-63	M-88	M-107P	D-1A	M-105P *	M-105P *	AM-38F	AM-42	ASh-82FN†	AM-37
Power at altitude – (hp)	820	1,100	1,100	1,100	950	1,100	1,050	1,050	1,100	1,100	1,400	1,100 +	1,050	1,050	1,500	1,750	1,450‡	1,400
– (kW)	611	820	820	820	708	820	783	783	820	820	1,044	2,425 +	783	783	1,119	1,305	1,081	1,044
Length – (m)	6.35	6.35	6.35	6.7	8.54	8.54	8.29	8.0	6.79	7.36	9.9	6.4	8.42	8.42	11.6	11.12	9.14	10.68
– (ft-in)	20-10	20-10	20-10	21-11¾	28-0	28-0	27-2¼	26-3	22-3¼	24-1½	32-6	21-0	27-7½	27-7½	38-0½	36-6	30-0	35-0
Wingspan – (m)	7.0	7.0	7.0	7.0	9.6	9.6	9.4	7.3	8.6	8.6	10.2	6.48	11.5	10.1	14.6	13.4	13.5	10.0
– (ft-in)	22-11½	22-11½	22-11½	22-11½	31-6	31-6	30-10	23-11	28-2½	28-2½	33-5½	21-4	37-8½	33-1½	4710½	43-11½	44-3½	32-9½
Wing area – (m²)	18.0	18.0	18.0	18.0	16.5	16.5	15.46	9.57	20.83 =	20.83 =	18.7	7.0	19.0	17.0	38.5	30.0	26.0	20.0
– (ft²)	193	193	193	193	177	177	166	103	224	224	201	75	204	182	414	322	279	215
Empty weight – (kg)	–	–	–	–	–	–	–	–	1,400	–	3,285	790	2,495	2,480	4,397	4,285	–	3,742
– (lb)	–	–	–	–	–	–	–	–	3,086	–	7,242	1,741	5,500	5,467	9,693	9,446	–	8,249
Gross weight – (kg)	1,950	1,950	1,850	2,200	2,660	2,730	2,670	2,300	2,300	2,180	3,980	1,650	2,875	2,860	5,383	5,320	4,360	4,610
– (lb)	4,298	4,298	4,078	4,850	5,864	6,018	5,886	5,070	5,070	4,805	8,774	3,637	6,338	6,305	11,867	11,728	9,611	10,163
Speed at sea level – (km/h)	387.0	397.0	428.0	–	412.0	439.0	488.0	585.0	400.0	–	508.0	800.0	–	–	401.0	525.0	480.0	–
– (mph)	240.4	246.6	265.9	–	256.0	272.7	303.2	363.5	248.5	–	315.6	497.1	–	–	249.1	326.2	298.2	–
Speed at altitude – (km/h)	436.0	423.0	486.0	–	545.0	566.0	573.0	660.0	453.0	–	610.0	–	641.0	638.0	415.0	580.0	680.0	–
– (m)	–	–	–	–	6,000	7,000	5,000	4,900	4,900	–	6,000	–	10,000	–	1,300	3,260	–	–
– (mph)	270.9	262.8	–	–	338.6	351.7	356.0	410.1	281.4	–	379.0	–	398.3	–	257.8	360.4	422.5	–
– (ft)	–	–	–	–	19,750	23,000	16,500	16,000	16,000	–	19,750	–	32,750	–	4,250	10,750	–	–
Climb to 5,000m (min)	6.2	6.7	4.6	–	6.3	6.1	6.0	4.32	8.2	–	7.0	0.5	–	–	–	–	–	–
– to 16,400ft – (minutes)	6.2	6.7	4.6	–	6.3	6.1	6.0	4.32	8.2	–	7.0	0.5	–	–	–	–	–	–
Service ceiling – (m)	9,150	9,200	–	10,400	10,800	10,600	–	–	–	–	10,000	–	12,500	11,900	6,500	8,600	12,750	–
– (ft)	30,000	30,250	–	34,000	35,500	34,750	–	–	–	–	32,750	–	41,000	39,000	21,250	28,250	41,750	–
Operational range – (km)	700	–	–	–	450	760	–	–	–	–	–	–	720	700	–	–	–	–
– (miles)	434	–	–	–	279	472	–	–	–	–	–	–	447	434	–	–	–	–
Take-off run – (m)	196	–	–	–	325	282	–	250	–	–	–	–	–	–	275	–	350	–
– (ft)	643	–	–	–	1,066	925	–	820	–	–	–	–	–	–	902	–	1,148	–
Landing roll – (m)	–	–	–	–	–	–	–	–	–	–	–	–	–	–	–	–	–	–
– (ft)	–	–	–	–	–	–	–	–	–	–	–	–	–	–	–	–	–	–
Armament – (mm)	4 x 7.62	4 x 7.62	4 x 7.62	4 x 7.62	2 x 12.7 2 x 7.62	2 x 12.7 2 x 7.62	1 x 20 §	2 x 12.7	4 x 7.62	4 x 7.62	1 x 20 2 x 12.7 2 x 7.62	2 x 20	1 x 20 2 x 7.62	1 x 20 2 x 7.62	2 x 23	2 x 23	–	1 x 37 6 x 7.62
Page in main text	18	18	18	18	172	172	86	17	84	84	121	15	119	120	20	21	120	20

* with two TK-2 turbo-superchargers; † with RD-1Khz rocket booster; ‡ giving 300kg (661lb) extra thrust; + rocket motor, thrust given in kg and lb; § or 1 x 23; = upper wing.
See the Glossary and Notes, pages 13 and 14, for details of measurement units etc.

Table F

Yakovlev Fighters of the First Half of the Second World War

	I-26 No.2	Yak-1	Yak-1	Yak-1	Yak-1	Yak-1	Yak-1	Yak-1	Yak-1	I-28 (Yak-5)	I-30	UTI-26	Yak-7	Yak-7M	Yak-7A	Yak-7B	Yak-7-37	Yak-7PD	Yak-7M82	Yak-7B	Yak-7DI
Year of Production	1940	1940	1941	1942	1942	1942	1942	1943	1943	1941	1941	1941	1941	1941	1942	1942	1942	1942	1942	1943	1942
Powerplant	M-105P	M-105P	M-105PA	M-105PA	M-105PF	M-105PF	M-105PF	M-106-1sk	M-105PF	M-105PD	M-105P	M-105P	M-105P	M-105P	M-105PA	M105PF	M-105PA	M-105PD	M-82	M-105PF	M-105PF
Power at altitude – (hp)	1,050	1,050	1,050	1,050	1,180	1,180	1,180	1,350	1,180	1,160	1,050	1,050	1,050	1,050	1,050	1,180	1,050	1,160	1,330	1,180	1,180
– (kW)	783	783	783	783	880	880	880	1,007	880	865	783	783	783	783	783	880	783	865	992	880	880
Length – (m)	8.5	8.48	8.48	8.48	8.48	8.48	8.48	8.48	8.48	–	–	8.5	8.48	8.48	8.48	8.48	8.48	8.37	8.37	8.48	8.48
– (ft-in)	27-10½	27-9¾	27-9¾	27-9¾	27-9¾	27-9¾	27-9¾	27-9¾	27-9¾	–	–	27-10½	27-9¾	27-9¾	27-9¾	27-9¾	27-9¾	27-5½	27-9¾	27-5½	27-9¾
Wingspan – (m)	10.0	10.0	10.0	10.0	10.0	10.0	10.0	10.0	10.0	10.0	10.0	10.0	10.0	10.0	10.0	10.0	10.0	10.0	9.74	10.0	9.74
– (ft-in)	32-9½	32-9½	32-9½	32-9½	32-9½	32-9½	32-9½	32-9½	32-9½	32-9½	32-9½	32-9½	32-9½	32-9½	32-9½	32-9½	32-9½	32-9½	31-11½	32-9½	31-11½
Wing area – (m²)	17.15	17.15	17.15	17.15	17.15	17.15	17.15	17.15	17.15	17.15	17.15	17.15	17.15	17.15	17.15	17.15	17.15	17.15	17.15	17.15	17.15
– (ft²)	184.6	184.6	184.6	184.6	184.6	184.6	184.6	184.6	184.6	184.6	184.6	184.6	184.6	184.6	184.6	184.6	184.6	184.6	184.6	184.6	184.6
Empty weight – (kg)	2,318	2,364	2,429	2,394	2,412	2,350	2,395	2,257	2,316	2,450	2,550	2,181	2,477	2,638	2,450	2,490	2,694	2,452	2,745	2,528	2,360
– (lb)	5,110	5,211	5,354	5,277	5,317	5,180	5,279	4,975	5,105	5,401	5,621	4,808	5,460	5,815	5,401	5,489	5,939	5,405	6,051	5,573	5,202
Gross weight – (kg)	2,700	2,844	2,934	2,883	2,917	2,780	2,900	2,757	2,884	2,928	3,130	2,750	2,960	3,160	2,935	3,010	3,235	2,904	3,370	3,048	2,835
– (lb)	5,952	6,269	6,468	6,355	6,430	6,128	6,393	6,078	6,358	6,455	6,900	6,062	6,525	6,966	6,470	6,635	7,131	6,402	7,429	6,719	6,250
Speed at sea level – (km/h)	490.0	473.0	468.0	478.0	510.0	526.0	523.0	551.0	531.0	515.0	476.0	500.0	471.0	469.0	495.0	514.0	485.0	500.0	515.0	547.0	505.0
– (mph)	304.4	293.9	290.8	297.0	316.9	326.8	324.9	342.3	329.9	320.0	295.7	310.6	292.6	291.4	307.5	319.3	301.3	310.6	320.0	339.8	313.8
Speed at altitude – (km/h)	585.0	573.0	560.0	563.0	571.0	592.0	590.0	630.0	592.0	650.0	571.0	586.0	560.0	556.0	571.0	570.0	564.0	611.0	615.0	612.0	570.0
– (m)	4,800	4,860	4,800	4,850	3,650	3,800	3,850	3,400	4,100	9,000	4,900	4,500	5,000	5,100	5,000	3,650	4,730	7,600	6,400	4,000	3,900
– (mph)	363.5	356.0	347.9	349.8	354.8	367.8	366.6	391.4	367.8	403.9	354.8	364.1	347.9	345.4	354.8	354.1	350.4	379.6	382.1	380.2	354.1
– (ft)	15,750	16,000	15,750	15,900	12,000	12,500	12,600	21,000	13,500	29,500	16,000	14,750	16,500	16,750	16,500	12,000	15,500	25,000	20,000	13,000	12,750
Climb to 5,000m (min)	6.0	5.3	6.8	5.9	6.4	4.7	5.6	4.5	5.4	5.2	7.0	5.5	6.8	7.5	6.4	5.8	7.2	5.4	5.6	4.7	5.5
– to 16,400ft (minutes)	6.0	5.3	6.8	5.9	6.4	4.7	5.6	4.5	5.4	5.2	7.0	5.5	6.8	7.5	6.4	5.8	7.2	5.4	5.6	4.7	5.5
Service ceiling – (m)	10,200	9,300	9,900	10,400	10,000	11,000	9,500	–	10,050	12,000	9,000	9,400	9,250	8,750	9,500	9,900	8,250	11,330	10,000	10,000	10,400
– (ft)	33,500	30,500	32,500	34,000	32,750	36,000	31,000	–	33,000	39,250	29,500	30,750	30,250	28,750	31,000	32,500	27,000	37,000	33,000	33,000	34,000
Turn time – (seconds)	24	20-21	19-20	19	19-20	17-18	18-19	–	19	–	–	19-20	22	24	22	21-22	19-20	23	19-20	24	19-20	17-18
Operational range – (km)	700	700	–	650	650	–	–	–	700	–	975	700	643	750	643	645	550	575	700	700	600
– (miles)	434	434	–	403	403	–	–	–	434	–	605	434	399	466	399	400	341	357	434	434	372
Take-off run – (m)	300	340	–	320	320	285	320	–	340	–	303	310	375	440	410	435	–	–	–	350	300
– (ft)	984	1,115	–	1,049	1,049	935	1,049	–	1,115	–	994	1,017	1,230	1,443	1,345	1,427	–	–	–	1,148	984
Landing roll – (m)	540	540	–	530	520	530	500	–	560	–	525	550	550	650	610	620	–	–	–	540	580
– (ft)	1,771	1,771	–	1,738	1,706	1,738	1,640	–	1,837	–	1,722	1,804	1,804	2,132	2,001	2,034	–	–	–	1,771	1,902
Armament – (mm)	1 x 20 2 x 7.62	1 x 20 2 x 7.62	1 x 20 2 x 7.62	1 x 20 1 x 12.7	1 x 20 2 x 7.62	1 x 20	1 x 20 1 x 12.7	1 x 20 1 x 12.7	1 x 20 1 x 12.7	1 x 20 1 x 7.62	3 x 20 2 x 7.62	2 x 7.62	1 x 20 2 x 7.62	3 x 20	1 x 20 2 x 7.62	1 x 20 2 x 12.7	1 x 37 2 x 12.7	1 x 20	2 x 20 1 x 12.7	2 x 20 1 x 12.7	1 x 20 1 x 12.7
Page in main text	122	122	122	122	122	122	122	131	122	160	161	131	133	133	133	134	138	138	138	134	142

* with RD-1KhZ booster of 300kg (661lb) thrust; † time to climb to 10,800m (35,450ft); ‡ or 1 x 37 or 1 x 23   See the Glossary and Notes, pages 12 and 13.

Table G

Yakovlev Fighters of the Second Half of the Second World War

	Yak-9	Yak-9T	Yak-9D	Yak-9	Yak-9P	Yak-9TK	Yak-9K	Yak-9B	Yak-9DD	Yak-9M	Yak-9PD	Yak-9V	Yak-9S	Yak-9U prototype	Yak-9U prototype	Yak-9U production	Yak-9UT	Yak-9UV	Yak-9U	Yak-9P
Year of Production	1943	1943	1943	1943	1943	1943	1944	1944	1944	1944	1944	1945	1945	1943	1944	1944	1945	1945	1946	1947
Powerplant	M-105PF	M-105PF	M-105PF	M-106	M-105PF	M-105PF	M-105PF	M-105PF	VK-105PF	VK-105PF	VK-105PD	VK-105PF-2	VK-105PF-2	VK-105PF-2	M-107A	VK-107A	VK-107A	VK-107A	VK-107A	VK-107A
Power at altitude – (hp)	1,180	1,180	1,180	1,350	1,180	1,180	1,180	1,180	1,180	1,180	1,160	1,240	1,240	1,240	1,500	1,500	1,500	1,500	1,500	1,500
– (kW)	880	880	880	1,007	880	880	880	880	880	880	865	925	925	925	1,119	1,119	1,119	1,119	1,119	1,119
Length – (m)	8.5	8.65	8.5	8.5	8.5	8.65 §	8.87	8.5	8.5	8.5	8.5	8.6	8.5	8.5	8.5	8.6	8.6	–	8.6	8.6
– (ft-in)	27-10½	28-4	27-10½	27-10½	27-10½	28-4 §	29-1	27-10½	27-10½	27-10½	28-2½	27-10½	27-10½	27-10½	28-2½		28-2½	28-2½	28-2½	27-10½
Wingspan – (m)	9.74	9.74	9.74	9.74	9.74	9.74	9.74	9.74	9.74	9.74	10.74	9.74	9.74	9.74	9.74	9.74	9.74	9.74	9.74	9.74
– (ft-in)	31-11½	31-11½	31-11½	31-11½	31-11½	31-11½	31-11½	31-11½	31-11½	31-11½	35-2¾	31-11½	31-11½	31-11½	31-11½	31-11½	31-11½	31-11½	31-11½	31-11½
Wing area – (m²)	17.15	17.15	17.15	17.15	17.15	17.15	17.15	17.15	17.15	17.15	17.65	17.15	17.15	17.15	17.15	17.15	17.15	17.15	17.15	17.15
– (ft²)	184.6	184.6	184.6	184.6	184.6	184.6	184.6	184.6	184.6	184.6	189.9	184.6	184.6	184.6	184.6	184.6	184.6	184.6	184.6	184.6
Empty weight – (kg)	2,277	2,298	2,350	2,380	2,222	2,348	2,346	2,382	2,346	2,428	2,098	2,344	2,347	2,244	2,477	2,512	2,187	2,505	2,593	2,708
– (lb)	5,019	5,066	5,180	5,246	4,898	5,176	5,050	5,251	5,171	5,352	4,625	5,167	5,174	4,947	5,460	5,537	4,821	5,522	5,716	5,970
Gross weight – (kg)	2,870	3,025	3,117	3,050	2,820	3,246	3,028	3,356	3,387	3,095	2,500	3,107	3,130	2,900	3,150	3,204	3,260	3,128	3,227	3,550
– (lb)	6,327	6,668	6,871	6,723	6,216	7,156	6,675	7,398	7,466	6,823	5,511	6,849	6,900	6,393	6,944	7,063	7,186	6,895	7,114	7,826
Speed at sea level – (km/h)	520.0	533.0	535.0	531.0	505.0	518.0	518.0	507.0	522.0	518.0	503.0	506.0	513.0	558.0	600.0	575.0	578.0	564.0	569.0	590.0
– (mph)	323.1	331.1	332.4	329.9	313.8	321.8	321.8	315.0	324.3	321.8	312.5	314.4	318.7	346.7	372.8	357.2	359.1	350.4	353.5	366.6
Speed at altitude (km/h)	599.0	597.0	591.0	602.0	576.0	573.0	573.0	562.0	584.0	573.0	620.0	564.0	583.0	620.0	700.0	672.0	671.0	623.0	672.0	660.0
– (m)	4,300	3,930	3,650	3,250	3,950	3,900	3,900	3,750	3,900	3,750	10,500	3,600	3,950	3,850	5,500	5,000	4,900	4,100	5,700	5,000
– (mph)	372.2	370.9	348.5	374.0	357.9	356.0	356.0	349.2	362.8	356.0	385.2	350.4	362.2	385.2	434.0	417.5	416.9	387.1	417.5	410.1
– (ft)	14,000	13,000	12,000	10,750	13,000	12,750	12,750	12,250	12,750	12,250	34,000	11,750	13,000	12,750	18,000	16,500	16,000	13,500	18,750	16,500
Climb to 5,000m (min) to 16,400ft (minutes)	5.1 5.1	5.5 5.5	6.1 6.1	5.4 5.4	6.4 5.4	5.7 5.7	5.7 5.7	6.5 6.5	6.8 6.8	6.1 6.1	5.6 5.6	5.8 5.8	6.6 6.6	4.8 4.8	4.1 4.1	5.0 5.0	5.2 5.2	5.5 5.5	4.8 4.8	5.8 5.8
Service ceiling – (m)	11,100	10,000	9,100	10,100	–	–	–	8,600	9,400	9,500	13,100	9,900	9,750	10,400	–	10,650	10,700	–	11,100	10,500
– (ft)	36,500	32,750	29,750	33,000	–	–	–	28,250	30,750	31,000	43,000	32,500	32,000	34,000	–	35,000	35,000	–	36,500	34,500
Turn time – (seconds)	16-17	18-19	19-20	17-18	–	24	–	25-26	26	19-20	–	–	–	19.5	18.5	20	20-21	–	–	21
Operational range – (km)	660	620	905	–	–	–	850	–	1,320	950	–	–	930	850	884	675	690	650	590	1,130
– (miles)	410	385	562	–	–	–	528	–	820	590	–	–	577	528	549	419	428	403	366	702
Take-off run – (m)	305	380	370	360	–	380	305	440	400	420	–	390	–	320	380	375	–	390	375	540
– (ft)	1,000	1,246	1,213	1,181	–	1,246	1,000	1,443	1,312	1,377	–	1,279	–	1,049	1,246	1,230	–	1,279	1,230	1,771
Landing roll – (m)	450	500	550	530	–	500	450	580	500	550	–	560	–	575	535	530	–	560	530	582
– (ft)	1,476	1,640	1,804	1,738	–	1,640	1,476	1,902	1,640	1,804	–	1,837	–	1,886	1,755	1,738	–	1,837	1,738	1,909
Armament – (mm)	1 x 20	1 x 37	1 x 20	1 x 20	2 x 20	1 x 45 ‡	1 x 45	1 x 20	1 x 20	1 x 20	1 x 20	1 x 20	1 x 23	1 x 23	1 x 20	1 x 20	1 x 37	1 x 20	1 x 20	1 x 20
	1 x 12.7	1 x 12.7	1 x 12.7	1 x 12.7		1 x 12.7	1 x 12.7	1 x 12.7	1 x 12.7	1 x 12.7			2 x 20	2 x ?	2 x 12.7	2 x 12.7	1 x 20		2 x 12.7	2 x 12.7
Page in main text	142	143	145	146	147	147	147	150	151	152	153	155	155	155	155	155	158	158	158	158

* with RD-1KhZ booster giving 300kg (661lb) of thrust;   § or 8.87m (29ft 1in);   † time to climb to 10,800m (35,450ft);   ‡ or 37 or 23.
See the Glossary and Notes, pages 12 and 13, for details of measurement units etc.

Table G – continued

	Yak-1M	Yak-1M 'doubler'	Yak-3	Yak-3	Yak-3	Yak-3RD	Yak-3PD	Yak-3U
Year of Production	1943	1943	1943	1944	1944	1945	1945	1945
Powerplant	M-105PF	M-105PF-2	VK-105PF-2	VK-107A	VK-108	VK-105PF-2	VK-105PD	ASh-82
Power at altitude – (hp)	1,180	1,240	1,240	1,500	1,800	1,240 *	1,160	1,630
– (kW)	880	925	925	1,119	1,342	925 *	865	1,215
Length – (m)	8.5	8.5	8.5	8.5	8.5	8.5	8.5	8.17
– (ft-in)	27-10½	27-10½	27-10½	27-10½	27-10½	27-10½	27-10½	26-9½
Wingspan – (m)	9.2	9.2	9.2	9.2	9.2	9.2	9.2	9.74
– (ft-in)	30-2	30-2	30-2	30-2	30-2	30-2	30-2	31-11½
Wing area – (m²)	14.85	14.85	14.85	14.85	14.85	14.85	14.85	17.15
– (ft²)	159.8	159.8	159.8	159.8	159.8	159.8	159.8	184.6
Empty weight – (kg)	2,133	2,105	2,128	2,346	–	2,382	2,105	2,273
– (lb)	4,702	4,640	4,691	5,171	–	5,251	4,640	5,011
Gross weight – (kg)	2,655	2,660	2,697	2,984	2,830	2,980	2,616	2,792
– (lb)	5,853	5,864	5,945	6,578	6,238	6,569	5,767	6,155
Speed at sea level – (km/h)	545.0	570.0	565.0	611.0	–	–	–	–
– (mph)	338.6	354.1	351.0	379.6	–	–	–	–
Speed at altitude (km/h)	632.0	651.0	640.0	720.0	746.0	782.0	–	–
– (m)	4,750	4,300	4,400	5,750	6,000	7,800	–	–
– (mph)	392.7	404.5	397.6	447.3	463.5	485.9	–	–
– (ft)	15,500	14,000	14,500	18,750	19,750	25,500	–	–
Climb to 5,000m (min) to 16,400ft (minutes)	4.1 4.1	4.1 4.1	4.1 4.1	3.9 3.9	3.5 3.5	– –	13.2 † 13.2 †	– –
Service ceiling – (m)	10,700	10,800	10,400	11,800	–	–	–	–
– (ft)	35,000	35,500	34,000	38,750	–	–	–	–
Turn time – (seconds)	17	17	19	18	–	–	–	–
Operational range – (km)	845	900	850	1,060	–	700	–	–
– (miles)	525	559	528	658	–	434	–	–
Take-off run – (m)	290	275	290	345	–	–	–	–
– (ft)	951	902	951	1,131	–	–	–	–
Landing roll – (m)	485	485	480	590	–	–	–	–
– (ft)	1,591	1,591	1,574	1,935	–	–	–	–
Armament – (mm)	?	1 x 20	1 x 20	1 x 20	1 x 23	1 x 23	1 x 20	2 x 20
	?	2 x 12.7	2 x 12.7	2 x 12.7				
Page in main text	158	158	158	158	169	170	167	171

* with RD-1KhZ booster giving 300kg (661lb) of thrust; † time to climb to 10,800m (35,450ft);
See the Glossary and Notes, pages 12 and 13, for details of measurement units etc.

Yak-1s on alert, waiting for the signal to intercept.

Production Yak-3 from Plant No.292, Saratov.

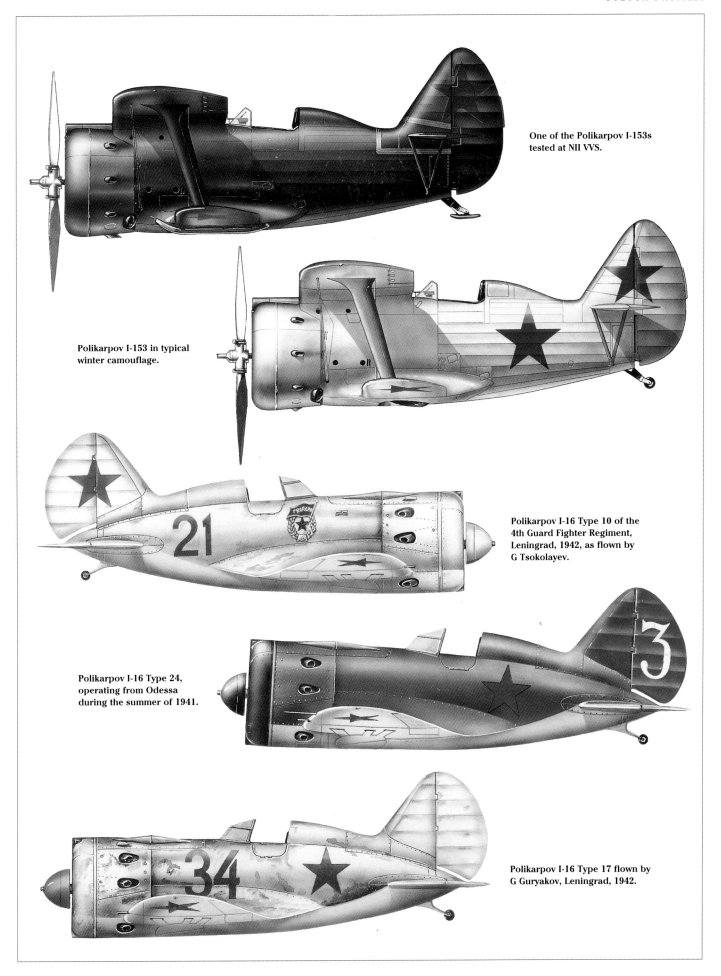

One of the Polikarpov I-153s
tested at NII VVS.

Polikarpov I-153 in typical
winter camouflage.

Polikarpov I-16 Type 10 of the
4th Guard Fighter Regiment,
Leningrad, 1942, as flown by
G Tsokolayev.

Polikarpov I-16 Type 24,
operating from Odessa
during the summer of 1941.

Polikarpov I-16 Type 17 flown by
G Guryakov, Leningrad, 1942.

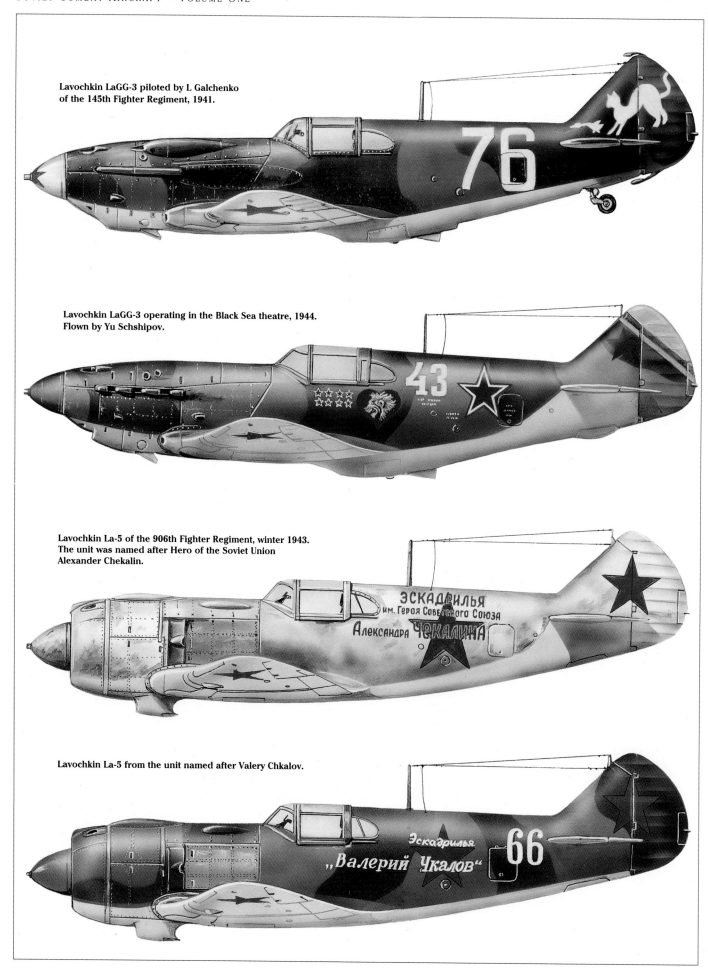

Lavochkin LaGG-3 piloted by L Galchenko
of the 145th Fighter Regiment, 1941.

Lavochkin LaGG-3 operating in the Black Sea theatre, 1944.
Flown by Yu Schshipov.

Lavochkin La-5 of the 906th Fighter Regiment, winter 1943.
The unit was named after Hero of the Soviet Union
Alexander Chekalin.

Lavochkin La-5 from the unit named after Valery Chkalov.

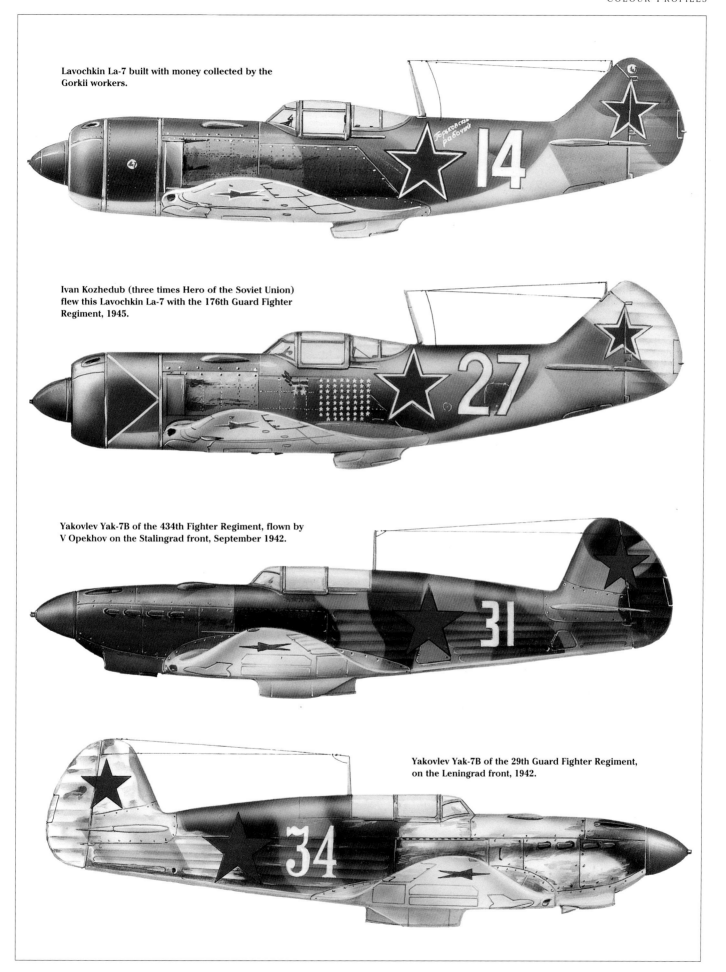

Lavochkin La-7 built with money collected by the
Gorkii workers.

Ivan Kozhedub (three times Hero of the Soviet Union)
flew this Lavochkin La-7 with the 176th Guard Fighter
Regiment, 1945.

Yakovlev Yak-7B of the 434th Fighter Regiment, flown by
V Opekhov on the Stalingrad front, September 1942.

Yakovlev Yak-7B of the 29th Guard Fighter Regiment,
on the Leningrad front, 1942.

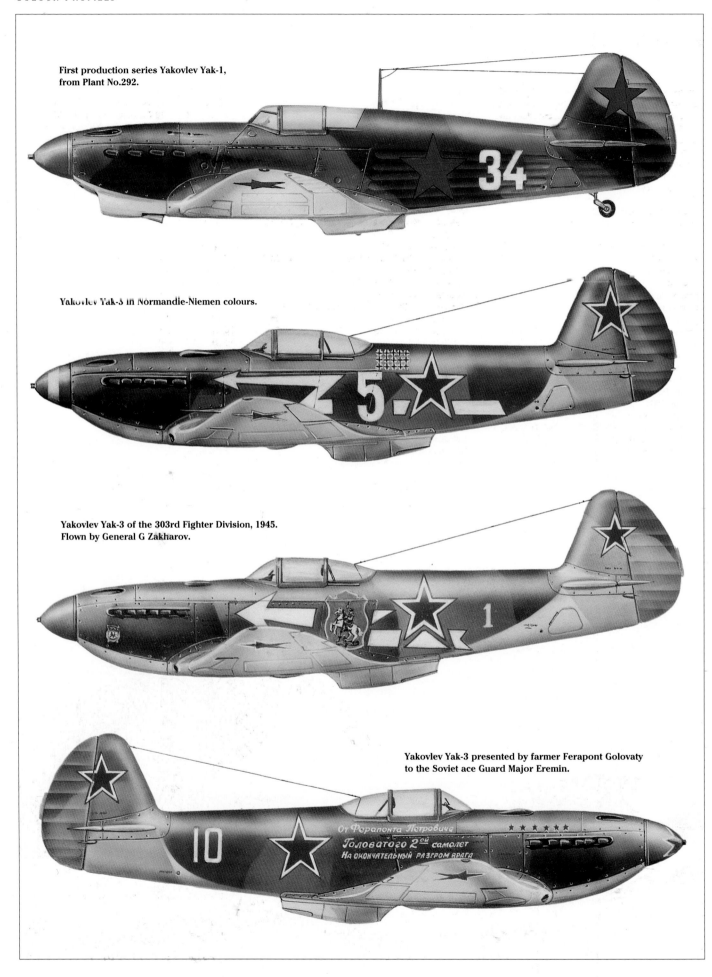

First production series Yakovlev Yak-1,
from Plant No.292.

Yakovlev Yak-3 in Normandie-Niemen colours.

Yakovlev Yak-3 of the 303rd Fighter Division, 1945.
Flown by General G Zakharov.

Yakovlev Yak-3 presented by farmer Ferapont Golovaty
to the Soviet ace Guard Major Eremin.

Index

In order to make the index as easy to use as possible, references to oft-quoted subjects, such as the single-engined fighter types, the designers, test pilots and their OKBs and the factories that built them, test elements of the air force and navy and operational pilots etc have all been omitted as they are readily accessible within each OKB section.

Soviet fighter types mentioned 'outside' of their own section *are* included in this index.

The ultimate iteration of the Yakovlev piston fighter line – the Yak-3. *Philip Jarrett collection*

To conclude, a trio of Yakovlev Yak-9Ds, a type which constituted the backbone of the VVS counter-offensive. *Philip Jarrett collection*